OUT O' TH' BUSHES

A Texas Preacher's Guide to Givin' Plumb Up!

TEX TONROY

WESTBOW
PRESS®
A DIVISION OF THOMAS NELSON
& ZONDERVAN

WestBow Press books may be ordered through booksellers or by contacting:

WestBow Press
A Division of Thomas Nelson & Zondervan
1663 Liberty Drive
Bloomington, IN 47403
www.westbowpress.com
1 (866) 928-1240

ISBN: 978-1-5127-2032-7 (sc)
ISBN: 978-1-5127-2033-4 (e)

Library of Congress Control Number: 2015918907

Print information available on the last page.

WestBow Press rev. date: 1/22/2016

Managing Editor: Dr. Kevin Hrebik
Consulting Editor: William Zinger

CONTENTS

CONCLUSION

DEDICATION

To the LORD GOD ALMIGHTY,
the God of my forefathers (and mothers),
who called me out of the bushes
back to His Marvelous Light

To my daughter, Lindsey
(Tonroy) Robertson, who said,
"I thank God and my Dad, that they both
ran to meet me when they saw me
coming out of the bushes."

ACKNOWLEDGMENTS

Thank God, who put this story in me, where it had to get out.

Thanks to Dr. Kevin Hrebik and Bill Zinger, my faithful editors.

Thanks to all those who prayed for me and encouraged me to keep on trying.

Thanks to my daughter, Lindsey, my son-in-law, Wes, and my son, Ian, who loved me and whom God has used to show me a multitude of things about discipleship.

Thanks to all the guys in prison, who opened their hearts and lives to show me how God works.

Thanks to all my family at John Wesley UMC, especially the "Utes," who let me teach and share the revelations God has given me, and who allowed me to practice making disciples.

Thanks to my wife, Gaye, who puts up with me through thick and thin.

Why call this book *Out o' th' Bushes*? I call it that because "the bushes" is my term for the wilderness where I've stayed most of my Christian life. You know, the secular world, often known simply as "the world," where Christians go, and sometimes stay for long periods, hiding from God and His call on their lives. It's that place where the cares of the world and the deceitfulness of riches (Matthew 13:22) rob us of the life that is in Jesus Christ. It's the place where we never really confess our sins, so God can't forgive us and cleanse us from all unrighteousness (1 John 1:9), so we stay separated from Him until He finally comes to deliver us, to pull us out and keep us "out o' th' bushes." Then, after we get out of the bushes and make the commitment to **be** Jesus' disciples, we accept His commission to **make** disciples. Making disciples is inextricably intertwined with coming out of the bushes.

If we're going to accept the commission that Jesus gave us just before He ascended into heaven, where He says, "God gave Me all power, so go, go into all the world, and make disciples, baptizing them in the Name of the Father, and the Son, and the Holy Spirit, teaching them to observe all things I have commanded you; [and know this], I am with you always, even to the end of the age" (Matthew 28:18-20), then we're going to have to draw near to God (James 4:8). And as part of our role in this commission, we must teach others (help others to learn) to draw near to God. That is the primary purpose of this book, and that is the primary purpose of discipleship.

Now I am convinced that the first phrase of the commission cited above is absolutely correct, that all power is, in fact, given to Jesus, in heaven and in earth, and if we are to take part in the making of disciples, we will only do it as Jesus gives us His power through the Holy Spirit. As it says in Luke 11:11-13, "If you, being evil, know how to give good gifts, how much more will your heavenly Father give the Holy Spirit to those who ask Him?"

This book is a combination of a "how-to" book and a study and discussion guide, but mostly it is a tool to use to draw ourselves nearer to God, so God will draw nearer to us. We then, in turn, share the love, the truth, the mercy, and the light of God with the disciples God puts us with. *Out o' th' Bushes* touches on what is really going on in our relationship with God, stressing six great themes of the Bible: Love, Humility, Thanksgiving, Trust, Obedience, and Service as the structure for the book. That's the message God gave me from the beginning.

Discipleship is all about building (growing) relationships, with God and with others, particularly with those God has put us with. Shine the light of this relationship concept on everything you read in this book. But more important, like Paul says in Philippians 2:5, "Let this mind (this attitude) be in you, which was in Christ Jesus." As we live our lives as disciples of Jesus, we are constantly involved in a process, a progression, a moving from being "natural" (like the world and the flesh) to being spiritual (more and more like Jesus). So it is with discipleship, a constant moving up the continuum from being more like me to being more like Jesus. As much as we're able, being like Jesus should be the focus of our lives in everything we do, especially in discipleship.

So how do we teach disciples? Just for clarity, I've deemed "make disciples" to mean "helping people develop a personal relationship with Jesus." On the other hand, "teaching them to observe all things whatsoever I [Jesus] have commanded you," sounds like we're supposed to be teaching rules and required activities and acceptable associations. My reading of the Bible indicates that is NOT what Jesus was talking about at all. I submit that "teaching them" (the disciples God has made through us) is all about teaching them the "mind" and the "attitude" that Jesus had when He was walking around on the earth, and even more, teaching them to discern the attitude that Jesus has right now, through the Holy Spirit, in the hearts of His people. So while I'd like to present a seamless dissertation about what Jesus thinks and says, a tome which has a beginning and an end and three major points with three sub-points under each point; that method just doesn't seem to fit the subject matter. How do you teach the "mind" or the "attitude" of Jesus? You do it one principle at a time, one story at a time, one shocking experience at a time.

In this book, I've used two sources for our material: **Passages** from the Bible, and **Stories** from the Bible and from my own experiences and those of others. In the end, I am hoping and praying that readers will not have acquired a list of answers to put on a test, but rather, that they will have acquired new and different attitudes, choices, and emotional responses to Jesus and His life that is in them. Finally, I pray that they will find new ways to see what God is doing in their lives and in the lives of others, along with new ways for them to respond to the life that is in Christ Jesus that has come to reside in them.

THEME 1: LOVE

THE GIFT OF THE MAGI

One dollar and eighty-seven cents. That was all. And sixty cents of it was in pennies. Pennies saved one and two at a time by bulldozing the grocer and the vegetable man and the butcher until one's cheeks burned with the silent imputation of parsimony that such close dealing implied. Three times Della counted it. One dollar and eighty-seven cents. And the next day would be Christmas.

There was clearly nothing to do but flop down on the shabby little couch and howl. So Della did it. Which instigates the moral reflection that life is made up of sobs, sniffles, and smiles, with sniffles predominating.

While the mistress of the home is gradually subsiding from the first stage to the second, take a look at the home. A furnished flat at $8 per week. It did not exactly beggar description, but it certainly had that word on the lookout for the mendicancy squad.

In the vestibule below was a letter-box into which no letter would go, and an electric button from which no mortal finger could coax a ring. Also appertaining thereunto was a card bearing the name, "Mr. James Dillingham Young."

The "Dillingham" had been flung to the breeze during a former period of prosperity when its possessor was being paid $30 per week. Now, when the income was shrunk to $20, though, they were thinking seriously of contracting to a modest and unassuming D. But whenever Mr. James Dillingham Young came home and reached his flat above he was called Jim and greatly hugged by Mrs. James Dillingham Young, already introduced to you as Della. Which is all very good.

Della finished her cry and attended to her cheeks with the powder rag. She stood by the window and looked out dully at a gray cat walking a gray fence in a gray backyard. Tomorrow would be Christmas Day, and she had only $1.87 with which to buy Jim a present. She had been saving every penny she could for months, with this result. Twenty dollars a week doesn't go far. Expenses had been greater than she had calculated. They always are. Only $1.87 to buy a present for Jim. Her Jim. Many a happy hour she had spent planning for something nice for him. Something fine and rare and sterling—something just a little bit near to being worthy of the honor of being owned by Jim.

There was a pier-glass between the windows of the room. Perhaps you have seen a pier-glass in an $8 flat. A very thin and very agile person may, by observing his reflection in a rapid sequence of longitudinal strips, obtain a fairly accurate conception of his looks. Della, being slender, had mastered the art.

Suddenly she whirled from the window and stood before the glass. Her eyes were shining brilliantly, but her face had lost its color within twenty seconds. Rapidly she pulled down her hair and let it fall to its full length.

Now, there were two possessions of the James Dillingham Youngs in which they both took a mighty pride. One was Jim's gold watch that had been his father's and his grandfather's. The other was Della's hair. Had the Queen of Sheba lived in the flat across the airshaft, Della would have let her hair hang out the window some day to dry just to depreciate Her Majesty's jewels and gifts. Had King Solomon been the janitor, with all his treasures piled up in the basement, Jim would have pulled out his watch every time he passed, just to see him pluck at his beard from envy.

So now Della's beautiful hair fell about her rippling and shining like a cascade of brown waters. It reached below her knee and made itself almost a garment for her. And then she did it up again nervously and quickly. Once she faltered for a minute and stood still while a tear or two splashed on the worn red carpet.

On went her old brown jacket; on went her old brown hat. With a whirl of skirts and with the brilliant sparkle still in her eyes, she fluttered out the door and down the stairs to the street.

Where she stopped the sign read: "Mne. Sofronie. Hair Goods of All Kinds." One flight up Della ran, and collected herself, panting. Madame, large, too white, chilly, hardly looked the "Sofronie."

"Will you buy my hair?" asked Della.

"I buy hair," said Madame. "Take yer hat off and let's have a sight at the looks of it." Down rippled the brown cascade.

"Twenty dollars," said Madame, lifting the mass with a practised hand.

"Give it to me quick," said Della.

Oh, and the next two hours tripped by on rosy wings. Forget the hashed metaphor. She was ransacking the stores for Jim's present. She found it at last. It surely had been made for Jim and no one else. There was no other like it in any of the stores, and she had turned all of them inside out. It was a platinum fob chain simple and chaste in design, properly proclaiming its value by substance alone and not by meretricious ornamentation—as all good things should do. It was even worthy of The Watch. As soon as she saw it she knew that it must be Jim's. It was like him. Quietness and value—the description applied to both. Twenty-one dollars they took from her for it, and she hurried home with the 87 cents. With that chain on his watch Jim might be properly anxious about the time in any company. Grand as the watch was, he sometimes looked at it on the sly on account of the old leather strap that he used in place of a chain.

When Della reached home her intoxication gave way a little to prudence and reason. She got out her curling irons and lighted the gas and went to work repairing the ravages made by generosity added to love. Which is always a tremendous task, dear friends—a mammoth task.

Within forty minutes her head was covered with tiny, close-lying curls that made her look wonderfully like a truant schoolboy. She looked at her reflection in the mirror long, carefully, and critically.

"If Jim doesn't kill me," she said to herself, "before he takes a second look at me, he'll say I look like a Coney Island chorus girl. But what could I do—oh! What could I do with a dollar and eighty-seven cents?"

At 7 o'clock the coffee was made and the frying pan was on the back of the stove hot and ready to cook the chops.

Jim was never late. Della doubled the fob chain in her hand and sat on the corner of the table near the door that he always entered. Then she heard his step on the stair away down on the first flight, and she turned white for just a moment. She had a habit for saying little silent prayers about the simplest everyday things, and now she whispered, "Please God, make him think I am still pretty."

The door opened and Jim stepped in and closed it. He looked

thin and very serious. Poor fellow, he was only twenty-two—and to be burdened with a family! He needed a new overcoat and he was without gloves.

Jim stopped inside the door, as immovable as a setter at the scent of quail. His eyes were fixed upon Della, and there was an expression in them that she could not read, and it terrified her. It was not anger, nor surprise, nor disapproval, nor horror, nor any of the sentiments that she had been prepared for. He simply stared at her fixedly with that peculiar expression on his face. Della wriggled off the table and went for him.

"Jim, darling," she cried, "don't look at me that way. I had my hair cut off and sold because I couldn't have lived through Christmas without giving you a present. It'll grow out again—you won't mind, will you? I just had to do it. My hair grows awfully fast. Say 'Merry Christmas!' Jim, and let's be happy. You don't know what a nice—what a beautiful, nice gift I've got for you."

"You've cut off your hair?" asked Jim, laboriously, as if he had not arrived at that patent fact even after the hardest mental labor.

"Cut it off and sold it," said Della. "Don't you like me just as well, anyhow? I'm me without my hair, ain't I?"

Jim looked about the room curiously. "You say your hair is gone?" he said, with an air almost of idiocy.

"You needn't look for it," said Della. "It's sold, I tell you—sold and gone, too. It's Christmas Eve, boy. Be good to me, for it went for you. Maybe the hairs of my head were numbered," she went on with sudden serious sweetness, "but nobody could ever count my love for you. Shall I put the chops on, Jim?"

Out of his trance Jim seemed quickly to wake. He enfolded his Della.

For ten seconds let us regard with discreet scrutiny some inconsequential object in the other direction. Eight dollars a week or a million a year—what is the difference? A mathematician or a wit would give you the wrong answer. The magi brought valuable gifts, but that was not among them. This dark assertion will be illuminated later on.

Jim drew a package from his overcoat pocket and threw it upon the table. "Don't make any mistake Dell," he said, "about me. I don't think there's anything in the way of a haircut or a shave or a shampoo that could make me like my girl any less. But if you'll unwrap that package you may see why you had me going a while at first."

White fingers and nimble tore at the string and paper. And then an ecstatic scream of joy; and then, alas! a quick feminine change to hysterical tears and wails, necessitating the immediate employment of all the comforting powers of the lord of the flat.

For there lay The Combs—the set of combs, side and back, that Della had worshipped long in a Broadway window. Beautiful combs, pure tortoise shell, with jewelled rims—just the shade to wear in the beautiful vanished hair. They were expensive combs, she knew, and her heart had simply craved and yearned over them without the least hope of possession. And now, they were hers, but the tresses that should have adorned the coveted adornments were gone.

But she hugged them to her bosom, and at length she was able to look up with dim eyes and a smile and say, "My hair grows so fast, Jim!" And them Della leaped up like a little singed cat and cried, "Oh, oh!" Jim had not yet seen his beautiful present. She held it out to him eagerly upon her open palm. The dull precious metal seemed to flash with a reflection of her bright and ardent spirit. "Isn't it a dandy, Jim? I hunted all over town to find it. You'll have to look at the time a hundred times a day now. Give me your watch. I want to see how it looks on it."

Instead of obeying, Jim tumbled down on the couch and put his hands under the back of his head and smiled. "Dell," said he, "let's put our Christmas presents away and keep 'em a while. They're too nice to use just at present. I sold the watch to get the money to buy your combs. And now suppose you put the chops on."

The magi, as you know, were wise men—wonderfully wise men—who brought gifts to the Babe in the manger. They invented the art of giving Christmas presents. Being wise, their gifts were no doubt wise ones, possibly bearing the privilege of exchange in case of duplication. And here I have lamely related to you the uneventful chronicle of two foolish children in a flat who most unwisely sacrificed for each other the greatest treasures of their home. But in a last word to the wise of these days let it be said that of all who give gifts these two were the wisest. Of all who give and receive gifts, such as they are wisest. Everywhere they are wisest. They are the magi.

Exodus 20:1-17

The Ten Commandments in Exodus 20:1-17 starts out with God talking to the Israelites, and He says (this is a paraphrase), "I am the Lord your God; I brought you out of the captivity in Egypt; I've been taking care of you (your families and your clan) since Abraham, and if you stick with Me, I will continue to take care of you. This first part says, without saying it in so many words, "I picked you out before the foundations of the earth to be Mine. I chose you to be my special people because I love you. I want you. I want you to be My people and I want to be your God. I love you. I've been putting up with you for a long time because I love you."

The above is sorta' the "why" of the Ten Commandments, or God's introduction. What follows is the list, divided in two parts. The first four are things God wants us to do to show our love for Him:

1. No other gods besides Me
2. No idols, no statues of anything to worship
3. Don't curse
4. Remember the Sabbath and keep it holy

The last six are the things we do to show our love for our neighbors:

5. Respect your momma and your daddy
6. Don't kill
7. Don't commit adultery
8. Don't lie
9. Don't steal

10. Don't covet (in case you don't know covet, in means wanting what somebody else has so much that you'd try to steal it if you weren't such a chicken)

Some people think that the Old Testament and the Ten Commandments were issued as edicts from a "hard" God, and that he's changed in the New Testament. To me, He's still the same. The Israelites were just pretty stubborn and hardheaded (maybe hardhearted, too) like us. Maybe God hasn't changed. He started out to love us, and He never gives up, in all kind of ways, reaching out to us and showing his love, hoping that someday we'll get it. This is where all the love that is in the world starts, with God (James 1:17).

John 3:16

This classic verse is a direct confirmation of all God shows us in the Old Testament about His love. The way I read the verse, and the parts of the Bible that support this verse (which is most of it), is as follows: God loved the world, the people in the world so much, that He came down to the earth in the body of a man, in the person of Jesus, and sacrificed Himself so that His blood would pay the penalty of sin (separation) for all of us (2 Corinthians 5:14). Also, Romans 8:32 says, "And if God loved us enough to give His own Son, won't He also give us all things?" That's how much.

Deuteronomy 6:4-9

This is the passage that the Jews call the "Shemah," and it deserves to be quoted, even if it's just in my paraphrase. It begins with, "Hear O Israel, the Lord our God, The Lord is the Only One." Just to let you know, the "Shemah" is the source of the "first and great commandment" that Jesus spoke when he said, "You shall love the Lord your God with all your heart and all your soul and all your mind and all your strength." And the last part says, "And these words which I command you today shall be in your heart [memorize them, know them by heart]. You shall teach them diligently to your children, and shall talk of them when you sit in your house, when you walk by the way, when you lie down, and when you rise up. You shall bind them as a sign on your hand, and they shall be as frontlets between your eyes. You shall write them on the doorposts of your house and on your gates," (Deuteronomy 11:18-20).

These are just some of the ways we show our love for God.

Leviticus 19:18

This is the verse that Jesus quotes when he says, "And the second is like unto it, 'You shall love your neighbor as yourself.'" Actually, the whole verse says quite a bit more: "You shall not take vengeance, nor bear any grudge against the children of your people, but you shall love your neighbor as yourself: I am the Lord."[7]

My paraphrase goes like this, "Don't seek revenge; don't hold a grudge; but love your neighbor as yourself." Holding a grudge and seeking revenge are things you do if you don't love your neighbor. If you hold a grudge then you are not forgiving, and if you don't forgive others, then God will not forgive you (because you won't let Him). And it's clear, even to me, that holding a grudge is the opposite of loving someone. It almost rises to the level of hating them. And seeking revenge is worse, if that were possible, because it is acting out the hatred you feel when you hold that grudge. This is all pretty easy to see if you think about it. So loving your neighbor as yourself is not some high sounding something they talk about in church. Holding a grudge and seeking revenge are things you cannot afford to do. They cut you off from God. If you don't get anything else from this book, please get this.

Oh, and did you notice the last line? "I am the Lord." This is not just some guy off the street; not some honyock who doesn't know anything. This is the Lord God Almighty, Maker of Heaven and Earth. This is the Person who is responsible for creating **you**. Hear ye Him! If I were a betting man, I'd bet Jesus was thinking about that when He reminded them that this verse was the second greatest commandment.

Luke 10:29-37

This passage is the story of The Good Samaritan. Most everyone knows this story.

A man was going on a trip, and he was attacked by bandits, who took all his stuff and left him naked and half dead by the side of the road. A priest came by, saw him, and passed by on the other side of the road. A Levite (church worker) came by, saw him, and passed by on the other side of the road. Then a Samaritan, a "low" class half-breed person, despised by the Jews, saw this Jewish man lying by the road, and what did he do? The Bible says, "He took pity on him." He bandaged his wounds, and doctored him, and took him to a hotel and took care of him. He even gave the innkeeper money to take care of the man when he left. And Jesus said to the lawyer, "Which one of these men was a neighbor to the man who was attacked by the robbers?" And the lawyer said, "The one who showed him mercy." And Jesus said, "Go and do likewise."

That must be what love is about.

1 Corinthians 13:4-8

This is a passage that deserves to be quoted. It deserves to be memorized and quoted every day, to God, to your family, and to your neighbors, whether they're lying in the road, or living in the house next door.

This passage is all about what love looks like in the real world, down here where the rubber meets the road, when things are not rosy, when everybody is struggling just to make it to the end of the day without going crazy. This is my version, found from several translations, too numerous to mention. So here goes:

> "Love suffers long, (yes, I know, modern versions say 'Patient,' but it means so much more than that) and is kind;
> It is not jealous, or boastful, or proud, or rude;
> It does not demand its own way;
> It is not irritable or grouchy, and it will hardly even notice when others do it wrong.
> Love doesn't rejoice in evil, but rejoices in the truth.
> It excuses all the faults of all the others,
> It believes the best about everyone,
> It hopes the best for everybody,
> Love hangs in there with you through thick and thin, forever.
> It never gives up. Love never fails."

I've got a few things to say about this passage. To me, the underlying core ingredient of love is "putting up" with people. Putting up with your husband or your wife. Putting up with your kids. Putting up with your momma and your daddy. Putting up with people when you've told them for the fourteenth time to do (or not do) something, and they keep on doing it wrong over and over (sometimes it's on purpose). 'Bout the third time I tell somebody something to do and they don't do it; or they don't get it; I'm ready to say, "Just go away!"

But that's not what God does. God pats us on the back and says, "Come on. You can do this. Try it one more time. I'm here. I'm helping you. You don't have to be afraid." And yes, it is "suffering long" when you do this with your kids and the people God puts you with. God puts up with us so He can teach us to put up with others. It's like that verse in 2 Corinthians 1:4 that says, "He comforts us so we can comfort others."

How many wives are there out there who have told their husbands 500 times that their mommas just don't live here, and they're going to have to pick up after themselves? Or the kids about doing what they say they're going to? About doing the homework and not waiting 'til the last minute? Isn't that what love is really about? Telling them over and over, and over, hoping, praying, believing that it will finally soak in? That's what God does.

That "putting up with 'em" love is also expressed in "Love excuses the faults of others." Some versions say, "Bears all things." Eugene Peterson's version, *The Message*, actually says for that phrase, "Puts up with anything." The New International Version of the Bible in Spanish uses the expression, *"Todo disculpa,"* which means, "Excuses all." Makes me think of those mommas out there, when their kids get in trouble, and somebody else starts saying bad things about them, the mommas say, "But he's a good boy; and he tries hard. He just messed up a little this time." She doesn't even remember this is maybe the 15th time he's messed up. God is just like that. Reminds me of the Prodigal Son (Luke 15:11-32).

My Daddy used the expression, "Chalk 'em off your list." It meant you weren't going to have anything else to do with someone. That's what you would expect the father in the story of prodigal son to do, isn't it? But he didn't do that. He treated his son like his son! That's what God does for us, if we'll just let Him.

Love means being humble. It means not thinking you have to "stick up for yourself"; letting the other person go first in line; not gigging 'em back when they gig you; giving 'em that "soft answer" that turns away anger (Proverbs 15:1). That's love. Not demanding your own way. Wow! How often do I feel like someone has stepped on my toes and I really need to get them stated. Talk about quenching that "loving feeling." Not irritable or grouchy. That really is love.

Like I saw one time on the menu in an old time café: "We hope you enjoy the even temper of our waitresses, mad all the time." Sometimes we act like that. The other side of that coin really offers some relief; when you go up to someone and ask them how they're doing, and you really care; you really listen when they tell you. Ya' think maybe they will notice?

2 Timothy 2:24-26

In this passage, Paul says to Timothy, "And a servant of the Lord must not quarrel but be gentle to all, able to teach, patient, in humility correcting those who are in opposition, if God perhaps will grant them repentance, so that they may know the truth, and that they may come to their senses and escape the snare of the devil, having been taken captive by him to do his will."

I want to highlight a few things: "The servant of the Lord must not **argue** with them, but be **gentle** to everybody, ready and able to **teach**, **patient** (there's that 'putting up with 'em again), **humbly** instructing those who oppose (you, God, themselves); maybe God will give them **repentance** to the recognition and acceptance of the **truth**, so they can withdraw themselves from the **trap** of the devil, by whom they are taken captive to do his will."

Do you feel the built-in love that is contained in this verse? It follows the "Love Chapter" of 1 Corinthians 13. "Don't argue with them" is the part about not demanding your own way. "Gentle" is all about being kind, not irritable or grouchy, not boastful or proud or rude. "Ready and able to teach" is being willing to put up with them "not getting it" and continuing to tell them the truth, to rejoice in the truth. "Humbly instructing" is about when they say something mean and tacky, you don't have to gig 'em back, because the Spirit in you can believe the best for them, hope the best for them, and never give up praying for them. When we do our part in love, they have the best chance of "repenting," finding the "truth," and escaping the "trap" they are in.

Ephesians 4:29-32: A Story about Sam

"Let no corrupt communication proceed out of your mouth, but that which is good to the use of edifying, that it may minister grace unto the hearers. And grieve not the Holy Spirit of God, whereby ye are sealed unto the day of redemption. Let all bitterness, and wrath, and anger, and clamour, and evil speaking, be put away from you, with all malice, and be ye kind one to another, tenderhearted, forgiving one another, even as God for Christ's sake hath forgiven you." (KJV)

In *The Message*, the passage goes like this, "Watch the way you talk. Let nothing foul or dirty come out of your mouth. Say only what helps, each word a gift. Don't grieve God. Don't break his heart. His Holy Spirit, moving and breathing in you, is the most intimate part of your life, making you fit for Himself. Don't take such a gift for granted. Make a clean break with all cutting, backbiting, profane talk. Be gentle with one another, sensitive. Forgive one another as quickly and thoroughly as God in Christ forgave you." What a beautiful message!

The above passage has been on my heart for some time. Like most married couples, my wife and I sometimes say mean things to each other. The problem is it doesn't just grieve (sadden) the Holy Spirit, but it grieves me and it grieves her and it grieves our son; it makes us all sad.

It's only recently that I began to understand that being kind and tenderhearted means that I'm supposed to show that kindness and tenderheartedness by talking nice to other people, especially my own personal, immediate family, saying encouraging things that make them feel good and enjoy being with me, instead of saying mean, sarcastic things. I must be slow. Bet I've read that passage 50 times, and I'm just now beginning to get it. Reminds me of Proverbs 15:1, "A soft answer turns away wrath (anger), but a harsh word stirs up anger." If I just talk nice to my wife, it's amazing how much nicer she is to me. Guess that must be what "kind and tenderhearted" is all about.

When my two oldest sons, Sam and Andy, were in high school,

they went to military school in New Mexico. Secretly, they said they wanted to go to military school because there was less discipline there than there was at home. I don't know. Maybe. All in all, I think they learned a lot there, both in education and in life experiences. Not all good, but certainly some was. They made good grades; they excelled in the military training; and they responded well to the military discipline (probably learned that at home?). 'Course they weren't perfect angels, but who is? Both of them got in some trouble from time to time, partly because they were a little resistant to authority. Can't imagine where they got that. As a matter of fact, both of them got kicked out for various reasons, but both of them got back in and graduated.

This little story is about Sam. One day, for some unknown reason, he decided he'd stick the fire hose in the window of the Tactical Officer's office (Tach Office) and fill it up with water while the Tach Officer was away doing his rounds one night. When he came back, the tach office was about 2½ feet deep in water (up to the bottom of the windows), and when he opened the door, the water knocked him down flowing out the door. He was a little hot.

Because there is a "secret code of honor," nobody squealed on Sam for several hours. Finally, the officers devised a way to put enough pressure on everybody that someone finally gave in and told them who did it. That was maybe 10:00–11:00 in the morning. Shortly after that, the Officer of the Day called me on the phone in our hometown, maybe 6 hours away. His first words were, "Come and get the sumbitch; we don't want him around here." After that, he gave me a short version of what happened and then told me that Sam and all his belongings would be waiting for me out on the curb, whenever I was able to get there. He knew how far I was away, and he didn't care. Then I said, "I want to talk to Sam." And the guy said, "He doesn't want to talk to you." But he put him on.

You know, my kids were used to me talking mean to them. That was what always happened whenever they did something they weren't supposed to do. That was what always preceded the whipping they usually got. So Sam was ready. He was always the one who knew that it wouldn't do any good to beg for mercy, so he just kept his mouth shut. Said only what was necessary to be respectful.

But that day was different. I was sitting there in my office and I heard these words coming out of my own mouth, "Sam, I don't know exactly what happened; but it's going to be all right. We'll figure out some way to work this thing out; take care of what happened; and get through it. You don't worry about it. I'll be there as soon as I can get there, and I'm leaving right now." He didn't say much. I don't think he was any more ready for what I said than I was.

I had time to think about the whole thing while I was driving out there. I decided it must have been God who intervened in that situation. God changed my heart, and the change in my heart made for a change in my speech. And on the way, I realized that I loved Sam, and Andy, that they were my sons, and I didn't have any business talking to them like they were dogs. I decided I should talk to my sons at least as well as I'd talk to my adult friends—and I'd never talk to any of them like that; I'd be afraid they'd whip my rear. And right there, driving out to New Mexico, I made a vow to God that I'd try to talk better to all the members of my family. I haven't always succeeded, but God is still working on me, and He's not finished with me yet.

The time writing this book has given me a renewed desire to focus my attention on surrendering my mouth to God so that He can be kind, tenderhearted, and forgiving through me to my family (and to others). I'm more sure than ever that this is what love is really about in terms of being a "doer" of His Word, in terms of obeying the direction of the Holy Spirit, in terms of being patient, and kind, never rude, not demanding, or irritable or grouchy, and hardly even noticing if others did me wrong.

You know, it's funny. My kids know what is right. They don't do it all the time, just like the rest of us, but they know. And the most telling thing I can say to them to get them to do right is this, "I'm not going to tell you what to do about this. I just want you to do what you know is right." Gets them every time. And it always works best when you say it very softly, almost at a whisper. That's love. That's God's Holy Spirit moving in us to will and to do His good pleasure. (Phil. 2:13)

Back to "The Gift of the Magi" story, toward the end, it says, "Here I have lamely related to you the uneventful chronicle of two foolish children in a flat who most unwisely sacrificed for each other the greatest treasures of their home. But in a last word to the wise of these days let it be said that of all who give gifts these two were the wisest. Of all who give and receive gifts, such as they are wisest. Everywhere they are wisest. They are the magi."

What does it mean when it says, "Of all who give and receive gifts, such as they are wisest. Everywhere they are wisest. They are the magi."? Why did the author call them "foolish children," and then say, "they are the wisest, they are the magi"? I suppose reasonable minds could differ, but it seems to me the answer to that question is contained in the same sentence. The reason they are wisest, the reason they are the magi, is because they "willingly sacrificed the greatest treasures of their house" for the one they loved.

That is what we are supposed to do if we really love; that is what we **do** for the ones we really love. That is exactly what God did for us—He gave, He sacrificed the Person He held most dear—for you and me, just because He loves us. That's just the kind of love He wants from us. Can we do any less?

A Few Words about Mercy

In modern versions of the Bible, there are a lot of times when the word "mercy" in the KJV is translated "love," "great love," or "compassion". And I guess mercy really is a facet of God's love, but it is such a special facet of God's love that it deserves some special attention. In the dictionary, the word "mercy" is defined as follows: "Kind or compassionate treatment of an offender, adversary, prisoner, etc, in one's power; compassion where severity is expected or deserved. A disposition to be kind, forgiving, or helpful. The power to show mercy or compassion: 'to throw myself on his mercy'. Antonyms of mercy are: harshness, severity, implacability, punishment, chastisement, vengeance."

So you might say that "mercy" is love, or just like love, but it has a depth of meaning that we don't usually associate with love, certainly not what we humans usually think about when we say love. In spite of the fact that we're worthless and don't deserve anything but punishment, don't deserve a thing except judgment and condemnation, God says, "I don't care. Because I love them and I want them to love me, I'm going to be nice to them." It's more than just regular, human love; it's **mercy**.

Psalms 100:6 (KJV) says, "For the Lord is good, His mercy is everlasting, and His truth endures to all generations." His mercy is everlasting. To obtain mercy, all you've got to do is accept it. He'll never quit giving it to you. He likes being merciful because He loves us and He wants us to have a relationship with Him. Right now, He's standing there with His hand out, waiting for you to come and take His hand. That's mercy.

Here's a poem from *The Merchant of Venice* by William Shakespeare:

The quality of mercy is not strain'd,
It droppeth as the gentle rain from heaven
Upon the place beneath: it is twice bless'd;
It blesseth him that gives and him that takes:
'Tis mightiest in the mightiest; it becomes
The throned monarch better than his crown;
His sceptre shows the force of temporal power,
The attribute to awe and majesty,
Wherein doth sit the dread and fear of kings;
But mercy is above this sceptred sway,
It is enthroned in the hearts of kings,
It is an attribute to God himself,
And earthly power doth then show likest God's
When mercy seasons justice.

That's mercy. While we're talking about mercy, we also need to talk about grace. Grace is a name of a sweet, mild-mannered, tenderhearted girl whose greatest pleasure is to be nice to the people she encounters (and their greatest pleasure as well). "With Grace" is the way we act when we're brought up right; when our mommas actually taught us, actually showed us how people are supposed to act when they act graciously; when they let us see what true manners are all about. Not so much about which fork to use as about how to make people feel comfortable and at ease in your home. Grace is a sign of how you really are down in your heart, when the Spirit of God is residing there.

Someone said that Grace is "unmerited favor," which is God being nice to you even though you don't deserve it; mercy is God being nice to you even when you deserve to be punished. Grace and mercy are just two faces of the same coin, and the coin is God. Oh, you've heard that expression haven't you? God is love . . . He's also mercy . . . and grace.

Talking about mercy also requires that we talk about forgiveness. In Ephesians 4:32, Paul says, "Be kind to each other, tenderhearted, forgiving one another, as God for Christ's sake, has forgiven you." Forgiveness is just another facet of God's love; another facet of God's personality. In 1 Corinthians 13:4-7, part of the Love Chapter, it doesn't exactly say the word forgiveness; but it does say, in the Living Bible, "[love] will hardly even notice if others do it wrong." And it says, love "bears all things (excuses all things)." What better actions can we use to show forgiveness than these?

There is a unique fact about forgiveness in the Bible that few people seem to notice. There's a qualification involved in obtaining God's forgiveness. In order to qualify to receive God's forgiveness, you must forgive others. If God is so merciful and forgiving, why would He withhold His forgiveness from us for any reason? You know, it makes this requirement crystal clear in Matthew 6:9-15. Everybody knows the first five verses of this passage; it's the Lord's Prayer. It says the way we're supposed to pray is to say, "Forgive us our debts (trespasses) as we forgive those who trespass against us." Hardly anyone mentions the next two verses after the end, where it says, "For if you forgive them, God will forgive you; but if you don't forgive them, neither will God forgive you."

I've thought this over a lot. Do you know why God won't forgive you if you don't forgive others? I'm sure there are a lot of Bible scholars and wise men and imminent preachers of the Gospel who might disagree with me, but I think the reason God won't forgive the unforgiving is because He can't. Yes, I know, God can do anything He wants to. And I'm absolutely convinced that's true. But He can't in this case, because the person who refuses to forgive is blocking himself from receiving God's forgiveness. It's just like in the situation about being converted and receiving salvation through Jesus. In order to be saved, we must receive the gift. If we're not willing to receive the gift, by grace, through faith, we just won't be saved. (Eph. 2:8-9) In forgiveness, if we don't open ourselves up, and surrender the hate and the bitterness that are involved in holding a grudge against someone, we're never going to reach the point where we can receive forgiveness. God is not going to **make** us do this anymore than He's going to **make** us trust Him. If we don't trust Him, we can't receive rest. If we don't forgive, we can't receive forgiveness (Matthew 6:15).

Are you familiar with Leviticus 19:18? That's the second verse that Jesus quoted when someone asked Him what was the first and great commandment. On the first one, He quoted Deuteronomy 6:4-5, "Love the Lord with all your heart and all your soul and all your strength." And he went on to say, "And the second is like it, 'Love your neighbor as yourself.'" That's the last part of Leviticus 19:18. The whole verse goes like this, "Don't seek revenge; don't hold a grudge; but love your neighbor as yourself." That whole verse has a lot of meat. How are you going to love your neighbor if you hold a grudge? Holding a grudge is saying, "I'm mad and I'm not getting over it. I'm not going to forgive that person for what they did to me. I'm going to harbor this anger and this pain and this hurt in me until I can do something about it." And revenge is just what a person does when they have kept on harboring these bad thoughts, lost all restraint, taken the law into their own hands, and decided to do something about it.

So here's the question, "How can you accept God's forgiveness, when you won't forgive, and release yourself from the bondage you've got yourself wound up in because of your vengeful thoughts against that other person?" That's why God can't forgive you. God's forgiveness is as all-enveloping as the air we breathe; but if you won't forgive, you can't take a breath. Unforgiveness kills people every day—it makes them physically ill; it hardens their hearts; it hardens their bones; it makes them so they can't breathe, physically or spiritually.

Forgiveness is so inextricably wound up with love that God can't help but give it to us, and forgiveness is so inextricably wound up with love, that if we don't forgive, we can't love, and if we don't love, we can't receive God's love.

1 Thessalonians 5:16-18

"Rejoice evermore. Pray without ceasing. In everything give thanks: for this is the will of God in Christ Jesus concerning you."

Another way to say it comes from the Amplified Bible, "Be happy (in your faith) and rejoice and be glad-hearted continually (always); Be unceasing in prayer (praying perseveringly); Thank God in everything (no matter what the circumstances may be, be thankful and give thanks), for this is the will of God for you who are in Christ Jesus (the Revealer and Mediator of that will)."

What does this verse have to do with love? I don't know. Sometimes I can't figure out whether this passage should be filed under "Love" or "Obey," or maybe even under "Serve." It sorta' fits under all three.

You know what? Like someone said, if you're happy and thankful and blessed because you believe in Jesus, send a message to your face. 'Course, if you're frowning all the time, it's probably (almost certainly) because your face knows the truth about what is in your heart. Like it says in Matthew 12:34, "Out of the abundance of the heart the mouth speaks." Same goes for your face. "Out of the abundance of the heart your eyes and your face speak." Being happy because you have an ongoing, growing relationship with God through Jesus, and the Holy Spirit is residing in your heart, is just not something you can't force or fake. And if you claim to have that relationship, but you're still unhappy, and it shows on your face, then most likely it's because you still haven't really surrendered your whole self to God, to let Him run your life. You're still trying to take care of everything for yourself, to stay in control. And as long as you're doing that, God is going to let you. But when you finally give up and let Him have your whole life and your whole self, then you'll get that sense of relief that only God can give. You'll know what rest is all about. You feel that sense of security, inside and out, that only Jesus can give. Then you'll be rejoicing all the time and giving thanks for everything that happens to you, good, bad or indifferent. And your face will be glowing with God. You just won't be able to hold it in. Like Peter said in Acts 4:18-20, "We just can't help but tell what we've seen and heard." You'll be saying, "I just can't help but grin because I'm so glad to get to be here, right in the middle of the hollow of God's hand! Hallelujah!"

And what about "Pray without ceasing" in verse 17? Or "praying perseveringly" from the Amplified? I don't know about you, but perseveringly sounds like work, like a duty, like something you have to do to stay in good graces with God. And that's not the way this passage feels to me. This passage feels like what Brennan Manning said in his devotional book, *Reflections for Ragamuffins*, "What masters of the interior life recommend is the discipline of 'centering down' throughout the day: a quiet, persistent turning to God while driving, cooking, conversing, writing, and so on. After weeks and months of practice, relapses, discouragement, and returns to the center, this discipline becomes a habit." Brother Lawrence called it "the practice of the presence of God."

That "persistent turning to God" doesn't seem like work to me, or even a duty; it's more like a privilege, an honor, an opportunity to draw closer to God in my spare moments; it's an act of love—especially if it turns into a habit of drawing near to God so He'll draw near to you. 'Course I guess you could use the word perseveringly as a substitute for persistent. Who am I to judge another's expression of his connecting with God? People say things a lot of different ways and still mean the same thing. What's that expression? Semantic differential? Maybe discipline is something disciples do, and they're happy to do it because they get to be closer and closer to Jesus.

1 Thessalonians 5: **18** says, "In everything give thanks: for this is the will of God in Christ Jesus concerning you." Let's see, that sounds almost exactly like Romans 8:28-29, "All things work together for good to them that love the Lord, to them that are the 'called' according to His purpose, whom He did foreknow and did predestine to be conformed to the image of His Son, so that He might be the first-born among many brothers and sisters." If we are sitting in the middle of God's purpose, and He is working everything out for good to us, we really can give thanks in all things, no matter what they may look like to the untrained eye, to the natural, non-Spirit-filled person on the street. And it sounds like giving thanks in all things puts us in the middle of God's will in Jesus. That's just another reason to "rejoice evermore" from verse 16. It's a festival of love and praise and worship and thanksgiving all rolled into one.

Of course everyone knows that everything is not sweetness and light all the time. And since it's not, we're going to have spells of sorrow, sacrifice, pain, maybe even an occasional doubt. But if I read this passage in 1 Thessalonians correctly, we're supposed to rejoice and pray and give thanks in all things all the time. I don't know about you, but I just can't get that done, in and of myself. I just can't be happy all the time, or good all the time, or obedient all the time.

So the only way I can get through to the "Festival of Praise" is if and when I surrender my whole self to God, and let Him take care of me and my problems, so I can focus on the solution of Jesus, the same Jesus who is my Lord and Savior, and who is my Brother; the One who is with me by His Spirit. That's what brings me back to God every time, to rejoicing, and praying, and giving thanks in all things.

God's Love

How much does God love us? Enough. Enough to come to earth in the Person of His Son, to die on the cross, to save us from our sins and from ourselves, so we will come to be one with Him, again.

And then, after He had paid all the price to reconcile us to Himself, He then devised a plan—a grand design to keep us in communion with Him forever by His Holy Spirit working in us, leading us, guiding us, keeping on wooing us, forgiving us, and cleansing us, all because He is faithful and just. (1 John 1:9) That's gotta' be love.

He is faithful and just because he does what he says He'll do. He practices what He preaches. Even when we mess up, when we confess, He forgives us. That is more than just faithful (trustworthy) and just (righteous). That's love. God really is love. You can't explain it. It's too overwhelming. You just have to trust Him and accept it. Guess we'll find out why and how when we get to heaven. "And this is God's love, that while we were still (unrepentant) sinners, Jesus died for us" (Romans 5:8). That's love. However much we love God, He loves us more. More abundantly. Pressed down, shaken together, and runnin' over. (Luke 6:38) Won't have enough barns to put it all in. (Malachi 3:10) Exceeding abundantly above all that we could ask or think. (Ephesians 3:20) That's how much.

THEME 2: HUMILITY

MOSES, HUMBLE?

Using parentheses, as if speaking in a whisper, Numbers 12:3 (KJV) says, "(Now the man Moses was very meek, above all the men which were upon the face of the earth.)" Just so you'll know, "meek" is the King James word for humble. Thus, "Moses was the humblest man on the face of the earth,." While it was true, he didn't start out that way. In the beginning, he thought he was pretty hot stuff. After all, he was royalty in Egypt. He was the adopted son of the Pharaoh's daughter, he grew up in the palace of the Pharaoh, and had everything that anyone could possibly want—the best of everything at that. He was the best cared for, the best educated, the most properly trained, and the most lavishly entertained person in the world of his time. His royal pampering wasn't just during childhood; he also spent the first 20 years of his adulthood as the Pharaoh's grandson. He had the run of the palace and the kingdom, and he did whatever he wanted to, whenever he wanted to, to whoever he wanted to. This is not to say that he did anything particularly bad; it was just that life was all about him. He was sorta' like John Wayne—he didn't take any crap off of anybody.

When he was about 40, Moses got to thinking about the fact that he was really an Israelite. He decided that God had called him to take care of "his" people, and because of his unique position in society, he was just the person to do it. Not long after that, he saw an Egyptian overseer beating an Israelite slave, and he decided enough was enough—he, Moses, would take care of his "brother." He started beating the Egyptian, and in the process of the beating, he killed him. He wasn't really too worried right then; he buried the guy in the sand and went on about his business. It was only after another incident a day or two later that he really got scared. He saw two Israelites fighting, and he said to the one who was winning, "Why are you beating your brother?" And the guy says, "This isn't your affair, leave me alone. Anyway, what are you going to do, kill me, like you did that Egyptian?" Then Moses got scared, because he knew that everybody in town already knew about it, or soon would, and he would be called to account. It was then that he ran away; knowing he was as good as caught.

The fact that Moses didn't come to a full repentance and conversion right away gives me some wry comfort. If it took God 40 years to get Moses ready for Him to use him, then maybe there's hope for me. Even though the Bible makes short shrift of the time between the killing and the Exodus, it makes it clear that it was a full 40 years.

Yes, there is little in the Bible about Moses and this "40 years in the wilderness," which is not to be confused with another "40 years in the wilderness" spent there with the Jews in their wanderings. I find it interesting that Moses spent 40 years living, learning, and leaving his past before embarking on another 40 years leading the Israelites through the wilderness—where they lived, learned from God, and left their past behind them. Just as he moved from out of his past (the "bushes" of ungodly royalty) toward God's plan, so they moved from out of their bondage (the "bushes" of slavery and Egyptian idols) toward God's promised land.

It was during his first 40 years in his wilderness that Moses became "the most humble man on the face of the earth." It was during this 40 years that he completely gave up himself and truly learned humility. It was in this wilderness that he completely gave up, humbled himself, and surrendered all his plans to save his people. His surrender was so complete that he had been delivered from all hope or desire of ever accomplishing anything for himself. It was then that God came to get him. After teaching him the ways of God, teaching him to listen and wait, and to hope and trust in the Lord, God came to deliver him from wandering in the bushes. It was then that Moses was ready, not to do what he wanted to do, but whatever God wanted him to do. It was then that Moses became "more humble than anyone else on the earth" (see Exodus 2 and 3 for the full story).

Moses was so humble that when God called him from out of the burning bush, he said, "I can't do that Lord. I can't lead those people. They won't listen to me. They won't believe what I say. I can't talk well at all. Even when God said, "I'll tell you what to say," Moses said,

"Please get someone else to talk for me." So God said He'd get Aaron to be Moses' spokesman. In fact, in Numbers 12:3 where is says that Moses was the most humble man on the earth, the story says that Aaron and Miriam, Moses' brother and sister, had spoken out against Moses because he had married an Ethiopian woman, and God was angry with them for it. God Himself defended Moses, and He even struck Miriam with leprosy for a little while. Moses was so humble that during the whole episode he never said a word, not one word, in his defense, nor anything bad about Aaron or Miriam. During the whole story, all that Moses did was to pray for Miriam to be healed from the leprosy. Pretty cotton-pickin' humble. The meekest man on the earth.

1 Chronicles 7:14

God said to Solomon, "If My people who are called by My name will humble themselves, and pray, and seek My face, and turn from their wicked ways, then I will hear from heaven, and will forgive their sin and heal their land."

Boy, this verse says a lot. God is not talking to just people in the Old Testament, nor is He talking to just anybody. He is talking to His people, to all those who claim the Name of Jesus—just us—not all the people who have not yet been touched by His Spirit.

What is the first thing He says to us? He says, "Humble yourselves." Quit thinking you're so great. Remember Who is really in charge here. Who is the Potter and who is the clay? (Isaiah 64:8) Who created the earth and everything in it? (Genesis 1) Oh, and quit thinking that you are in control! Quit thinking that you don't need Him to help you. If you really think that, you're just not paying attention; you are completely ignoring reality. Do you know why you think you don't need Him? For some, it is because of your affluence. The reason it is so hard for a rich man to get into heaven is because his money and his stuff insulate him from the hard facts of life. (Matt. 19:23) He begins to think that he really is in control, and he really doesn't need God.

Next, God says to pray. Pray for your needs. Pray that God will deliver you from all the bad things that are happening to people (sometimes to you) over which you have no control. Pray to God for His mercy to protect you from need, sickness, death, despair, divorce, and division in your family, your church, and your nation. Pray for God to help you realize how little and weak you are and how big and strong and loving He is. The real essence of prayer is coming to the realization of how humble you must be to have a genuine, enduring relationship with God. It is a great mystery that God makes you want to be humble, so you can be filled with His Spirit, grace, and power. (1 Timothy 3:16)

Next, He says, "Seek My Face." What does that mean? We do a lot of praying for stuff, and while this thought is not original with me, it bears repeating: "God didn't create us for what He could give us, even though it gives Him pleasure to give us stuff. He created us to be friends with Him; to talk with Him, to walk with him, to know Him for who He really is, to enjoy His Presence." That's probably the main reason that He loved Abraham, Moses, Elijah, Isaiah, and David; also Peter, Paul, James, and John—because they sought His Face. They didn't seek the stuff that He could provide; they already knew He would provide the stuff, so they didn't need to worry about that. They had time to think about, and feel, and know God for Himself.

John 17:3 says, "And this is eternal life, to know You, the one true God, and Jesus Christ, Whom You have sent." This verse really does talk about part of what God can give us, but even more, it talks about what "eternal life" is really all about, what life itself is all about. It is about knowing God for Who He is, not just for what He can give; to enjoy His Presence, every day, every hour, every minute, and every second. Only when we humble ourselves do we really come to know God and begin to and realize how big and strong He is, and how little and weak we are. Only then do we realize how badly we need to surrender ourselves and get out of the way, so God will come into our hearts and fill us up with His love, power, mercy, and grace, so we can truly experience what it means when it says, "Out of your innermost being will flow rivers of living water" (John 7:38). This is what it means when God says, "Seek My Face."

Continuing the passage, God says, "And turn from your wicked ways." That seems pretty simple, doesn't it? Quit doing all that bad stuff, which includes all the "works of the flesh [such as] adultery, fornication, uncleanness, lewdness, idolatry, sorcery, hatred, contentions, jealousies, outbursts of wrath, selfish ambitions, dissensions, heresies, envy, murders, drunkenness, revelries, and the like" (Galatians 5:19-21). Whew! When I read that whole list I think maybe the things I do aren't quite so bad after all. I only do a few of those things (now), and they're not too bad, right? Well, a sin is a sin, and the biggest Sin, the one with the "Big S," the one I'm always the most guilty of, is control, which is wanting to run my own life and not pay any attention to what God wants me to do.

As I've said before and will say again, I just cannot overcome my sinful nature by my own strength. The only way I can exhibit the "fruits of the Spirit" (Galatians 5:22) and give up the "works of the flesh" is to surrender my whole self to God, let Him fill me up with His Spirit, and let Him live His eternal life in me. Maybe the best I can do is to forgive those who sin against me, so God will forgive me for all the times I sin against Him. 'Course I guess it doesn't hurt to **try** to do right; to try to trust God and obey Him; to try to be obedient on a moment by moment basis. Maybe that's what it means when it says, "Turn from your wicked ways" in this passage. Mostly, what God wants for us is to humble ourselves before Him. When we do this, we will turn from our wicked ways, and He will hear our prayers, forgive our sins, and heal our land.

Micah 6:8

"What does the LORD require of you, but to do justly, to love mercy, and to walk humbly with your God?"

This verse makes me think of what someone said about getting down to the essence of things. In this case, how **do** you have a real, long-lasting (read 'eternal') relationship with God?

First, "do right" (more on this later). Second, "**love** mercy" (note the emphasis). In other words, **love** to receive mercy from God, and **love** to pass it along to others. Love not judging others, but leaving judgment to somebody else, and focus your whole attention on giving everyone as much mercy as you can. With forgiveness, we're supposed to forgive others in the same measure that we have been forgiven—likewise, mercy is both sides of the same coin. Give mercy abundantly, overflowing, not holding back, with all your heart and soul and strength. Love cutting everyone some slack, a lotta' slack, all the time. If they need judging, the world and ultimately God will see to it—not me; not you.

Third, "walk humbly with your God." What does that mean? The simple, clear part is that it means you are supposed to maintain an attitude of humility in relation to God, one that says, "Without God I'm a worthless piece of manure; so I better continually keep in mind

Who God is, and what a great privilege it is for me to get to know Him, and have a relationship with Him."

The harder part is what "walk humbly" means in relation to other people. What would it mean if we said, "Walk humbly, with your God," inserting a comma for clarification (to find the fuller, truer meaning). Then it would mean something different, perhaps something like, "Realizing that we are with God all the time, and He is with us all the time (whether we're paying attention or not), we should "walk humbly" with everyone around us. Don't think more highly of yourself than you ought to think (Romans 12:3). Don't take the best table at the banquet (Luke 14:8). Like it says in 1 Corinthians 13, "Don't demand your own way. Don't be jealous or boastful or proud or rude. Be patient [put up with them] and kind." Funny, that passage is supposed to be talking about love, but notice how it is all intermeshed with what it really means to be humble? What a blessing we'd all be to those around us if we just acted out that passage in our everyday, normal, ordinary lives. Surely that is what Micah is talking about when he says, "Walk humbly[,] with your God."

Matthew 5:3-12

Jesus said, "Blessed are the poor in spirit, for theirs is the kingdom of heaven. Blessed are those who mourn, for they shall be comforted. Blessed are the meek, for they shall inherit the earth. Blessed are those who hunger and thirst for righteousness, for they shall be filled. Blessed are the merciful, for they shall obtain mercy. Blessed are the pure in heart, for they shall see God. Blessed are the peacemakers, for they shall be called sons of God. Blessed are those who are persecuted for righteousness' sake, for theirs is the kingdom of heaven. Blessed are you when they revile and persecute you, and say all kinds of evil against you falsely for My sake. Rejoice and be exceedingly glad, for great is your reward in heaven, for so they persecuted the prophets who were before you."

This passage says a whole lot—far more than we can properly deal with in this small book. Within it is the verse, "Blessed are the meek [the humble], for they shall inherit the earth." We'll look at that more in a minute, but first, let's look at the whole passage.

What is the attitude of this passage? You know that line, supposedly gleaned from airplane pilots, "It is not the aptitude, but the attitude, which determines the altitude." What that seems to mean is, "It is not how good you are at something (or how powerful your engine is), but how your wings are adjusted (actually called the "attitude" of the wings), that determines how high you get." In flying, it's not the size of the motor but the angle of the wing flaps that determines the altitude. This passage is just full of attitude and all of it is humble.

"Blessed are the poor in spirit." Blessed people—happy and well spoken of, but who realize they're not much good and don't amount to much; they know they don't perform very well. Theirs is the kingdom of heaven. Did you hear that? They have heaven. Not later but now. This makes me think of another passage in 1 Corinthians 1:26, "For you see from your calling, brethren, that not many wise according to the flesh, not many mighty, not many noble, are called." The point is that if you realize you're not very wise, not very mighty, not very noble (I just figured out that means, "of high birth," which isn't me), then you are already a lot closer to God and to the attitude He wants all of us to have.

"Blessed are they that mourn." Blessed are you if you are in mourning for the way you are. If you are truly sad about the way you are, both inside and out, then you are ready, prepared, to let God comfort you. There's that attitude again, that humble attitude.

"Blessed are those who hunger and thirst after righteousness, for they shall be filled." Blessed are you if you've realized that you have no righteousness, no goodness, in and of yourself, because then you are ready, like an empty vessel, devoid of righteousness, to be filled with God and His righteousness. It's the only way we're going to get righteousness from God. Only when we've humbled ourselves, denied ourselves, and died to our sinful nature will we be filled with God and His righteousness. (Luke 9:23)

"Blessed are the merciful, for they shall obtain mercy." Like I said earlier, give forgiveness, get forgiveness; give mercy, get mercy. Give a little, get a little. Give a lot, get a lot. Remember that with mercy, "the same measuring stick you use to measure others will be used to measure you!" (Luke 6:38). If you regularly excuse the faults of others, and even *make excuses for them* to others, God will do the same for you. If you don't, then God won't do it for you (Luke 6:37). Remember, it's not really that He isn't willing to show you mercy; rather, it's that you are not willing to receive His mercy, because you are unwilling to share His mercy with others.

"Blessed are the pure in heart." Is there anybody out there who is really pure in heart? I don't know, but I do know I have met very few, and the few I've met have been little old people who have long ago given up thinking they're somebody. They gave up any illusions of how great they were; they surrendered their whole hearts to God, and God poured a full dose of His purity into them. They were all about God and not about them; they were about pure, unadulterated, whole, entire love. That's humble.

"Blessed are the peacemakers." Why them? Why does God bless them? Maybe it's because in order to be a peacemaker, you have to know about being humble. You have to attribute the best motives to both sides in order to find the middle ground of peace. Maybe it's because you can't be the "ruler" and expect either side to genuinely agree to peace. Maybe peace only comes from God (really), and if you're going to "make peace," you're going to have to get yourself and all of your selfish stuff out of the way, because that's the only way God can or will use you to "make peace." Did you ever think about the word "selfish"? We always think it means some attitude about possession, usually of property, stuff, things. But "self-ish" really is a lot more about me having my way. It's not just about stuff; it's more about control—my ball, my game, my goal posts, my way. If you don't do things my way, then I'm not going to play with you anymore. I'm just going to pack my stuff and go home. Not much humble in that, is there?

"Blessed are you who are persecuted for righteousness sake." First, what does that mean? Condemned for being good? Condemned for being godly? I don't know for sure, but it seems as if God is saying, "You are approved by me if you allow yourself to be talked bad about, without saying anything back, without cursing the people who persecute you, being willing to turn the other cheek, to walk the mile (and the extra mile), to give up your coat and your cape (Matthew 5:40-41). Maybe that's adding some to the passage, and I have no intention of doing that, but it definitely says something about your attitude if you are persecuted for righteousness sake, and that attitude is all about being humble.

"Blessed are you when men shall revile you and persecute you, and say all manner of evil against you falsely, for My sake." I don't know why, but every time I read this verse I think about the martyrs, those who were burned at the stake, stoned to death, thrown to the lions, or tortured in the Inquisitions. In Hebrews 11:37-38, it even talks about these special people: "They went about in sheepskins and goatskins, destitute, persecuted and mistreated—the world was not worthy of them." And I always think of the story about the stoning of Stephen, where he is in the middle of being stoned to death, and he says, "Lord, do not charge them with this sin." How's that for an attitude? It's nothing if it's not humble and forgiving. Whew! Just a regular man, like me and you, and he thought so little of himself that he could pray for his attackers at a time like that. Must've been God in his heart!

"Blessed are the meek, for they shall inherit the earth." I guess when I was a kid, I used to think that meant if you were really mild mannered and easy going, and wouldn't say anything bad about anybody ever, and always put others ahead of yourself, and you were just genuinely happy about it too; that in some miraculous way, after a long, long time, you would get to rule the earth (along with the other really meek people) while everybody else went to heaven (or hell). Confusing, you say? Maybe. Maybe it's about the new heaven and the new earth, and when the new Jerusalem comes down out of the sky, and it's 1,500 miles long and 1,500 miles wide (Revelation 21); the meek, along with the apostles, will rule the "new earth." What do I know? Whatever is going to happen, why the meek? Why the humble? Why are they going to be blessed? What if "inherit the earth" means something spiritual as opposed to something physical. Maybe that's a pretty good bet, but for purposes of this discussion, let's just say that the rewards for being meek (humble) will be pretty good. It will be a high level of reward. Being humble makes God happy with you; He will be glad to talk nice to you and about you. So humble is good. Why? I guess it must come back to the attitude. If you humble yourself, give up yourself, deny yourself, die to yourself, surrender yourself, and give plumb up (daily), then Jesus by His own Holy Spirit will come into your own private little heart and fill you up to overflowing. I can say without reservation that you will be blessed!

Luke 9:23

"If anyone would be My disciple, let him deny himself, and take up his cross daily, and follow me."

This is one of the central verses in the message of Jesus while He was on the earth in bodily form. If we're talking about learning humility, what does it mean for someone to "deny himself" and "take up his cross"? Learning humility is all about giving up self. And giving up self is about denying what you want and making the willing choice to do whatever God wants, even if you don't know what it is going to be. Willingly stopping seeking what you want in lieu of whatever God wants is definitely a humbling experience. It's kinda' like Abraham (then known as Abram) having the following conversation with God (see the story in Genesis 12):

"Abram, get on your camel and ride off into the desert," God said.

"Where we going Lord?" Abram asked.

"I'll tell you when we get there," God answered.

Humility is about giving up control of your own life so God can take control of it.

But an even clearer indication of the humility involved in becoming Jesus' disciple is the phrase, "take up your cross." What does that mean? Galatians 2:20, says, "I have been crucified with Christ; it is no longer I who live, but Christ lives in me; and the life which I now live in the flesh I live by faith of [trust in] the Son of God, who loved me and gave Himself for me." What does this verse have to do with being humble? Well, how much more humble can you get than being crucified? This verse is all about surrendering, humbling yourself, and letting Jesus live His life in you so that His faith (trust), His love, and His humility come to dwell in you. It's kinda' like Philippians 2:5-8 where it talks about, "Jesus, being found as a man, humbled Himself and became a slave, and was obedient unto death, even death on a cross." The whole passage starts out with, "Let this mind [this attitude] be in you, which was also in Christ Jesus." He humbled Himself and became a slave, and He was obedient unto death, even death on a cross. The start is "Be like Jesus!" and Galatians 2:20, says, "I am crucified with Christ"; on purpose, because I want to be like Jesus.

James 4:6, 10 (and parallels)

"But He gives more grace. Therefore He says: 'God resists the proud, but gives grace to the humble'" (v. 6). "Humble yourselves in the sight of the Lord, and He will lift you up" (v. 10).

"God resists the proud . . . But gives more grace to the humble, therefore humble yourselves under the mighty Hand of God, that He may exalt you in due time" (1 Peter 5:5-6).

"The Lord mocks the mockers [scorns the scornful] but gives grace to the humble" (Proverbs 3:34). The Greek version says the same thing: "The Lord opposes the proud, but favors the humble."

Do you think there might be something to it? Do you think that maybe this is a real promise that we could rely on? You've probably heard some of the prosperity preachers who say that you've got to claim the promises of God and that if you don't, then He may not realize you need that promise in your life, and He won't do anything about it, even though He has made this promise in no uncertain terms. Well, I'm not absolutely convinced that we have to claim God's promises in order to avail ourselves of them. While it may apply sometimes, I am absolutely sure that you can claim this promise, and you can enjoy the promise of these verses, just by giving up yourself, denying yourself, surrendering to God, and letting Him lift you up.

This particular promise is a "two for one." What does it mean when it says, "grace," "favor," or "more grace"? And what does it mean when it says, "lift you up"? Somebody said that grace is "unmerited favor." Sometime when I was pretty young, I figured out that "unmerited favor" means this: When you do something that is really bad, something you know you weren't supposed to do, something your momma lectured you about over and over, something you are really ashamed of because you knew going in that it was wrong, and that you were going to have to pay if anybody found out—but you did it anyway (on purpose, not accidentally). Then, when you got caught, you were really sorry, and you were ready to admit it, confess it, accept the punishment, and pay the penalty.   Even though you're willing and prepared to pay, God says, "This is your lucky day! You don't have to pay! Even though you deserve all the punishment I could give you, you don't have to pay!"

I know, there's a bunch of highly respected theologians and spiritually astute, truly surrendered ministers who would disagree with my interpretation, my extreme explanation of the time and circumstance of grace, but that is it anyway. The short version is this, "By grace are you saved through faith [trust in God], and not of yourselves, it is the gift of God, not of works [anything you did, good or bad], lest any man should boast" (Ephesians 2:8-9). God just forgives you because He wants to, not because you deserve it, not because you're sorry, not because of any reason you could ever dream up, but just because He loves you.

As if that wasn't enough, he admonishes everybody else to forgive you, to cut you some slack, and basically just forget it ever happened, just because He can. He's God, He's sovereign, and He can do whatever He wants, even stop the orderly succession of His own rules. That to me is even better than I ever expected. I've had this happen to me over and over in my life—stupid habits; stupid business decisions; stupid personal decisions; saying the wrong thing at the wrong time to the wrong person. Of course, I didn't get delivered from my stupidity every time, but it happened a whole lot more than I deserved. Sometimes, God lets me stand close to the fire so I can feel the heat and learn something that I wouldn't have known otherwise, and then He lets me up.

Of course, I guess you can't tell your children this, for fear they'll run off and do a bunch of very stupid stuff, and you'll lose all control. The question is, "Did you ever have any real control anyway, beyond trusting God?" You might be wondering what happened to the rule that sooner or later we all have to take responsibility for our own actions. We can't run around thinking God is going to save us every time we do something stupid. Even though God does forgive us for our sins, the consequences of our actions are something we have to deal with every time, because that's the way God designed the universe, to run according to rules, just like gravity. Yet that's not exactly what these verses say, which is that if we'll humble ourselves, God will give us "more [unmerited] favor." In a hundred different ways throughout the Bible, it says the same thing—if we'll just trust Him, He'll take care of us. It seems to me like that's the central theme of the Bible, and it is certainly a central theme of this book. So even though this is against all the rules, I still believe that God is God, and He can do whatever He wants, even help us when we don't deserve it. The God I serve is a God who really does deliver me from evil, even when I've done something really stupid. That's grace. I like grace!

What does it mean when it says God will "lift you up"? I used to think it meant that He will lift you up in the eyes of the world, before other people, that he will make you look good, maybe even better than other people. I must've missed the whole point. Sometime back God told me that it means, "Lift you up to Me." Since I came to my senses, the only thing I ever wanted anyway was to be close to God and to get to spend every day with Him. I want to be there when God moves, in my life and in the lives of other people; I want to see God touch people's hearts and see them changed forever. Wow!

So the simple version of these verses is that if I will only recognize reality—how little I am and how big God is; how smart He is and how stupid I am; how weak I am and how strong He is—then He will give me grace, even "more grace" than he's already given me, and He will lift me up to Himself, starting right now; not later, not when we all get to heaven, but right now!

1 Corinthians 1:25-31

"Because the foolishness of God is wiser than men, and the weakness of God is stronger than men. For you see from your calling, brothers and sisters, that not many wise according to the flesh, not many mighty, not many noble, are called. But God has chosen the foolish things of the world to put to shame the wise, and God has chosen the weak things of the world to put to shame the things which are mighty; and the base [dirty] things of the world and the things which are despised God has chosen, and the things which are not, to bring to nothing the things that are, that no flesh should glory in His presence. But of Him you are in Christ Jesus, who became for us wisdom from God—and righteousness and sanctification and redemption—that, as it is written, 'He who glories, let him glory in the LORD.'"

Do you want to hear something funny? Until the third century, sometime after 200 A.D., the Church wouldn't even let lawyers be members (probably because they didn't trust them!). In fact, until Constantine the Great became Emperor and then converted to Christianity, very few of the wealthy, educated, high-born people (royalty) were members of the church. Mostly Christianity was a "Way" for the poor, sick, slaves, servants, criminals, and don't forget tax-collectors. "The Way" was for the hated and despised people, the strangers, foreigners, half-breeds, prostitutes, bastards, lepers, and even the blind, lame, orphans, and widows—it was for all those who were rejected by the in-crowd.

This verse, however, says that God chose those exact people to represent Him on this earth; He chose them on purpose to let all the rich, powerful, smart, well educated, and royal people know that they weren't such hot stuff after all. He chose society's rejects to let in-crowd know that God is God, and for all their natural advantages, God is the real Source of life, power, and authority over all, and that He bestows His blessings on whomever He wants.

This goes to show you what a sense of humor God has. He showed "those guys" that they didn't have a corner on the market of acceptability. He also showed that He is going to use the little people to accomplish His purposes in this world, whether the big guys like it or not.

Why is that? Because God likes humble people. He likes to bless people who know they are humble. Luke 5:31-32 says, "Jesus told the Pharisees, 'The healthy people don't need a doctor, but the sick. I came not to call the righteous [those who think they're good], but to call sinners [those who know they're sinners] to repentance." The humble know they need help, so they're receptive. The people who think they're righteous don't need God. It's like the verse that says, "It is easier for a camel to go through the eye of a needle than for a rich man to enter the kingdom of God." (Matt. 19:24) Why? 'Cause a rich man thinks he doesn't need God. He doesn't need heaven. He's got money. What does he need with God? Wait and see.

So it sounds to me like there's going to be a bunch of formerly poor, uneducated, and ignorant but supremely happy people in heaven praising and giving all the glory to God for His mercy and grace. All because they were humble. Maybe they didn't like things much when they were on the earth, but they knew God was going to deliver them from this world. Or maybe, because they were humble, they really surrendered to God and let Him take care of them, inside and out, and He let them enjoy heaven beginning while they were still here on the earth. That's what being humble will do for you—if you humble yourself before God, He will lift you up!

The passage says "not many wise." After Peter and John spoke to the Sanhedrin (the High Priests, Pharisees, and Sadducees), Acts 4:13 says, "13 Now when they saw the boldness of Peter and John, and perceived that they were uneducated and untrained men, they marveled. And they realized that they had been with Jesus."

"Not many mighty"? How's David and Goliath to support that concept? A boy, maybe a 15-year-old, turns a whole army to flight by killing one 9-foot tall giant? Must be God (see the whole story in 1 Samuel 17).

"Not many noble"? Mostly, Jesus used the blind, lame, demon-possessed, and lepers to bring glory to God. He liked to tell stories, like the one about the Pharisee and the tax collector, asking, "Who do you think was justified? The Pharisee who extolled himself before God; or the tax collector who said, 'Have mercy on me, a sinner'"? (Luke 18:10-14).

It's all about being humble. God loves people who are humble. He loves them so much that He willingly puts all the "big guys" to shame just to lift up the humble. Like when Jesus said, "He who exalts himself will be humbled; but he who humbles himself will be exalted." (Luke 14:11)

The best part for us is the last part of the passage, "Christ Jesus, who became for us wisdom from God—and righteousness and sanctification and redemption" Jesus became all these things for us, that is, we receive all these things through Him, by His Spirit working within us. God is glorified because everybody standing around watching knows for sure that we couldn't possibly have become all those things by ourselves. If it can't be us doing it, then it must be God!

Baptism (Matthew 3)

It is in the spiritual order of things that in our spiritual lives we must follow the example of Jesus in His ministry on this earth. He submitted Himself to baptism, which is a symbol and example of his submission to death and resurrection as ordained by God, to fulfill all prophecy, and then the Holy Spirit came upon Him and He began to fulfill God's will and purpose for Him.

So, in order for us to fulfill God's plan for each of our lives, we must submit ourselves, we must surrender ourselves, we must humble ourselves to death and resurrection with Jesus, so we can receive the Holy Spirit and fulfill God's will, which is God's ministry for us. It is only when we humble ourselves, when we willingly and daily submit to dying to our natural selves, that we can fulfill the calling of God for each of our lives. Only when we become humble will He raise us up to Himself, just like He raised Jesus up, lifting Him up to Himself.

THEME 3: THANKSGIVING

THE VALLEY OF THE SHADOW

In May 1970, a boy, call him Jim, 21, was inducted into the U.S. Army. He was married to Glenda almost a year and they had a five month old son, Tom. On May 5th, Jim caught a bus from Colorado Springs to Denver, where he was sworn in that afternoon. He was at Fort Lewis, Washington, before dark.

He shouldn't even have been there since he'd been in school on a 2-S deferment that kept him out of the Army. But when Glenda got pregnant they got married and he dropped out of school. As soon as the draft board found out, he was promoted to 1-A. I don't know what he was thinking; certainly he wasn't thinking much or clearly. Maybe he thought he'd dodge that bullet, but no such luck.

Then he got a letter from the draft board to go take a physical, which he passed. A month or two later, he got a new job, traveling sales, and they moved to Colorado. He thought that he'd get lost in the system and Viet Nam would be over before he got drafted. Right. When his birthday was assigned number 47 in the first draft lottery, he knew he was toast. Rumor had it that everyone under number 100 was going. Jim and Glenda tried not to think about it, but it didn't go away, and soon came the letter to report. They packed all their stuff in two days, so Glenda and their infant son Tom could move in with the in-laws 'till after basic. It was a sad goodbye.

Jim figured he'd be going to the infantry and straight to Nam, since that was the path of most draftees. He long ago decided that he was not going to join any military organization to avoid being drafted, and have to serve four years instead of two. I guess he thought he'd get lucky and they'd send him somewhere, anywhere, but Nam. But God was looking out for him. He made a perfect score on his Army language aptitude test, and they gave him a choice. He could go to Vietnamese language school and become an interpreter, or he could go to the infantry—it didn't take him long to figure that one out. So he was on orders for Viet Nam from the seventh day of his service. Things were getting darker and darker.

It took them a long time to get his papers straightened out, so he had to hang around his basic training unit for three weeks after it was over. Then he had a two-week leave during which he flew to Knoxville, Tennessee, to get Glenda and Tom, and then drive to Ft. Bliss in El Paso, Texas, to the Defense Language Institute of the Southwest for Vietnamese language school. Talk about culture shock—seven months of eating, sleeping, and breathing Vietnamese, the desert, and cheap Mexican food. It must've been God though because Glenda's sister and brother-in-law lived in El Paso. Glenda got pregnant again, and she was due with their second child in May, a month or so after the school was over.

About April Fool's Day, Jim was on a plane for Baltimore, to go to another school at Ft. Holabird, Maryland, for interrogation training. Glenda, Tom, and the "baby to be" stayed in El Paso. That was the last three months before going to Nam, and during that period Jim became friends with some Friends from the Quaker church who told him about becoming a conscientious objector. By this time, he was pretty much totally depressed with life. Long before he got drafted, he had been convinced that Viet Nam was wrong, and he had been against the war. Even before being inducted, he'd thought about going to Canada as a political statement. Of course he didn't want to go— he had a family; a wife and a son, and he was scared some, too. The reason he filed though was because he had done a lot of thinking about all this: the theory, the practice, the politics, the right and the wrong. What would God think?

At the time, the authorities told him that if he wanted to succeed in his application for conscientious objector status, he would have to establish that he was against **all** wars; not just against the Viet Nam war. When he sat down to write his application, he began to think about who he really was and what he really believed. It would have been a lot easier if this were WWII. Then there had been a clear and noble cause—a real evil enemy that had sworn to take over the world, and the Americans were almost the only thing standing between the world and oblivion. This time, there were a lot of "little" enemies; this time, it wasn't so black and white. A paradigm shift in political thought had led people astray. We were no longer true believers in the "American Way." This time millions of people were saying the government was wrong.

Jim spent a lot of time wrestling with his religious beliefs. He came from a long line of true-blue Americans who believed in God, country, and family. In the end, his application sounded a lot like a sermon in support of doing what the Bible said, which was not exactly what he learned at school or in Sunday school. Everybody knew that all patriotic Americans obeyed their leaders without questioning, such as in Alfred Lord Tennyson's, *The Charge of the Light Brigade,* "Ours is not to reason why, ours is but to do or die," or like Patrick Henry said, "Give me liberty or give me death."

The only problem this time was that American liberty wasn't threatened; the Domino Theory didn't really hold water. Jim had been studying history and political theory nearly his whole life, and the voices of the Founding Fathers kept coming back to him. All men are created equal, with certain inalienable rights, including life, liberty, and the pursuit of happiness. They have a duty to defend their liberties against the government. Unlike in WWII, this time it was the government that had become the most egregious recurring threat to American lives and liberties, much more than foreign aggressors. In this situation, somebody had to stand up against the government. Even one voice crying out could not ultimately be silenced. This was more than a theory; this was something for which people went into exile; indeed, this was a belief for which young men went to prison. Yes, conventional wisdom said they were fools. Conventional wisdom be hanged!

Then Jim thought about his spiritual upbringing, which, sad to say, was like that of many other people in the world. Many questions were subject to interpretation, and there were a lot of gray areas. Lots of times you just have to leave it up to God and let Him take care of it. You get to wait to see what He's going to do. In the meantime, there's a lot to think about: what you believe, what you trust: about God, about the church, about people who claim to be Christians, about the ones who really **act** like they believe. You get to see what happens when you are really in a bind, and there's actually nowhere to go except to lean on God. Then you hope to goodness that all that stuff you **said** you believed is really true.

In the end, Jim wrote down what it said in the Bible. He wrote down the line where Solomon said, "Trust in the Lord with all your heart and lean not to your own understanding" (Proverbs 3:5). He wrote down the story about Shadrach, Meshach and Abednego, where they said to King Nebuchadnezzar, "[God] will deliver us from your hand, O king. But if not, let it be known to you, O king, that we do not serve your gods, nor will we worship the gold image which you have set up"'" (Daniel 3:17-18). He wrote down the stories about how God delivered the Israelites from their enemies when there was absolutely no hope. He wrote about Gideon, Hezekiah, and Abraham, and others in the 11th chapter of Hebrews such as David and Goliath, and David when he said in Psalm 20:7, "Some trust in horses and some in chariots, but we will remember the name of the Lord our God, they are struck down and fallen, but we are risen and stand upright."

At the end of his discourse, Jim said, "If we really believed what it says in the Bible, we wouldn't need armies, because we could trust God." It may sound silly now, or cowardly, like he didn't have any choice, like he was cornered, so he would say something stupid and hope that a miracle happened. But that's what he said, and that's what he did. His letter was a prayer of faith. He had gotten himself into this corner where he had nowhere else to go, so he put all his money on God. He laid down his life at God's feet and prayed that something good would happen.

Because of Army procedures, Jim had to go through three consultation/examinations. One was with a chaplain/pastor, one with a psychiatrist, and one with a board of review. The pastor said that while he understood Jim's position, he did not agree with it and suggested he reconsider. The psychiatrist found Jim to be mentally stable but told him he was asking for a lot of trouble.

It was the review board that was the crowning blow for the Army. Seven officers and six senior enlisted men manned the board, and the chairman was the executive officer of the company Jim was in. The review started in mid-afternoon and continued long into the night. It started with a statement by the chairman, which was followed by a very short statement by Jim. Then there was an unending succession of questions by each of the 12 board members—what did Jim expect to gain; what he was trying to prove; what would he do with the rest of his life after being branded a traitor. There were two or three "recesses," during which one or another of the senior enlisted men would take him aside and tell him all the good things he'd be missing, and then he was brought back to the full board and told what a worthless piece of manure he was for filing a Conscientious Objector (C.O.) application. They even told him that it was almost certain that his application would be rejected, as that was the case for nine out of ten.

Jim held on. By this time in the process, he was convinced that he was right, and he wasn't going to give up. He was determined to see the application through to the end, but he remained respectful, continuing to answer the questions while absorbing the attacks. Finally, it was over, and they had not persuaded him to change his mind. In fact, they had consolidated his position. Looking back after the review, he was sure that had his application been rejected, he would have refused to continue to participate in the system, resulting in being sentenced to some term of imprisonment (usually five years) and a dishonorable discharge from the Army. Positively crazy how your life looks sometimes.

They took him out of the interrogation classes and assigned him as a clerk to the commanding colonel of the post. Usually, it took a month or two for the Army to review an application and make a ruling. After that, if they rejected your application, you could appeal the rejection to the local U.S. District Court, and they might overturn the ruling but that was rare. In the meantime, Jim was treated as a regular soldier—no punishment, no imprisonment, nobody berating or condemning him. Instead, he was imprisoned by the thoughts of what awaited him. Just when he thought everything bad that *could* happen *had* happened, a whole new unexpected development reared its ugly head.

While Jim and Glenda were waiting for the news about the ruling on his application for a C.O. discharge from the Army; waiting to see if he was going to prison, or go free; they were blind-sided by another catastrophe. Jim got a call saying his second son had been born with a rare and serious facial birth defect. Still in the hospital after the delivery, Glenda was in shock. His name was Ben, and he was generally healthy, with good weight and good length, but he had an external nasal proboscis. One of his nostrils had separated from the other and grown out on his face like a little finger attached at the top of his nose. None of the doctors at the Army hospital in El Paso had ever seen anything like it, and they didn't know what to do. Jim was in shock, too. In his 21-year-old mind, the world was falling in on his 19-year-old wife, and he was more than 2,000 miles away and couldn't help.

He went out on the porch at his office and cried out to God; and God was gracious. His commanding officer allowed him an emergency leave to visit his family in El Paso. For many reasons, he and Glenda decided that in four weeks Jim would come back and they'd drive back to Baltimore, over a weekend. It would be a strain, but at least they'd be together. They rented a third floor walkup apartment with no furniture but an old baby bed they carried with them on top of the car. It only fell off once, sliding down the highway, coming to rest in the median, still in one piece. Another small miracle. They found a couch in a junk heap behind the apartment and Glenda covered it with railroad engine upholstery fabric. Jim built a table and four chairs at the craft shop on the post.

Ben was happy and healthy except for his "problem." Jim and Glenda were young and clueless, so the Army doctors suggested they take him to Johns Hopkins University Hospital, because it was a teaching and research facility and had more resources than any place around. Johns Hopkins had a doctor who correctly diagnosed the condition and offered them a course of treatment, or at least a vision of what would be involved. They were still in shock, but they were beginning to think there might be hope for Ben. With the C.O. ruling still hanging over them like the shadow of death, all they could do was wait.

Waiting, on the salary of a Spec 4 in the Army, meant they had nowhere to go; they were strangers in a strange land. They managed to gather up enough gas money to drive to Washington, DC a couple of times and walk around and see the sights (at least those that had free admission). Once, they even drove to New York, camping in the back of their car at a park in New Jersey on the way; again, it was to see only the sights that were free. Their one luxury was a ferry ride to Staten Island, round trip for ten cents apiece.

They didn't realize it then, but God had given them enough faith and enough hope in their hearts to keep them through a very dark time. Hope does spring eternal, even in the worst of times. God didn't give them more than they could bear. So they waited for almost two months, and then, finally, the clouds broke. On August 2, while Jim was working at his desk in the Commanding Officer's office, the Colonel's secretary said, "The Colonel wants to see you." Jim went to the Colonel's door and knocked.

The Colonel said, "Come in." Jim entered, approached the desk and stood at attention. "Sit down," said the Colonel.

Jim said, "Yes Sir," and did.

The Colonel said, "We received a letter today from the Headquarters of the First Army about your case. Your application for Conscientious Objector discharge has been granted. You will be given an Honorable Discharge from the Army." The Colonel handed the letter to Jim.

It was all Jim could do to keep from jumping up and down, laughing and crying all at the same time. All Jim could say was, "Thank God."

Things went fast after that. It usually took about a week for someone to "process out" of the Army. Jim had to have an exit physical, a dental exam, fill out all the papers, turn them in, get them approved; only then would the orders be issued. For a few days, it was like walking on air for Jim and Glenda, but then the reality of their situation began to soak in.

Even though they were celebrating a major event in their lives, they were still young, uneducated, and unemployed, with a very large burden of debt staring them in the face. They didn't know what they could do about treatment for Ben. The doctors estimated all the treatments at $200,000, clearly a lifetime of debt. During that time, the Army recruiter even called Jim in and told him that, in spite of his C.O. discharge, he should re-enlist. At least that way the Army would pay for all the treatments for Ben. After all they'd been through, it seemed like a cruel joke.

It seemed like God had been taking care of them pretty well so far, however, and the Army was just not the place to be when it was the height of Viet Nam, especially for a guy with Jim's sentiments. When the recruiter told him he should re-enlist, he actually laughed. It wasn't loud or long but just a chuckle. He told the guy, "No thanks, we'll figure something out."

On August 10, 1971, Jim was given his discharge papers and officially discharged from the U.S. Army. The CO came out to his desk, gave him the papers, and said, "Here is your discharge. You are free to go. I have enjoyed getting to know you, and I wish you well in your future life. Have a safe trip back to Texas."

Jim said, "Thank you, Sir. Thank you for your nice treatment of me under difficult circumstances." (He had spent two hours thinking about what he would say; he even practiced it in front of the mirror.)

They spent the first night in Knoxville, Tennessee, at the home of Jim's dad, and the next morning they headed for Houston, Texas. The doctor they had seen at Johns Hopkins University Hospital in Baltimore, Dr. John Cooper, had recommended they go to Baylor Medical School in the Texas Medical Center in Houston to consult with them about what to do about Ben. They drove all day and all night, and they pulled into the parking lot at the Medical Center about 9:00 am. Since Jim had been in the Army for more than a year, he didn't have any civilian clothes that were presentable. He had sworn he wouldn't ever wear Army clothes again, even the Army boots, so he and Glenda, Tom, and Ben, walked into the waiting room of the Plastic Surgery Department with Jim in yellow and white striped bell bottoms and a pair of sandals! They told the receptionist who they were, why they'd come, on whose recommendation, and they showed the nurse Ben's nose.

In about two minutes, a Doctor Melvin Spira came out into the waiting room and invited them back to an examining room. They later found out that he was the head of the Plastic Surgery Section for the whole medical school. He examined Ben, took some pictures, and told them he would arrange for a meeting with a number of doctors the next morning. He said he'd like for them to come back at that time; they agreed they would do whatever he said. He said this was a very rare condition and it deserved special attention.

Jim said, "We just got out of the Army. We know this is going to be very expensive and we don't have any money."

Dr. Spira said, "Don't worry about that at all. We have access to financial assistance, and we'll see that everything is taken care of. Y'all go to a motel and get some rest, and we'll see you in the morning."

When they arrived at the hospital the next morning, they were ushered into a conference room in Dr. Spira's office. There were seven or eight doctors there besides Dr. Spira, all of whom were very interested in Ben. They were all discussing various aspects of the treatment, after which they sent Jim, Glenda, Tom, and Ben to get some X-rays of Ben's head. While they were gone, the doctors came up with a plan for the first surgery and said to come back in one month. It would be the first of many, maybe as many as ten or twelve. Dr. Spira told them they would stay in the hospital for several days after the surgery to make sure that Ben was healing properly. He told them to go home and get settled.

The conversation between Jim and Glenda on the way back to Lubbock went something like this. Jim said, "I can't believe how nice they're being to us."

Glenda agreed, saying, "They were so nice. They just took care of everything. Dr. Spira kept saying they will pay for everything. We won't have to pay for anything."

Jim kept thinking and saying, "This whole thing is just a miracle. A few days ago we were still wondering if we were ever going to get out of the Army, and we were worried sick about what would happen to Ben. Now, we're out of the Army, and we have the best doctors in Texas looking after our son for **free**! It just must be God. Nobody but God could possibly have arranged such a deal as this. Praise the Lord! Hallelujah!"

It was a trip from Houston to Lubbock full of praise and thanksgiving for all the things that God had done. It was a time of celebration such as neither of them had ever known. It was almost like being high, except better, because they still had their senses about them. For a day or two, they didn't think about any of their troubles because they were so astounded at their good fortune.

Even though they knew they'd have bad times in the future, this was a time of such rejoicing; it was such a memorable event in both of their lives that they'd never forget what God had done. He gave them a real sense of how much He loved and cared for them. It really made them think that if He would do all this for them in such a short time, they could count on Him to take care of them in the future. So they began to trust him more and more, in the good times and even in the bad times. Thank God! Thank God! Thank God!

What is the moral of this story? There are several morals. One is that though we often don't understand what is happening or why, God really is working all things together for good to those who love Him (Romans 8:28). Another moral is that even though we do inexplicably stupid things that get us into worlds of trouble, God uses those specific events to teach us wonderful lessons and draw us closer to Him and to each other. And what about the moral that some of us, maybe most of us, never really trust God, and call on Him for deliverance from all our self-imposed difficulties until we have nowhere else to go? Yet God loves us anyway, and comforts us, and protects us, and fixes our lives for years to come, and takes care of us "exceeding abundantly above all we could ask or think, by His power that is at work within us" (Ephesians 3:20), because we finally came back home, hat in hand, and trusted Him.

It is almost an afterthought to say that Jim and Glenda had **great** thanksgiving and rejoicing! Praising God from whom all blessings flow! Making a joyful noise to the Lord (Psalm 100:1)! They were really whooping it up all the way from Houston to Lubbock. If you had been there, it would have done your heart good.

TEX'S THOUGHTS ON THANKSGIVING

This section of the book is simply called "Thanksgiving" for the sake of brevity, but it talks about three areas of our relationship with God and each other: 1) Worship, 2) Praise, and 3) Thanksgiving. The reason it's all rolled into one is because each of those actions expresses the same attitude of the heart that God wants us to carry around with us all the time. The attitude of the heart that God wants us to give Him is one of happy, thankful, loving, humble trust, knowing beyond a shadow of a doubt that He is taking care of us and loving us even when it looks like the world is falling apart all around us.

We all need to feel that sense of mutual admiration and love between us and God that is expressed in each of those concepts. So what do you do to get God to come close to you? What do you do to please God and make Him happy? You worship Him and praise Him and thank Him!

Matthew 5:11-12

In the Sermon on the Mount, Jesus said, "Blessed are you when they revile and persecute you, and say all kinds of evil against you falsely for My sake. Rejoice and be exceedingly glad, for great is your reward in heaven, for so they persecuted the prophets who were before you."

You might ask, how is that possible? Blessed often is translated "happy." How can you possibly be happy when people are reviling (insulting) you and persecuting you, and saying all kinds of lies about you because you trust in Jesus? Well let me tell you. It may sound pretty crazy, but when you're standing there enduring the ridicule and the insults and the lies, you get this feeling in your heart, and you get this thought in your mind (must be God) that this is a little bit funny! These people are so far off in the bushes they don't even think God exists, and you start to think that you *are* happy, that you really are getting a blessing from God right then. Pretty crazy, isn't it?

That brings up the meat of Jesus' sermon. Rejoice when these things happen! Whoop it up, because it is so very neat that you love God and God loves you, and it really doesn't matter what those other people think—certainly not when you compare to what God thinks, and how great it is to have a close personal relationship with the one true God! Hallelujah!

As for the last part of this verse, that "your reward is great in heaven," I like that. I also I keep wondering how it could be any better than this, knowing that it's heaven to have the Spirit of the Lord God Almighty, of our Lord Jesus Christ, right here in our hearts and souls and bodies, right now, in spite of all the people out there who just don't get it. It is nice to be compared favorably to the prophets, most of whom were genuinely intelligent, courageous, faithful men and women, and I'd like to be put in the same category with them, but the real reason I'm rejoicing is that I get to have a close, personal relationship with God and Jesus and the Holy Spirit, just like them. To me, that's the best evidence of how God feels about you and how you feel about God, when you can rejoice even when you're being persecuted. (Think about Stephen, Acts 7:59-60)

1 Corinthians 13:6

Talking about what love is like, in this passage Paul says that love "does not rejoice in iniquity, but rejoices in the truth."

Do you know the word "iniquity"? Iniquity is hidden sin—those sins that only you and Jesus know about, those that don't show much to other people, the hidden sins that damage you inside. "Transgressions" are sins that are open to the public. In Isaiah 53:5-6, prophesying about Jesus, Isaiah says, "He was pierced for our transgressions; He was bruised (crushed) for our iniquities; the punishment that brought us peace was upon Him, and by His stripes we are healed. All we like sheep have gone astray, everyone into his own way, but the Lord has laid upon Him the iniquity of us all." Pierced refers to the time when they stuck a spear in Jesus side when He was hanging on the cross. Crushed refers to the bruises He sustained from the beatings he suffered. Those bruises were evidence of **our** hidden sins He carried for us.

So people who love God, people who love others with God's love, shouldn't rejoice in iniquity. We shouldn't rejoice in hidden sins, those of other people or of our own. We should turn away from iniquity; we should be saddened by it, and we should pray for God to forgive us and deliver us from our iniquities, and deliver others from their iniquities as well.

But there's more! We should rejoice in the Truth that Jesus is the King of kings, and that "God is the Light, and in Him there is no darkness at all." (1 John 1:5) We should rejoice that His love and light are spread abroad in the world; rejoice in the Truth of the Gospel that Jesus died for us and for our sins; rejoice that He rose from the dead and lives forever in the universe and in us. And that's the Truth!

Romans 12:9-17

In this passage, Paul talks about how if we claim to be Christians, we should act like it. He goes on to state some specifics of what that means, with characteristics like, "Don't be a hypocrite. Be genuine. Be kind and affectionate to each other; put others first. Be passionate about worshiping and serving the Lord. Rejoice in hope, be patient in tribulation, keep on praying. Take care of the needy. Entertain people in your home, especially humble people. Be nice to those who are mean to you. Don't cuss them or fight back. Rejoice with those who are happy, be sad with those who are sad. Be agreeable and humble; don't be conceited." Paul sounds almost human (not like an apostle) when he says, at the end, "Be nice to your enemy, because by being nice you heap coals of burning fire on his head." This may not be exactly the correct motivation for Christian behavior, which makes me think that God has a sense of humor, maybe even Paul as well.

Have you noticed from this verse that "acting like a Christian" is mostly about our attitude? It's about just being nice, and not being all bound up trying to "make out like" we're fine up-standing citizens, when we're really all just a bunch of sinners saved by grace. That we should act humble, instead of acting like we have all the answers that we're going to bestow on those poor ignorant people below us.

The right attitude is just being glad to get to be here, rejoicing that

God loves us, being willing to share that love with others, rejoicing in hope that God provides (the peace we have in our hearts) even at the worst of times, and being truly thankful that God has called us out of the darkness, the deep terrifying darkness, into the light of His unending love. Praise the Lord! (1 Peter 2:9-10)

Psalm 118

In this Psalm, David offers praises to God in all kinds of ways. In the middle, verse 22, he says, "The stone which the builders rejected has become the chief cornerstone. This was the Lord's doing; it is marvelous in our eyes. This is what the Lord has done; we will rejoice and be glad in it." David is talking about Jesus—He is the stone the builders rejected. The builders are the Jews, especially the leaders of the Jews. Jesus is the cornerstone of the living church, the Body of Christ. God did it. It is marvelous! Praise the Lord! We will rejoice and be happy! In verse 24, some versions say, "This is the day the Lord has made, we will rejoice and be glad in it." Other versions say, "This day the Lord has done this [He has made Jesus the cornerstone of the church], we will rejoice and be glad in it." Either way, we can **rejoice** at what the Lord has done, for us, in us and through us, **today**!

There are all kinds of reasons for us to be happy about our relationship with God through Jesus, and David doesn't mind saying so, especially about God's special plan for us, which is to be saved from ourselves so we can **really live**! Hallelujah!

Psalm 5:11-12

In this Psalm, David says to God, "But let all those rejoice who put their trust in You. Let them ever shout for joy, because You defend them. Let those who love Your Name be joyful in You. For You O Lord will bless the righteous with favor. You will surround him as with a shield." Just who are the righteous? It's those who have Jesus' righteousness, because they **trust in Him**.

So why should we rejoice? One reason is because we have put our trust in the Lord, and we know He is taking care of us. He **is** defending us, so we have this great reason to be joyful. Another reason we have to rejoice, to be thankful, and to praise and worship God is because we know He is blessing us—because we are righteous and because we have the righteousness of those who trust God, like Abraham (see Genesis 15:6, "Abraham believed [trusted] God and it was counted to him for righteousness").

How do you like that line, "With favor You will surround him with a shield." This makes me think of an invisible shield, a bulletproof, electron shield, so the galactic invaders can't touch you. Even better, this shield comes with God's favor. When you have God's favor, it means that God likes you and almost everyone else likes you, too, because God influences them on your behalf. Yes, I know you may think I'm kidding. You may say that doesn't happen, certainly not in this day and age. *Au contraire!* I have personally experienced favor and witnessed it in the lives of others. It's almost like being golden; for no apparent reason, good things just happen. Why? Because God enjoys granting favor to people, especially to those who trust Him. It's like 'ole David says in the end of the 23rd Psalm, "Surely goodness and mercy shall follow me, all the days of my life, and I will dwell in the house of the Lord forever." That's what favor feels like.

So rejoice! Be happy! Be thankful! Enjoy God's favor!

1 Thessalonians 5:16-18

In Paul's first letter to the Thessalonians, in the farewell portion, he says, "Be cheerful no matter what; pray all the time; thank God no matter what happens. This is the way God wants you who belong to Christ Jesus to live" (*The Message*)." In the NKJV for this passage it says, "Rejoice always, pray without ceasing, in everything give thanks; for this is the will of God in Christ Jesus for you." If, as it says in *The Message*, this is the way God wants you to live (if you belong to Jesus), isn't it interesting that it makes such a point about being happy in your life with Jesus? It makes you think that God really expects that if we have a close personal relationship with Him we are actually going to be **happy**. Novel concept, huh? Diverges substantially from the way many garden variety Christians act, doesn't it?

I hear stories about people in many other nations, who claim to be happy, even ecstatic, about the fact that they know Jesus as their Lord and Savior. I hear stories that when they get saved they go out in the streets and tell everyone they meet about how **great** it is to know

Jesus, to have His own personal Spirit living in their own personal hearts. Some of them stay up all night listening to each other tell stories about all the miracles that Jesus has done and is doing in their lives. It reminds me of the stories of how Paul would stay up until the wee hours of the morning, after he'd been preaching all day, still telling stories about how **great** his God was! (Acts 20:7-12) They have these great revivals in Africa, for example, where tens of thousands of people walk, yes **walk**, miles and miles, from all over the country, just to hear people talk about Jesus, and sing, and worship God. Many then are saved, healed, and delivered from demons, and their lives are changed **forever**. Whole families get saved at once, and people are rejoicing like you never heard. Talk about happy! In one way, I think it's a great testimony to the presence of God in their lives and their churches, that some churches in Africa, Asia, and South America are sending missionaries to the U.S. to tell people **here** about Jesus!

When I read this passage that says, "Rejoice always," the above kind of happiness is what I think of. Of course, just as important is being happy in the quiet times in life, like David writes in Psalm 46:10, "Be still and know that I am God." It's like when you're walking home from school on a Friday afternoon, thinking about how nice it is that you're not going to have to go back to school for two whole days, and no homework before Sunday evening, and you can play all day tomorrow. That is definitely what "Be cheerful" is all about. You're even happy to do a few chores before your mom tells you to. Whoa.

Rejoice always . . . be cheerful all the time . . . these verses also apply when you're visiting someone in prison, when you're sitting in the surgery waiting room at a hospital, or when you're visiting people in the old folks home. Being happy is a tool that God uses to lift the gloom and doom that often hangs in the air in such places. Everyone needs a little relief, and sometimes it is truly a relief to meet someone who is genuinely happy in their hearts. That's exactly how God wants us to live. That's light—it's a small stream of living water flowing out from you to those people with a semi-permanent state of depression—that's the life and love of Jesus is one human package.

What does "Pray without ceasing" mean, in the context of being happy and thankful? Lots of people seem to think that praying is a fairly formal event, something that is usually only done by preachers, priests, or missionaries; or something only done on special occasions, like weddings, funerals, ordinations, or inaugurations. Some of us still pray at meals and at bedtime if we have small children. A few still pray out loud before going on a trip or before starting a new job. All those times are great for making contact with God. I thank God that He is alive and well in our country and in our culture so that we still think enough of Him to pray and talk to Him at great events. To humble ourselves, and pray, and seek His face, and maybe even turn from our wicked ways for just a moment, to acknowledge His presence in our lives. Thank God.

But that's not exactly the kind of praying I'm talking about. That's kind of like what my daddy used to call "light bread." Some people say that bread made with refined flour doesn't have much nourishment left in it. I always say it's a whole lot better than no bread at all. You'll live a lot longer on light bread and water than you will on nothing. So thank God for public praying. It's a whole lot better than nothing.

The kind of prayer I'm talking about, the kind of prayer I think this passage is talking about, is substantially different from that. It's not exactly like an activity where you're actually focusing your conscious mind on God and specifically talking to Him about specific issues, or events, or material things in your life. It's more like an attitude, an awareness of God's presence, a knowing down deep in your heart, that God is here inside you, and that He's listening to what's going on, not just in your public life, but also in your heart. It's something you can feel. You feel it when you hear a certain song, read a story, or hear someone speak a truth, and God, who is still there in your heart, smiles and says, in that still small voice, "Wow, isn't that a great line!" Sometimes you feel it when you see a little baby, a puppy, a kitten, or the bud of a small flower that is the first to open in your flowerbed. That's God. I don't guess you actually hear words, but you certainly get the message.

There's a funny thing about this kind of praying. You kinda' get in a zone where you're waiting to hear Him say something, when you're actually expecting Him to say something; and when you least expect it, He does! It's like those times when you ask someone how they're doing, and they actually start to tell you something real like, "I'm really scared. My momma is in the hospital and she's had a stroke, and they don't know if she's going to live," or "My wife just told me that she's leaving, and she wants a divorce," or "Our son is on hard drugs and he just got arrested." Let me tell you, you never know what to say, but you try to listen, and when you open your mouth, you hear yourself saying things like you never heard before. You hear life (Jesus' Life) coming out of your mouth.

I guess this kind of praying is more about listening than it is about talking, and the more you listen, the better it gets. Then when you do say something, it's amazing how it touches the person you're talking to, and touches you, too—truly amazing, truly miraculous.

The question then is, "How do you get into this zone?" In my experience, it takes some time. It takes a lot of "Seeking the Lord where He may be found, call on him while he is near" (Isaiah 55:6). It takes a lot of "Seeking His Face," (2 Chronicles 7:14) and getting to know Him, not just what He can do for you. It takes a lot of "drawing near to God so He'll draw near to you" (James 4:8). It doesn't happen overnight, but if you persist, you'll wake up some day, and you'll notice that things are a little different. You'll begin to hear and see things in a little different way. You'll begin to hear yourself saying different things in a different way than before, and you'll notice that your words are having a different effect. You'll know that something is definitely going on, even if you can't express it in words. That's God moving in your life.

You'll also find, after you've been in this zone awhile, that you've quit thinking about asking God for stuff, and you're just waiting on God to show you more of Himself. I'm beginning to think this is what Jesus was talking about in His prayer in John 17:20-23, "My prayer is not for them alone. I pray also for those who will believe [trust] in me through their message, **that all of them may be one, Father, just as you are in me and I am in you. May they also be in us** so that the world may believe that you have sent me. I have given them the glory that you gave me, that they may be one as we are one—I in them and you in me—so that they may be brought to complete unity. Then the world will know that you sent me and have loved them even as you have loved me."

Now that I think about it, I think this "oneness" with God, Jesus, and each other, this "complete unity" that God and Jesus and the Holy Spirit are bringing us to, this love that God has loved Jesus (and us) with, is the condition that Paul is talking about when he says "pray without ceasing," "pray continually," or "pray all the time."

I'm convinced that if you get up in the morning, get down on your knees beside your bed, and tell God/Jesus/the Holy Spirit that you love Him, that you want to give yourself and your life completely to Him again today so He can do whatever He wants to do with you, and if you listen for what he says and do it, that you will gradually come to the place Jesus is talking about in His prayer in John 17. I'm praying that you'll do it, and I'm thanking God that it's going to happen.

The next question is, in this passage, why is "pray without ceasing" bracketed with "be happy" on one end and "give thanks" on the other?" Is it because this attitude, this condition of being in unity with God and each other, is just that—much more a state of being than an activity? I've decided that is what I think. It really is a state of being, rather than, or more than, an activity or activities. Do you notice what these three apparent "activities" have in common? In all three is the expression of totality—rejoice all the time, pray all the time, and give thanks in all things, no matter what happens. In this light, it sounds like "as your life goes along, from now 'til the end, give thanks, in the ups and downs, good and bad, happy or sad, light or dark, easy or hard." That sounds like "all the time" to me.

What I want to know is, how in the world can we "give thanks all the time," in every event, irrespective of its apparent goodness or badness relative to our lives? The short answer is that there is only one way, and that one way is that we don't really focus our lives, our emotional "center," on the outcome of events in our lives, because we're focused on something else. The only way we can do that is if we are focused on God, on His presence, on His life in our lives. We can only do that when we truly surrender ourselves, deny ourselves, die to ourselves, and focus our entire attention on Jesus and what He wants. When we do that, we begin to be able to fulfill Jesus' expectations for us, to fulfill His prayer in John 17, and to become one with Him and the Father and with each other as He is one with the Father. That's the only way, the only condition, the only state of being in which we can experience what this passage says about rejoicing, praying, and being thankful **all the time**. That's what Jesus wants for us, just like He said in John 17. So we can't give up; we've got to keep on keeping on, asking, seeking, knocking, surrendering, trusting, rejoicing, praying, and giving thanks.

Philippians 4:4-8

"Celebrate God all day, every day. I mean, revel in him! Make it as clear as you can to all you meet that you're on their side, working with them and not against them. Help them see that the Master is about to arrive. He could show up any minute! Don't fret or worry. Instead of worrying, pray. Let petitions and praises shape your worries into prayers, letting God know your concerns. Before you know it, a sense of God's wholeness, everything coming together for good, will come and settle you down. It's wonderful what happens when Christ displaces worry at the center of your life. Summing it all up, friends, I'd say you'll do best by filling your minds and meditating on things true, noble, reputable, authentic, compelling, gracious—the best, not the worst; the beautiful, not the ugly; things to praise, not things to curse. Put into practice what you learned from me, what you heard and saw and realized. Do that, and God, who makes everything work together, will work you into his most excellent harmonies" (*The Message*).

NKJV translates the passage this way: "Rejoice in the Lord always. Again I will say, rejoice! Let your gentleness be known to all men. The Lord is at hand. Be anxious for nothing, but in everything by prayer and supplication, with thanksgiving, let your requests be made known to God; and the peace of God, which surpasses all understanding, will guard your hearts and minds through Christ Jesus. Finally, brethren, whatever things are true, whatever things are noble, whatever things are just, whatever things are pure, whatever things are lovely, whatever things are of good report, if there is any virtue and if there is anything praiseworthy—meditate on these things."

So what is this passage about, really?

> *It's about the war that's going on in our hearts and minds, the struggle between good and evil, between the flesh and the Spirit, between the peace of Jesus and the worry of the devil, between fear and happiness, between life and death.*

It focuses on the eternal questions: How are you going to live your life? Are you going to live under the cloud of worry, stress, care, and doubt? Are you going to continue to try to take care of yourself? Are you going to let the cares of this world, and the deceitfulness of riches (see Matt 13:22); read: [work, houses, cars, trips, fame and fortune] choke out the presence of God and leave you a shriveled shadow? Do you realize how badly you need some relief?

If you want relief, do you know where that relief is going to come from? Do you know how to access that relief? Do you know how to get the relief to come, stay, and never go away? This is your lucky day! If you're looking for relief, have I got a deal for you! The short version of what this passage is about is, "What are we going to do about fear and worry?" In this short passage, it tells us exactly what to do.

1. **Rejoice.** Celebrate God and delight yourself in the fact that God is in your life, all the time, in every way. Be happy and glad that you get to be here where God is, because you know that He is taking care of you. Remember all the time that God is near, that the Master is about to arrive; he could show up any minute! Worship God in your heart and with your mouth for all the truly touching things He does for you all the time.

2. **Let your gentleness be known to all men.** Make it clear to all that you're on their side, helping them and not hindering them. Let all men see your unselfishness, your consideration, your forgiving, merciful spirit. In general, be nice, be kind, be tenderhearted and forgiving (Ephesians 4:32), like God is to you because of what Jesus has done for us.

3. **Pray.** Let praises and definite requests shape your worries into prayers, letting God know your concerns. Ask for what you need, be thankful for what you get.

4. **Be thankful.** Give thanks for what God has done and is doing for you; give thanks in all things because you know that God is working all things together for your good (Romans 8:28). You *can* be thankful if you trust that ultimately God loves you and He's going to take care of you forever. Like Jesus said, just before His ascension, "Know this, I am with you always, even to the end of the age [the world as we know it]" (Matthew 28:20). God also said, "I will never leave you nor forsake you" (Hebrews 13:5).

5. **Think about Good Things.** Think about all the good things that are in your life (in all of our lives) because of God and His

grace in providing "for all of our needs by His riches in glory by Christ Jesus" (Philippians 4:19). What good things? Truth, Honor, Justice, Purity, Love, Kindness, Grace, Virtue, things that are authentic and genuine—the best, not the worst; the beautiful, not the ugly; things to praise, not things to curse. Fill your mind and your heart with all the good things that come down from God (James 1:17), which He decided to give us before time began. (Ephesians 1).

So if you want to give up worry and get peace, that's all you have to do. Yeah, but I can see you sitting there thinking, "Whew, that's a big order!" That it is, but what it really requires is completely giving up your whole self to God, Jesus, and the Holy Spirit, trusting Him with complete control of your life. All you have to do is surrender and trust, but it's going to take renewing your commitment to Him every day for the rest of your life. The good news is, you don't have to do it all at once. You can make a small start, and God will use that small start to ultimately fill your life with Himself. Once you begin to surrender, pray, trust, and obey, you will know the peace that passes all understanding (Philippians 4:7).

Do you know the verse from Proverbs 3:5, "Trust in the Lord with all your heart, and lean not to your own understanding"? That's what this kind of peace is all about, the kind that you get when you quit, stop, cease and desist from leaning on your own understanding. Praise the Lord!

Praise the Lord!

I'm decided that David, the son of Jesse, anointed by Samuel to be the King of Israel and Judah, is (and was) the champion at praising the Lord God Almighty. He was far and away above all the other individuals in the Bible at praise. The book of Psalms has by far the most verses about praising the Lord of any in the Bible, with the bulk of them coming from David's pen.

In fact, according to *Strong's Exhaustive Concordance*, in Psalms alone there are 158 instances of the use of the word praise. In 1 Chronicles 16 is David's song of thanksgiving to the Lord after the Israelites finally got the Ark of the Covenant back from the Philistines and put it in the Tabernacle at Jerusalem. In that chapter alone, David says praise to the Lord, gives glory to God, sings to Him, worships Him, gives thanks to Him, remembers Him, and proclaims the Good News of his salvation, including that memorable verse in 16:34, "O, give thanks to the Lord, for He is good! For His mercy endures forever." In 1 Chronicles 29:10-20, at the end of his reign, we find "David's Praise to God," in which he blesses the Lord God of Israel, exalts Him, and extols His greatness. Other places, such as 2 Chronicles 29:31, say that King Hezekiah commanded the Levites to use the words of David to praise the Lord. David offered more praise to the Lord than all the other people, in all the other verses, in all the other books of the Bible, put together, Old Testament and New.

One of David's most oft repeated praises was, "O give thanks unto the Lord, for He is good, His mercy endures forever" (KJV). He uses this exact phrase at the beginnings and/or the ends of Psalms 105, 106, and 118. Combinations and variations of this theme are recorded in Psalm 136, where he recites the creation of the world, the miracles preceding, during and after the Exodus, and he ends declaring, "O, give thanks unto the God of heaven, for His mercy endures forever." Some say that the God of the Old Testament was a wrathful god, a god of judgment and not mercy. In Psalm 136 alone David says, 26 times, in combination with various praises for God's multitude of good works and great qualities, "His mercy endures forever!" Do you remember what mercy is from the first chapter? Mercy is when God blesses us when we deserve to be punished. I don't know about you, but at the end of my prayer time every morning I say, "Thank you for being merciful to us, please keep on doing it."

Most people interlace their prayers with thanksgiving, praise, giving glory to God. Often, there is more worship than supplication (asking) or intercession (prayers for the needs of others). Whenever we pray together, in worship services or in small groups, He is with us, as it says in John, "Where two or three are gathered together in My Name, there am I in the midst of them" (Matthew 18:20). That's talking about prayer, but it ends up being a time of praise, worship, and thanksgiving, just as much, if not more than prayer, because Jesus' Holy Spirit is right there in the middle of it.

THEME 4: TRUST

INTO THE FIRE

I've spent a lot of time trying to pick the right story to exemplify what I'm thinking about when I say trust. I've tried to find a modern day story that really conveys the message as well as all those "faith-full" stories in the Bible, and I'm still searching. I guess my "fall back" stories about men and women trusting God come mostly from the Old Testament, some of the best ones from the Torah, like Noah, Abraham, Joseph, and Moses. 'Course there's all the stories about Joshua, David, Hezekiah, and Elijah. And what about Sarah, Rahab, Deborah, Bathsheba, Esther, and Ruth, not to mention Daniel and Shadrach, Meshach, and Abednego. Wow!

I guess right now I'm thinking about Hananiah, Mishael and Azariah, which were the Jewish names for Shadrach, Meshach, and Abednego. This is their story, from the third chapter of Daniel, verses 1-30:

> King Nebuchadnezzar made an image of gold, ninety feet high and nine feet wide, and set it up on the plain of Dura in the province of Babylon. He then summoned the satraps, prefects, governors, advisers, treasurers, judges, magistrates and all the other provincial officials to come to the dedication of the image he had set up.
>
> Then the herald loudly proclaimed, "This is what you are commanded to do, O peoples, nations and men of every language: As soon as you hear the sound of the horn, flute, zither, lyre, harp, pipes and all kinds of music, you must fall down and worship the image of gold that King Nebuchadnezzar has set up. Whoever does not fall down and worship will

immediately be thrown into a blazing furnace." Therefore, as soon as they heard the sound of the horn, flute, zither, lyre, harp and all kinds of music, all the peoples, nations and men of every language fell down and worshiped the image of gold that King Nebuchadnezzar had set up.

At this time some astrologers came forward and denounced the Jews. They said to King Nebuchadnezzar, "O king, live forever! You have issued a decree, O king, that everyone who hears the sound of the horn, flute, zither, lyre, harp, pipes and all kinds of music must fall down and worship the image of gold, and that whoever does not fall down and worship will be thrown into a blazing furnace. But there are some Jews whom you have set over the affairs of the province of Babylon—Shadrach, Meshach and Abednego—who pay no attention to you, O king. They neither serve your gods nor worship the image of gold you have set up."

Furious with rage, Nebuchadnezzar summoned Shadrach, Meshach and Abednego. So these men were brought before the king, and Nebuchadnezzar said to them, "Is it true, Shadrach, Meshach and Abednego, that you do not serve my gods or worship the image of gold I have set up? Now when you hear the sound of the horn, flute, zither, lyre, harp, pipes and all kinds of music, if you are ready to fall down and worship the image I made, very good. But if you do not worship it, you will be thrown immediately into a blazing furnace. Then what god will be able to rescue you from my hand?"

Shadrach, Meshach and Abednego replied to the king, "O Nebuchadnezzar, we do not need to defend ourselves before you in this matter. If we are thrown into the blazing furnace, the God we serve is able to save us from it, and he will rescue us from your hand, O king. But even if he does not, we want you to know, O king, that we will not serve your gods or worship the image of gold you have set up."

Then Nebuchadnezzar was furious with Shadrach, Meshach and Abednego, and his attitude toward them changed. He ordered the furnace heated seven times hotter than usual and commanded some of the strongest soldiers in his army to tie up Shadrach, Meshach and Abednego and throw them into the blazing furnace. So these men, wearing their robes, trousers, turbans and other clothes, were bound and thrown into the blazing furnace. The king's command was so urgent and the furnace so hot that the flames of the fire killed the soldiers who took up Shadrach, Meshach and Abednego, and these three men, firmly tied, fell into the blazing furnace.

Then King Nebuchadnezzar leaped to his feet in amazement and asked his advisers, "Weren't there three men that we tied up and threw into the fire?" They replied, "Certainly, O king." He said, "Look! I see four men walking around in the fire, unbound and unharmed, and the fourth looks like a son of the gods."

Nebuchadnezzar then approached the opening of the blazing furnace and shouted, "Shadrach, Meshach and Abednego, servants of the Most High God, come out! Come here!" So Shadrach, Meshach and Abednego came out of the fire, and the satraps, prefects, governors and royal advisers crowded around them. They saw that the fire had not harmed their bodies, nor was a hair of their heads singed; their robes were not scorched, and there was no smell of fire on them.

Then Nebuchadnezzar said, "Blessed be the God of Shadrach, Meshach and Abednego, who has sent his angel and rescued his servants! They trusted in him and defied the king's command and were willing to give up their lives rather than serve or worship any god except their own God. Therefore I decree

> that the people of any nation or language who say anything against the God of Shadrach, Meshach and Abednego be cut into pieces and their houses be turned into piles of rubble, for no other god can save in this way." Then the king promoted Shadrach, Meshach and Abednego in the province of Babylon."

When I read a passage or a story from the Bible to my kids, I usually ask them, "What are the one or two phrases or sentences that best express the essence of this story?" Sometimes they have to read it over to themselves a time or two, but they usually find the right one. Before you read on, see if you can pick out the essence of this story. In this case, the moral of this story is about trust.

Oh, before we go on about the story, there's one thing I've discovered since I've been thinking about God and trying to surrender to Him. Every time I see the word "believe" or "faith" in the Bible, I substitute the word "trust." It works almost every time, except in that verse that says, "Even the devils believe, and tremble" (James 2:19). For example, "For God so loved the world, He gave His only begotten Son, that whoever believes [trusts] in Him, will not perish, but have eternal life" (John 3:16). And, "Abraham believed [trusted] God, and it was counted to him for righteousness" (Genesis 15:6). And, "For it is by grace you have been saved, through faith [trust], and that not of yourselves. It is the gift of God, not of works, lest anyone should boast" (Ephesians 2:8). Like I say, it works almost every time.

In Hebrew and Greek, the original languages of the Old and New Testaments, respectively, the word for "believe" is the same as the word for trust. In Greek, the root word is *pisteuo*, which means "to believe, to have confidence in, to trust": the same root with a different ending, *pistis*, means faith, and *pistos* means "trustworthy" or "faithful."

Today in the U.S., "believe" is a different word with a different meaning from "trust." Believe is something we do with our heads; trust is something we do with our hearts. Believe is mental assent to a fact or to the truth of something; trust is reliance on the object of our belief. So James 2:19 quoted above is right. The demons do believe, they do recognize that God exists, and they do tremble. But they don't trust Him. They give mental assent, but they don't rely on

Him to take care of them. Oh, and if trust is something we do with our hearts, we should remember one other thing, which it says over and over throughout the Bible, "Men look at outward appearances, but God looks at the heart" (1 Samuel 16:7). So God knows, He knows very well, whether we trust with our hearts, or we just believe with our heads.

What about the word "faith"? In Hebrews 11:1 and following, it says, "Now faith is the substance of things hoped for and the evidence of things not seen. . . . Without faith it is impossible to please God, for whoever comes to God must believe that He exists, and that He is a rewarder of those who diligently seek Him." Please substitute trust, highlighted for effect: "Now **trust** is the substance of things hoped for and the evidence of things not seen. . . . Without **trust** it is impossible to please God, for whoever comes to God must **trust** that He exists, and that He is a rewarder of those who diligently seek Him." It still fits, and it still conveys the true message of what God wants from us, which isn't something you do with your head.

Proverbs 3:5-6

In this passage, Solomon says, "Trust in the LORD with all your heart and lean not on your own understanding; in all your ways acknowledge Him, and He will direct your paths." Some versions say in the last line, "and He will make your paths straight." It may just be semantics, but to me the first version is more all-encompassing, says more, covers more, and has more depth and breadth about what God does if we'll trust Him and surrender to Him in all our ways.

This is my verse. It expresses the essence of my understanding of what our relationship with God is all about. My experience has been that even when I really try, when I really work hard at seeking the Lord's Face, and work hard at trying to do what God wants me to, I still have things happen that I didn't expect; i.e., things that at the time seem hard, hard to live with, hard to understand, and hard to reconcile with my understanding of who God is and who I am in Him. But you know, our sight is so limited, we think "all my ways" is just what *I* expect, just what *I* think God wants for my life, and for my family, my ministry, my country, and my church. Notice how minutely focused I am on my stuff? A little *my*opic, ya' think? And maybe, once in a while, God has been thinking about somebody else. Maybe He's been spending a little time thinking, dare I say it, about you. Your life may require a little attention, too. In fact, you may think your life is as complicated as I think mine is.

I just love this verse. As I said, this really is my verse. Maybe out of the whole Bible, this verse fits my situation best. I really need, in all my ways, to trust the Lord. Not just a little bit. I need to throw myself at His feet and beg Him to keep on taking care of me, like He's been doing from the beginning. Every day, I need to thank God for

His overwhelming mercy and ask Him to keep on giving it to me; and I need to tell Him I'm trusting Him to keep on doing it, because otherwise, I'm sunk.

I'm talking with all my heart, no reservations, with no forethought, with no doubt, with no prior planning about what I'm gonna' do if it appears He might not take care of me. Sorry, but if He doesn't do it, it's not gonna' get done. I am just too flaky. Even on the days when I think I'm the smartest person I know (which is less and less often, LOL), without God's TLC I don't have a prayer. This involves the same thought as the verses "with all your heart, and all your soul, and all your strength, and all your mind" (Deuteronomy 6:5; Matthew 22:37). Whatever there is in me that I count as me, I've got to turn it over to God. That's praying with "all your heart."

'Course then comes the hard part, "lean not to your own understanding." The hardest thing about truly trusting is giving up our death grip on reality. From the very beginning of our lives, we learn to trust in and rely on only what we can see, touch, taste, feel, and hear to carry us through; to keep us out of trouble, for example, "Look both ways before you cross that street!"

As we grow, it quickly becomes a struggle between trusting in what we can see versus trusting in what God says, and it's especially hard when most of the people standing around are saying, "Logically, you must be a fool to trust in stuff you can't see." ('Course, in 2 Corinthians 4:16, it says something like, "But we don't trust in the seen, but in the unseen; 'cause the stuff we can see is temporary, but the unseen is eternal").

Be a fool, be a fanatic, be an idiot; but do it for God. Most of the time I'm not ready to do that, not whole hog. I'm still holding back. What are they gonna' think, the people I care about, the people I care about what they think? There I go again. Who do I care more about? Do I care more about what God thinks, or about what I think? 'Cause you know I just use the idea of "others" as a front for me.

"Lean" means "rely on" or "put your weight on." "Your own understanding" means "everything you know about everything," which in the case of some people is quite a lot. But in the grand scheme of things, is it really? I can only speak for myself, but my understanding is pretty limited when compared with what is "known" in the world. Think about all the stuff that is available on the 'Net.

You can research quickly almost any topic, and what you find out can be used to increase your knowledge and your understanding, so that hopefully you can make better decisions that will affect your life positively. My conclusion, based on what little I do know, is that I pretty much don't know anything; and I don't even want to learn much that I don't already know. At least, I don't want to know it bad enough to spend the time and energy it takes to do the research. Now this may be an exaggeration, but I'd say that the 'Net encompasses, one way or another, all that can be known on the earth, or soon will. Maybe not, but we'd all agree that it encompasses a lot. Let's say, just for discussion's sake, that everything on the 'Net is co-equal with "your" understanding, or with "my understanding." At least as it regards me, that is a gross exaggeration. But let's just pretend it is. How do you think that compares with what God knows?

I doubt you'd even be reading this book if you didn't buy into the basic premise that God exists, and that He created everything that exists, inside and out, whether we know about it or understand it, or not. So wherever we are on the continuum of knowledge and understanding (K&U), between zero K&U and what God knows, our K&U is limited. How limited is subject to discussion, but when I start thinking about my K&U compared to God's, my Daddy's expression, "dumber than a stump" comes to mind. Or maybe "dumber than a box of rocks." You can insert your own culturally significant phrase, but that's me. You know why? There's two reasons—I'm so very limited, and I'm so focused on myself.

I'm limited by time, space, culture, education, national origin, gender, age, race, ad infinitum. Just take one—I'm a man—because it has a little humor in it. Talk about a limiting factor. My wife says I don't understand anything, and she's pretty much right, but whatever I do understand has very little to do with the magnificent realm of what it means to be a woman: like having a baby, being a momma, or having the depth of understanding that produces the tender, loving care of a woman's heart. The woman's perspective adds tons of quality to every area of our lives, from education, to science, to athletics, to the arts, and especially our relationships with each other and with God. I'm a mere man, but God created all those women, and put within them all the gifts of their hearts, minds, bodies, souls, and spirits. In this light, men are blessed to share life with them!

Some days we all think men and women come from different species. In my job as a lawyer, I've been involved in accident reconstruction based on eyewitness testimony. It is amazing how often and how much the account of a particular event differs based on whether it comes from a man or a woman. Sometimes you wouldn't even recognize that they were talking about the same event. There's all kinds of explanations, usually pointing back to "perspective," but I'm sticking with different species!

Point being, there's a lot of things I don't know. When it comes to "leaning on my own understanding," I'm weak. My understanding is weak, and leaning on it is like walking on a crippled foot. It just doesn't work; I fall down when I put my weight on it. Leaning on God is like sitting down and putting your feet up; it's like getting up on a solid rock. I am reminded of the verse from David, "The Lord is my rock, my fortress and my deliverer" (2 Samuel 22:2).

You get to choose. Do you want to keep on relying on yourself? Or have you reached the point where you're really tired, really sick and tired of trying to run your own life? Are you falling farther and farther behind, wondering why things are still not working, sorta' praying that some miracle will happen to deliver you from a bad job, or a failing marriage, or the bottom of a bottle?

That's the question. How tired are you? Are you tired enough to trust God? Are you tired enough to admit that you just can't trust yourself, that you're unreliable? Are you tired enough, sick enough, to trust God, even when you have no idea how even God can fix all the stuff that's wrong with you? I'm sure you've heard that line about insanity: it's "doing the same things over and over expecting different results." Are you ready to trust God even if you have to give up—give up trying to control your own life; maybe even give up your insanity?

That is what this leaning thing is about. If you're tired enough that you're ready for a little rest from your own understanding, your own abilities, and your own results, all you've got to do is stop trusting you and start trusting (leaning) solely on God. It'll change your life.

Well, maybe that's not all you've got to do. Now comes the other half of the verse, "In all your ways acknowledge Him, and He will direct your paths." Of course, "All your ways" means everything— all your hopes, dreams, desires, heartaches, frustrations, and disappointments. It means all your ways in your job, school, church politics, the dance on Friday night, your wedding day, and when your kid dies. It means all your relationships, your momma and daddy, your brothers and sisters, your friend that's closer than a brother, and especially your spouse and kids (the good ones and the ones that went astray), for better or worse, for richer or poorer, in sickness and in health, forsaking all others, forever.

Sounds like getting married to God, doesn't it? It is, except more so, because this doesn't just last 'till "death do us part." It's forever. Unless you've thought about this a whole lot in the past, you're not even ready to start thinking about having this much to do with God. This much trusting is just outside the realm of reason. 'Fraid so.

Well don't go away yet. You may see something that'll really get you, something that'll make you think there's a chance that God might actually be able to do what some folks have said He can do.

I've looked up "acknowledge" in the dictionary, and it is defined as, "1) to admit to be real or true; recognize the existence, truth, or fact of: 2) to show or express recognition or realization of: to acknowledge an acquaintance by nodding. 3) to recognize the authority, validity, or claims of: 4) to show or express appreciation or gratitude for: 5) to indicate or make known the receipt of."

To "acknowledge Him" then, must mean to admit that He's real and true, and that you recognize His existence. Hebrews 11:6 says, in part, "anyone who comes to God must believe [trust] that He exists, and that He is a rewarder of those who diligently seek Him." It means to recognize His authority, to show gratitude for what He's done. It's a big call, but that's what this trusting is about.

The passage ends with, "And He will direct your paths." I guess the simple version is, He'll tell you what to do, and when, and how, and when you mess up, He won't let you sink in the quicksand. It helps if you ask Him what to do. He answers when we ask Him because we're actually listening for an answer. But sometimes, even when we didn't ask, and we weren't even trying to listen, much less listen for an answer; He breaks through and snatches us back from the brink of destruction. This is 'cause He's got a plan, and He's going to see to it that His plan succeeds, even when we're not paying a bit of attention. That's how much God wants us to trust Him.

Psalm 23:1-6

"The LORD is my shepherd; I shall not want. He makes me to lie down in green pastures; He leads me beside the still waters. He restores my soul; He leads me in the paths of righteousness For His name's sake. Even though I walk through the valley of the shadow of death, I will fear no evil; For You are with me; Your rod and Your staff, they comfort me. You prepare a table before me in the presence of my enemies; You anoint my head with oil; my cup runs over. Surely goodness and mercy shall follow me all the days of my life; and I will dwell in the house of the LORD forever."

What is this famous Psalm of David really about? Why does it appear in the section about trust? Maybe it's because it falls in the category of "trust results." It's about what happens when you really trust God. The Bible says that David was a man after God's own heart (Acts 13:22). What did he do to touch God's heart? He trusted Him. He fought lions and wolves without fear, because he knew God was taking care of him. He fought Goliath, calling him an uncircumcised Philistine, and whipped him, because he knew that God was taking care of him (read the whole story in 1 Samuel 17). He trusted that God would take care of him his whole life, even when he did really stupid things like go to bed with Bathsheba and then have her husband Uriah killed in battle. But in spite of David being a "regular" human being who sinned just like the rest of us, God called him, "A man after My own heart," mostly because he trusted Him. The 23rd Psalm is David telling what it feels like when you trust God, when you really and truly, whole hog, trust God.

Saying, "The Lord is my Shepherd" in 1,000 B.C. meant a whole lot more than it does today. Most of the Israelites were shepherds then, and even those who lived in the cities went down on holidays to visit the kinfolks in the country, who were still herding and raising sheep. When Jesus was born, God had the angels make the first announcement to the shepherds. The whole society was wrapped up in herding sheep, and many of the parables and the symbols are related to sheep, all the things they mean, and all the ways the people shared the lessons learned from herding sheep. This included everything from going and finding them when they're lost, to staying in the pen or the barn with them when they're having their lambs, to putting their blood on the doorposts to ward off the avenging angel and make him "pass-over"; all those things had a profound effect on the way the people looked at and thought about shepherds. The whole subject was deeply ingrained in them.

So what does the Lord do for you when He is your Shepherd? First, let me ask another question. What do the sheep do when they have a good shepherd? Well, they trust him for everything: food; a nice warm, secure place to rest; protection from the elements and the wild animals; care when they're sick; coming to find them when they're lost; and help with bearing and raising their young. If you have personally observed them, or studied them in books, sheep are a pretty dependent lot. They really need help to get along. So what do the sheep do when they have a good shepherd? Well, they trust him. Sometimes they do what he says, sometimes they don't. Sometimes they do stupid stuff like run off in the bushes away from the flock, but they still expect that the shepherd is going to come find them and get them back home safe and sound. There's a lot to be said for looking at sheep when you're talking about humans; there are lots of similarities in behavior. Sheep trust, and shepherds take care of sheep. Trust is a primary element in the sheep getting along with the shepherd and the shepherd being able to do his job.

So back to the original question: What does the Lord do for you when He is your Shepherd?

1) "I shall not want." He provides for all your needs (and some of your wants) 'by His riches in glory in Christ Jesus' (Phil. 4:19)

2) "He makes me lie down in green pastures." Tex's version has this, "He lets me rest, really rest, and feeds me very well at the same time." This rest is a major benefit of trusting. In fact, in Hebrews 3:11, it says that the Lord told the Israelites that they would **not** enter into His rest because they didn't trust Him. So the only way you can really rest is if you "put all your cares over on the Lord, because He cares for you". (1 Peter 5:7) You have to really trust Him to take care of them, whatever they are, so you don't have to. That is what real rest is about; that is what real trust is about. As my Daddy would say, "You can write it down in your book." Whenever you get sick and tired of being sick and tired, and you're finally ready to let God take care of

you, remember that verse in Peter (Tex's version), "Put all your cares on God, 'cause He cares for you." Hallelujah! Amen!

3) "He leads me beside still waters." Still waters, not raging streams, a place where you can go stand in the water and really take a long slow drink of cool refreshing water and just enjoy the cool breeze blowing off the cool water, and think about how nice it is just to get to be here. A place where you don't have to worry about the lions and the wolves coming out of the bushes to get you, because you know the Shepherd has your back.

4) "He restores my soul." When you're tired and worn out, when you've walked too far, worked too hard, and you need time to heal up, the Shepherd gives you the time and the place to do it. Just when you thought you never were going to get any relief, here comes the Shepherd to pick you up and carry you. Talk about security! That's what "restores my soul" means—a little relief, usually when you need it the most.

5) "He leads me in the paths of righteousness for His Name's sake." What this means to me is that I can even trust God to help me to do right just to make me and Him both happy. It makes both Him and me happy that I do what I'm supposed to, and it makes us grow even closer together when I don't have to feel guilty, because I can totally trust and rely on Him. It's just another thing about the security we have in a trusting relationship with God, both inside and out. This goes back to what we said earlier about when we surrender ourselves to Him, He puts His own Spirit in us, and we are *able* to do right, instead of falling back in it.

6) "Even though I walk through the valley of the shadow of death, I will fear no evil, for You are with me." David was up against it a number of times in his life; he had plenty of "near death" experiences of a different kind, where they were fixin' to cut him to pieces with a sword, or run him through with a spear, or knock his brains out with a big rock. It's like when someone is very sick and not expected to recover, and you get this sense of peace in your heart that everything is going to be okay. That's what it means if you really trust God. You start to realize that no matter what happens, God is taking care of everything, and He's going to keep on taking care of. everything. That's what trust is all about. I read a quote by Ben Stein that fits here, "Faith (trust) is not believing God can, but knowing God will."

Even when you're up against it and have nowhere to go; when you're between a rock and a hard place, God is still there and He's still in control.

7) "Your rod and your staff they comfort me." The Amplified Version says, "Your rod [to protect], and your staff [to guide]." When I was a kid I always believed that the rod was for discipline. But I must've had a cognitive disconnect. Discipline for sheep? I think the "protect and guide" message fits a lot better. In the Spanish Bible, it says *"vara de pastor,"* which translates loosely as "shepherd's crook." That's what they use to fish the lambs out of the water after they fall in, and to turn the sheep back when they get too near the cliff. That's protecting and guiding; that's comfort.

8) "You prepare a table before me in the presence of my enemies." Some say banquet, some feast. The scene is one of a victor come home from the battle and being fed well, being wined and dined. But what's with the enemies? What are they doing here? Maybe they're chained to the table leg with manacles, waiting for the scraps with the dogs? In any case, David is not in that condition. He's being well cared for by his Shepherd—it's just another result of trusting the Shepherd.

9) "You anoint my head with oil." I don't know about y'all, but to me, "anointed with oil" has always been a universal sign of the blessings of the Holy Spirit being poured out; a sign that you're being treated as a king, as when Samuel anointed David to be king, long before this Psalm was written (1 Samuel 16:13). We know that after King Saul was anointed king, he received the Holy Spirit, because when he later disobeyed God, God "withdrew His Spirit" from Saul (1 Samuel 16:14). That was one thing that always made Saul mad, even crazy, that David always exhibited God's Spirit in almost everything he said and did, from even before the time when Samuel anointed David to be the future king.

It sure doesn't look like all of us are as "anointed" as David. Maybe it's because we don't trust God as much as David. I dare say we could all have that same anointing, if we surrendered and trusted God with all our hearts, like David did, because now God's Spirit is available to everyone who believes (trusts)—it says so in the John the 14th chapter.

10) "My cup runs over." This may not be last, but it's certainly not least, either. This is about the abundance that comes from trusting in God. It's about, "My Lord shall provide for all of your needs by His

riches in glory in Christ Jesus" (Philippians 4:19), and "God is able to do exceedingly abundantly above all we could ask or think, by His power that works within us" (Ephesians 3:20). See, that's what this is all about, "exceeding abundance." That is what God gives to those who trust Him. It says in the passage about giving gifts, "If your son asks you for bread, you won't give him a stone . . . how much more will God give the Holy Spirit to them that ask Him?" (Luke 11:11-13).

11) "Surely goodness and mercy shall follow me, all the days of my life." David had a way with words, didn't he? Like the little kid in school said, "Surely good Mrs. Murphy shall follow me." What's really great about ol' David is that he took such great joy in knowing God. He actually believed the stuff he was saying. Makes me grin. You know why he said all that? Because he had experienced it over and over all his life. In all kinds of situations, God had pulled his fat out of the fire. He delivered him from evil and gave him great abundance in experiences, relationships, heights, depths, and earthly possessions; He gave him great stories to tell his multitude of grandchildren. David knew that he knew that God had been taking care of him, was taking care of him, and was gonna' keep on taking care of him, just like it says in the marriage vows we mentioned earlier. While in this phrase David says, "all the days of my life," he really means what he says in the last verse:

12) "I will live in the house of the Lord forever." I may be crazy, but I think David understood that he would continue to experience God's presence, love, and grace, even after he died. I really believe that David knew what few of us figure out while we're still here on earth, that heaven begins right here on earth, when we surrender our whole selves to God through Jesus, and really begin to trust Him. Like Jesus said, "The kingdom of heaven is at hand" (Matthew 4:17), and "Seek first the kingdom of God, and His righteousness, and all this stuff shall be added unto you" (Matthew 6:33, paraphrase). When you really decide to trust God and quit worrying about taking care of yourself, you actually begin to feel what it's like to experience heaven. Get ready.

Psalm 37:39-40

"But the salvation of the righteous is from the Lord. He is their strength in the time of trouble, and the Lord shall help them and deliver them. He shall deliver them from the wicked, and save them, because they trust in Him."

You probably picked up the main point of this verse, "Because they trust in Him." We all know what salvation is, right—where you go to heaven when you die? Maybe it's also saving us from something here on earth, like the demons and the devil, the Philistines, maybe the Nazi concentration camps, or alcohol, drugs, or communists. You might call it salvation if you're delivered from those things.

But the verse says "the salvation of the righteous." Who are the righteous? Most of my life I understood that the righteous are those who do right, who live up to God's standards of behavior; they are people who don't "drink or cuss or dance or chew, or ever run with them that do." People who almost always follow the Golden Rule (Matthew 7:12), who act according to 1 Corinthians 13:4-8, the chapter about love, by being "patient and kind, never jealous or boastful or proud or rude; they don't demand their own way, aren't irritable or grouchy; they hardly even notice when others do them wrong; they don't rejoice in evil but rejoice in the truth; and they put up with other people, and believe the best about them, and hope the very best for them, and they endure all kinds of bad things just to show how good they are; and always for the right reasons" (paraphrase). Oh, and they always produce and exhibit the "fruits of the Spirit" which are love, joy, peace, patience, kindness, goodness, faithfulness, gentleness and self-control (Galatians 5:22). When it says, "Be ye perfect even as your Father in heaven is perfect" (Matthew 5:48), they almost always fill the bill. Those people are the ones who are really righteous. They're the ones who really deserve "the salvation that comes from the Lord."

If you listen to a lot of "good" people, they're really trying to lead orderly lives and raise their children to be honest, law abiding citizens; they are people who work hard, pay their bills, take responsibility for their own actions, and contribute something positive to society. Those people understand that "righteousness" is doing good and right, and if you don't do good and right, then you're just not very righteous. You may get by in this world, and because of God's mercy, you may even get to heaven, but you're really just not doing right. God may forgive you and deliver you anyway, but it will be in spite of the way you act rather than because of it.

You may have detected a slight tone of sarcasm in that last paragraph. Sorry, I just couldn't help it. What you've just heard is Tex's version of the doctrine of works. It's about counting your good deeds versus your bad deeds and seeing if you measure up so that you've done more good than bad, and you haven't hurt anybody on purpose, you'll be okay. You're in good company, because most of the people who have lived on the earth from the beginning, have believed in and practiced the doctrine of works. Oh, the rules vary from society to society. In some places in the past, you had to sacrifice your firstborn son or your virgin daughter in order to appease the gods. Nowadays, we don't practice such barbarities; now it's mostly about money. 'Course if you don't have the right amount of money, you can still live up to the standards if you sacrifice yourself to your job and spend your whole life working your fingers to the bone; providing you maintain the proper posture before your boss, of course.

Now that we've established what righteous means, let me just tell you, we're not talkin' about that kind of righteousness. What we're talking about is a completely different kind of righteousness. This is the righteousness that comes from the Lord. It doesn't come from working hard, long, well, and diligently. This is exactly the same kind of righteousness it talks about it Genesis 15:6, where it says, "Abram believed [trusted] God, and it was counted to him for righteousness." God counted it to Abram and to David that they were righteous, with God's righteousness, because they trusted Him. So we might paraphrase this verse to say, "The salvation of the righteous, (read: the people who trust God) is from the Lord, because they trust in Him.

Just so you'll know, all those people who have been, and are now, trusting in themselves and their works to make them in right standing with God so He'll take them to heaven, are going to be sorely disappointed. Even right here and now, they are going to live under almost insupportable burdens because they're trying to do it all by themselves.

So if you want what this verse offers, that is: 1) **strength** in your time of trouble, 2) **help and deliverance** from the wicked, and 3) **salvation**, then you would do well to heed what this verse says, "The salvation of the righteous is from the Lord . . . and they will be delivered . . . **because they trust in Him."**

Isaiah 26:3

"You will keep him in perfect peace, whose mind is stayed on You, because he trusts in You."

If you focus on God, He will keep you in perfect peace, because if you stay focused on God, you will trust Him, which is the main thing. I guess the "Tex" interpretation of this verse is, "All you have to do to get perfect peace (not fear, anxiety, worry, depression, anger, frustration, guilt, hatred, or any of those other negative emotions that keep crowding in on us, every day and night) is to keep your mind stayed (focused) on God." But it doesn't really sound like focus is the only ingredient; the real primary ingredient is trust. Focus is something you do with your head (your mind, your brain); trust is something you do with your heart, and God looks at your heart. You can focus all you want, but because it is something you do, it'll never give you perfect peace. But if you trust (with your heart), God sees that trust in your heart, and He keeps you; He keeps you in perfect peace, because He is responding to the trust He sees in your heart. So trust is the miraculous, supernatural key ingredient that draws man to God, and God to man.

Matthew 25:14-30

This passage is usually called the "Parable of the Talents," but I call it the "Parable of the Unfaithful Servant," because that is what the story is about. Y'all know the story: Three servants (really slaves) whose master, referred to as "lord" in the story, goes on a long trip. Before he leaves, he calls his slaves in and says, "Slave 1, I'm giving you 10 talents; Slave 2, 5; Slave 3, 1. Y'all see what you can make for me while I'm gone." A talent of gold was a great deal of money in those days. Someone said it was several lifetimes of wages for the average man; estimates have one talent at $300,000 in today's currency.

Then the lord is gone for a long time and finally comes back. The more "talented" guys were lauded and rewarded by their lord because they doubled their money; but the last guy, who only returned the lord's one talent, was lambasted and cursed, his talent was taken from him and given to Slave 1, and he was "cast into outer darkness" (you might say damned). Pretty harsh treatment, wouldn't you say? Why did his lord do that? I mean this guy was pretty much a wimp, hardly worth the arrow it would take to shoot him. What he did doesn't seem like such a big deal, either. I mean he didn't lose it betting on the horses, or spend it on wine, women, and song. So why did his lord condemn him so bitterly?

In the passage, Slave 3 says to the lord, "You're a hard man . . . and I was afraid." His lord says, "You're wicked and lazy (you didn't even try). If you cared at all, the least you could've done was put the money in the bank and make a little interest." But the "outer darkness" command was a little over the top. So I've got a theory about why the lord was so angry. It's about the servant's attitude. He's afraid of the lord; he's afraid the lord is going to do something bad to him. His attitude is the personification of distrust; he's convinced something bad is fixin' to happen, and it's a self-fulfilling prophecy. It's like John 3:18, when Jesus says, "For he who believes [trusts] is not condemned, but he who does not believe [trust] is condemned already, because he has not believed [trusted]." Slave 3 even told the lord to his face that he was a thief, saying, "You harvest where you didn't plant, and you reap where you didn't sow."

What does the lord say to that? He calls him a "wicked and lazy slave," and an "unprofitable servant." He says, "The least you could've done was put the money in savings, and you didn't even do that." He's saying, "You didn't even try; you'd already given up from the beginning."

Why did he call him wicked? Wicked means Slave 3 accused the lord of being a thief; it means he was afraid of the lord and didn't trust him. What does lazy mean? It means he didn't even try. He could have made money without any risk. Just the interest on $300,000 would have been some substantial change, which makes it a pretty big deal to take that kind of money and bury it in a coffee can (a bunch of coffee cans) in the back yard.

How much did his lord dislike this guy's attitude of fear and distrust? He sent him to, "Outer darkness, where there'll be wailing and gnashing of teeth." That's how much he hated it. It reminds me of Adam and Eve, when they got thrown out of the Garden. Guess we oughta' let this be a sign unto us, about how much God, our Lord, dislikes it when we are afraid of Him and don't trust Him. Guess we oughta' remember that God looks at our hearts, and what He enjoys most is when we trust Him.

John 5:24

This passage is the most basic expression of the Gospel. "Most assuredly, I say to you, he who hears My word and believes [trusts] in Him who sent Me has everlasting life, and shall not come into judgment, but has passed from death into life." Here's Tex's paraphrase: "I guarantee you, anyone who pays attention to what I say, and trusts in Him who sent Me, has eternal life. They will never be condemned. They have passed from death to life."

"I guarantee you" is usually translated, "Truly, Truly," or "Most assuredly," like the above version (read "Utmost certainty"). Like my daddy used to say, "You can write it down in your book." This is Jesus talking, not just any regular human. This is Jesus, God in the flesh, God's perfect gift to us. In John 5, just before this verse, Jesus goes to great lengths to explain his relationship with God, and then He says, "If you pay attention to what I say," "If you do what I say," "If you follow what I'm telling you." He doesn't just say, "Listen," or "Think about this." He says, "Pay attention. Trust Him who sent Me." Trust is becoming the central issue of this book, particularly trust in Him who sent Jesus, who of course is God. What happens when you trust God? You have eternal life. When? Right now; it starts today, not later. "You have passed from death to life." It's a done deal, a completed action; it has already happened.

"They will never be condemned." What does that mean? I can only report the meaning of the words—never means never. "Be condemned" means to be judged guilty and sentenced to punishment. It doesn't say what kind of punishment, but you can use your imagination. Some translations say, "Never be judged"; others say "condemned." It's a finished act. What can stop the punishment? Trust in God.

"They have passed from death unto life," which means eternal life. How do you receive eternal life? Trust God. Earlier, I said that this is the most basic expression of the Gospel, the Good News, of Jesus

Christ. When I say basic, I'm focusing also on what this verse does not say. It does not say anything about confessing your sin, repenting, confessing that Jesus is Lord, or being baptized. It only says, in essence, trust God and you will be saved, which means two things to me: 1) This is not a denial that we need to do the other things mentioned in this paragraph, and 2) "trust God" means sooo much, both to God and to us.

"Trust God" means that we surrender our whole selves to God. We surrender all that we have done, right or wrong; all that we have, in material and personal possessions as well as emotional and social connections; all those we love; and most of all, we surrender our natural, sinful self; we surrender control of our lives to Him. We deny ourselves, and we die to our sinful nature, so God can live His eternal life in us. (Luke 9:23) That is what it means to trust God. When we fully trust God, we also confess and repent of our sins, we also claim Jesus as our Lord and Savior, and we also are baptized in obedience to His command. But all of those things do not make you "right" with God. They will not, in and of themselves, "reconcile" you to God. The only thing we can do to get "right" with God is to trust Him. Trust that He loves you! Yes, I mean you! He loves you enough to send His Son (for God to come to earth in the person of Jesus Christ (2 Corin. 5:19)) to die as the sacrifice for you (Ephesians 5:2). Trust that no matter what happens, God, the Creator and Ruler of the universe, is taking care of you. Trust. That's what seals our relationship with Him. Just like the verse says, "If you'll pay attention, and trust in Him who sent Me . . . You have passed from death unto life."

Philippians 4:6-7

"Don't fret or worry. Instead of worrying, pray. Let petitions and praises shape your worries into prayers, letting God know your concerns. Before you know it, a sense of God's wholeness, everything coming together for good, will come and settle you down. It's wonderful what happens when Christ displaces worry at the center of your life" (*The Message*).

Tex's paraphrase: "Don't worry about anything, be thankful for what you have, ask for what you need, and leave it in His hands. When you do that, His peace, the peace that gives you comfort and rest, the peace that passes all understanding, will guard and protect your hearts and your thoughts through Christ Jesus."

In contrast to the previous passage about the "unfaithful servant" showing the attitude **not** to have toward the Lord, this passage is about the attitude **to** have toward the Lord. The King James version says, "Be careful for nothing." Tex's translation, "Don't worry about anything." Matthew 6:34 says, "Take no thought for the morrow," which liberally translated would be, "Don't worry," but Tex's translation is, "Don't even think about tomorrow at all." That's what this verse starts out saying as well, "Don't worry about anything; don't even think about it."

Like Scarlet O'Hara in *Gone with the Wind*, whenever she'd run up against some problem she couldn't deal with, she'd say "I'm just not going to think about that right now. I may have to deal with it later, but I'm just not going to think about it now." That's what God wants us to do. He wants us to turn all our problems over to Him, and not even think about them anymore, just let Him take care of them.

Then the KJV says, "And the peace of God, that passes all understanding, will keep your hearts and your minds through Christ Jesus our Lord." That's "the sense of God's wholeness about everything coming together for good that comes and settles down on you and settles you down." *(The Message)* What's that about the attitude again? The attitude God is looking for is this: When you're really worried, when you've got lots of things to be worried about, when you're at the end of your rope and your grip is slipping, when you're absolutely certain there isn't a cotton-pickin' thing you can do, you just make up your mind that you're going to stop worrying, trust God, and receive the peace that God has for you, right in the middle of the biggest storm of your life. That's the rest that David was talking about in the 23rd Psalm, "He makes me rest in green pastures. . . . Even when I'm walking through the valley of the shadow of death I will fear no evil, for You are with me." That is exactly the attitude you get when you take this verse to heart, "Don't worry about anything, but pray and ask God for what you need," and leave the results up to him. What'd ya' get? Peace. The air is full of God's peace. All we have to do is take a deep breath.

Hebrews 11:6

"Without faith [trust] it is impossible to please God, because anyone who comes to Him must believe [trust] that He exists and that He rewards those who earnestly seek him."

This is more about the attitude of trust in God. You just don't have a chance with God unless you trust Him. Since you can't see Him, you must trust that He exists. It's the funniest thing though, when you start trusting Him, you start seeing the things He does, and feeling His presence all around. He reveals Himself to you. You must trust that He'll reward you if you diligently seek Him, like it says in James 4:8, "Draw near to God, and He'll draw near to you." This "drawing near" could be translated, "diligently seek Him."

Farther down in Hebrews 11, it talks about all the great men and women of faith in the Old Testament, who we mentioned earlier in this book, like Abraham, Moses, Elijah, Noah, Isaac, Jacob, and Joseph, plus many more:

"And what more shall I say? I do not have time to tell about Gideon, Barak, Samson, Jephthah, David, Samuel and the prophets, who through faith conquered kingdoms, administered justice, and gained what was promised; who shut the mouths of lions, quenched the fury of the flames, and escaped the edge of the sword; whose weakness was turned to strength; and who became powerful in battle and routed foreign armies. Women received back their dead, raised to life again" (Hebrews 11:32-35).

All these people trusted that God exists, and that He is a rewarder of those who diligently seek Him—and surely He rewarded them. These people exhibited the attitude that God likes, the attitude that makes Him happy. No matter what circumstances we may find ourselves in, when we exhibit it, it makes us happy, too! Trust.

Genesis 15:6

"And he [Abram] believed in (trusted in, relied on, remained steadfast to) the Lord, and He counted it to him as righteousness (right standing with God)" (AMP).

Tex's Translation, "Abram trusted the Lord, and the Lord accepted his trust, and that trust made him right with God."

This covenant, sometimes known as the "Abrahamic Covenant," starts with this statement about Abram's (later known as Abraham) trust and what God thought about it. God goes on to say that because of his trust, God is going to give him and his descendants all the land between the "River of Egypt" (the Nile) and the "Great River Euphrates" (Genesis 15:18). That's the covenant, the agreement God made with Abram, because God liked the fact that he trusted Him.

What I've always thought was interesting about this passage is why God made this great promise to ol' Abe. It was not because he loved and worshipped Him, because he sacrificed half of his flocks to Him, or because he promised to dedicate his son to Him; **it was because Abram trusted God.** Like it asks in Micah 6:8, "What does the Lord require of you?" It looks like from Hebrews 11:6, that what the Lord requires is for us to trust him. If Abraham is recognized as the "Father of the Faith," why is it? It's because he trusted God.

My sense of Genesis 15:6 is that before Jesus died for our sins, even before God instituted the law, God's provision for reconciliation to Him was one thing, trust. After Jesus came and died for our sins, the way we access the gift of God, the path for reconciliation to God, is trust in the atoning sacrifice and the resurrection of Jesus. "For God so loved the world, that He gave His only Son, that whoever trusts in Him, will not perish, but have eternal life" (John 3:16). Trust is still the way, as Ephesians 2:8-9, says, "For by grace are you saved, through faith [trust], and that not of yourselves, it is the gift of God, *not of works,* lest any man should boast."

Romans 4:3 quotes Genesis 15:6 in its discussion of whether Abraham was counted righteous (reconciled to God) because of his faith (trust), or because of his works (being circumcised); and concludes that "Abraham was justified by his faith [trust]." Romans 4:5 says it even more clearly, "But to him who does not work, but believes [trusts] in Him who justifies the ungodly, his faith [trust] is accounted for righteousness."

I'm glad to say I qualify as one among the "ungodly" who trusts because I sure don't live up to God's standards of perfection under the law. Eminent theologians and religious philosophers call this concept "justification by faith," and it is one of the central tenets of the

Christian religion, one that's right up there with "salvation by grace." No doubt, Jesus is the central figure in human history, and what He did while He was on earth, dying on the cross, is the act that reconciles us to God. It was definitely God's grace that brought all this to happen.

Trust is the only way we can accept the gift that God offers us. Trust is the way we start our relationship with God, and trust is the way we maintain our relationship with God. In fact, trust is the only way to maintain your relationship with God.

There are multiple warnings in the Bible about how the early Christians started by trusting God every day, but they slowly fell back and returned to a doctrine of works, where they tried to prove they were worthy enough to have a relationship with God. They (and we) weren't worthy in the beginning, and we (and they) won't be worthy in the end. The only way to maintain our relationship with God is to daily surrender ourselves to Him, trust Him to save and justify us, and allow Him to live His life in us. It's like it says in Luke 9:23-24, "If you want to follow Me [be My disciple], you must deny yourself, and take up your cross daily [that's the cross of death to me, and life from Jesus] and follow Me. For whoever would save his life will lose it; but whoever will lose his life for My sake, will find it."

Trust is about getting up every morning and saying to God, "Dear Lord, I just want You to know that today, I'm surrendering again; I'm giving my whole self to You again, today. I pray that you'll help me to deny myself more, to die to myself more, so You can live more of Your eternal life in me." If you're ready to do that, God is ready to come into you, more and better and with more power and revelation than before. It's a growing and developing that never ends. I wasn't there, but I'd say it's a better than even bet that is what Abraham, Moses, Daniel, Samuel, David, and Shadrach, Meshach and Abednego did every morning of their lives (at least their "post-conversion" lives). Part of the reason they did that every morning is because they didn't want to drift away from God.

I heard a speech by a lady named Karen recently, who said the reason she maintains a daily, moment-by-moment relationship with God is because she has this vision of an astronaut working on the outside of a space capsule. He's attached to the capsule by a "tether," and if the tether comes loose from the ship or from the astronaut, he just sorta' slowly drifts off into space (forever). I'm with Karen; I don't want to drift away and be lost forever. Not renewing your relationship with God every day has an adverse affect on your relationship with Him, and a seriously negative affect on what God has planned for you to be and become in Him. I, for one, just don't want to mess that up.

So to round up this verse, "Abram believed God and it was counted to him for righteousness"; it was as if he had done right. His trust was counted as if he had perfectly satisfied all of God's requirements—and we all know that he didn't satisfy them, he just trusted.

Psalm 91:9-12

"Because you have made the LORD, your refuge,
Even the Most High, your dwelling place,
No evil shall befall you,
Nor shall any plague come near your dwelling;
For He shall give His angels charge over you,
To keep you in all your ways.
In their hands they shall bear [hold] you up,
Lest you dash your foot against a stone."

This passage is in here to discuss what it means to "make the Lord your refuge," to make "the Most High your dwelling place." "Refuge" in the dictionary is defined as: "shelter or protection from danger or distress; a place that provides shelter or protection; something (or some place) to which one has recourse in difficulty." "Dwelling" in the dictionary is defined as: "a shelter (as a house) in which people live." Refuge is about being protected, secure, or sheltered, a place to hide from danger or distress. Dwelling means your home—the place where your family is, your castle, your den, the place where you live (physically, and also down inside your heart). That's what it means when you make God your refuge and your dwelling place.

The feeling you get down in your heart is rest, but the only time you really get to rest in this life is when you find someone you can trust to protect you. Most of the time, the only one you can trust completely is God. Everyone else, sooner or later, comes up short; they're just not there when you really need them most. God is the only One who is really trustworthy, and when you have God to protect you, it's a lead pipe cinch that nothing bad is going to happen to you. No evil will befall you, no catastrophe, no earthquake, no hurricanes, no swine flu, no cancer, and certainly no plague will come near your dwelling.

Yes, I also know people who know, love, and trust God who have dread diseases, who have experienced floods, tornados, hurricanes, and tidal waves, and I don't know why. It sounds like it's directly contrary to this verse, and it raises the age-old question of why bad things happen to good people, and I don't know why. But I do know that God loves me (and them), and that He is taking care of them, even if, to the untrained eye, it doesn't look like it. I know that in the midst of illness, catastrophe, and even death, the peace of God that passes all understanding is keeping their hearts and their minds through Christ Jesus our Lord. And God is using all those things to bless those very people in more ways than we can imagine.

You know why? *Because down in their hearts, where they live, God is there, because that's where God lives, too.* See, that's what it means when it says, "You have made God your refuge and your dwelling place." It means that **God has made you His dwelling place, the place where He lives**. What a flash that is for me! You just can't get any better than that! When you've got God inside you, you really are fully protected, fully sheltered, fully hidden, fully home, in Him.

So when it says in verse 11, "He shall give his angels charge over you," it's a little easier to believe in them because it says so right here in the Bible. I grew up in a church where they talked a little bit about angels, and they sang a few songs about angels, mostly at Christmas, singing praises. But they didn't talk much about personal angels. In fact, if anyone really talked about your "guardian" angel, it was only a manner of speaking, and not anything you could really depend on. Oh, I don't know, I guess maybe some people thought a little baby might have a personal guardian angel, or maybe a small child on her first day of school, out in the big world. But not any big children, or teenagers, and certainly not any adults could expect to have a personal guardian angel. I think maybe some of my Irish forefathers might have bought into the whole angel idea, but that was only because they were kinda' crazy. They also believed in "the little people," fairies, trolls and such, so angels weren't too big a stretch for them. But in this modern age, where hardly anyone believes in anything they can't see, touch, or explain with reasoning and logic, angels are just waaaay out there.

But you know, there may be something to it. Even Billy Graham wrote a book about angels, saying they're everywhere. I've also checked several different translations of this verse, and they all say, "He [God] will give His angels charge over you." The Bible talks about angels in a number of different places as well, and it goes to some lengths to explain the different kinds of angels, good and bad. Some of them even have names and special duties. So who am I to say that angels aren't for today? I've heard that some of the experts in the field say that the specific purpose of angels is to take care of our physical beings, to protect us from danger and distress, and to keep the demons and evil spirits away from us. Whoa! Here I am again, holding onto my traditions of not believing in all that stuff about angels and demons. But don't be too sure. I've never seen an angel or a demon, but on more than one occasion, I have heard stories from credible people who say they have.

So if God wants to give His angels charge over me, well, I'm ready. Like I said, I've never seen one, but I've had some things happen to me personally that I shouldn't have lived through, and I'm still here. From car wrecks, to driving incidents, to childhood accidents, to near misses, to medical emergencies—so many inexplicable things have happened, seemingly just to let me know that I am not really in control of my life; so it must be God. The same has happened to almost everyone I know well—everyone I've spent much time talking to, all those people with whom I've sat on the back porch and had a toddy and shared stories—they've all had similar experiences. They haven't said too much about angels, but they've all had those "miraculous" experiences, like when they should've died but came out smellin' like a rose. Like I said, maybe it's not angels; maybe it's just a coincidence, or maybe it's luck. I don't know, but I'm goin' with angels. I happen to believe in (trust) God, and God said He's gonna' give His angels charge over me, so I'm gonna' trust what He says. Oh, and God has also said on numerous other occasions that He is going to take care of me if I trust Him.

By the way, in the end, after circling all the wagons and beating around the bush, that's what it means when it says, "Because you have made God your refuge and your dwelling place, nothing bad is gonna' happen." It means, "If you trust God, He'll take care of you."

I believe it's partly because of those angels. They're gonna' keep you in all your ways. With their hands they will hold you up, so you won't hurt your foot on a stone, so you won't get tripped up—not just in the major catastrophes, but in the little, everyday events of life, you won't even hurt your foot.

There's something interesting about this verse. It comes from Psalms, and it's one of those not clearly attributable to David. The one right before it, Psalm 90, is attributed to Moses. And this one, Psalm 91, sounds a lot like Psalm 90, both in style and substance. Ol' Moses, like David, knew a lot about trusting God. He had spells of wandering in the wilderness, both alone and with the Israelites, and he knew a lot both about being lost and about being found. He knew some about needing someone to watch over him; he probably needed angels, if anyone did. Or maybe it was David, who was a whole hog truster in God too. As my daddy would say, "David was a man who would stick his neck out for God, far enough to get it chopped off" (willing to take a risk!). Now there's a man who needed God to send him some angels to take care of him, a man who was willing to take a chance on God.

The other interesting thing about this verse is that it is one of the verses Satan quoted to Jesus during the temptation in the wilderness (see Matthew 4:6). This is a paraphrase, but it went something like this: "Satan took Jesus up on the pinnacle of the Temple and said to Him, 'If you're the Son of God, throw yourself off'; for as it is written, 'He shall give His angels charge over you, and in their hands they shall bear you up, lest you dash your foot against a stone' (that'll prove that you really are who you say you are)." Funny thing is, Jesus did not say that the verse did not apply to him, and He did not deny that God had the angels there to protect Him. He just said that we're not supposed to tempt God (by doing stupid stuff). So I just have one more thing to say about this verse. If it applies to Jesus, and Jesus is in you and me, and God is protecting Jesus, then it seems reasonable to think that God is protecting you and me, too. Praise the Lord!

In conclusion, this passage is just another way of saying what we've been trying to say all along: If you trust God, He'll take care of you. This time they say it a little differently, a little more specifically, "He won't just take care of you; He'll send angels!"

Isaiah 40:31

"They that wait on the Lord will renew their strength, They shall mount up with wings as eagles, They shall run and not be weary, They shall walk and not faint."

I call this the "Old People's Prayer," because right before this it says, "Even the youths shall faint and be weary, and the young men shall utterly fall, but they that wait on the Lord [the old people] shall renew their strength."

In Spanish, the word for "wait" is *esperar*, which also is the same word for hope. So in Spanish (and other Romance languages) whenever you're waiting for someone, you're sitting there hoping they're gonna' come. Even in English, though there are some situations where "wait" and "hope" are different ideas, in this one, if you're waiting on the Lord, you're usually, definitely, hoping He's coming, hoping He's going to do what needs to be done, and soon. Maybe it's just me, but it's a small step between hoping He's coming, expecting He's coming, and trusting that He's coming. The more you think about it, the less difference there is. In fact, in this case, about the only difference is the timing; it's about the degree of the feeling and not the quality.

So now when I quote this verse, I usually say, "They that wait, hope and trust in the Lord." Since trust is such an attitude of the heart, and since waiting (and being willing to wait) is such good evidence of the trust in your heart, and since God looks at our hearts, the evidence is pretty overwhelming that wait, hope, and trust are just the same idea in different clothing. Sorta' the same way belief, faith, and trust are the same. So "they that trust in the Lord shall fly like eagles, run and not be weary, and walk and not faint." Isn't it neat? It says the youths will faint, but the old people who trust the Lord will run circles around them. I claim this verse every time my arthritis starts to kick in. Praise the Lord! Bible verses for every occasion!

Hebrews 3:1-19 (with parallels)

The book of Numbers, written by Moses as part of the Torah in the Old Testament, contains the story about what happens to people who, after God chooses them as His own people, end up not trusting

Him. They spent 400 or 500 years calling themselves the "children of Abraham." They saw with their own eyes all the miracles that God did in delivering them from the hand of Pharaoh and his Egyptian armies. They experienced all the miracles of God that He did in leading them and guiding them, maybe 2 or 3 million of them, and providing for all their needs. This story is about what happens to people who, after all that, still don't trust God. Is it just me, or are they sorta' like us?

During their journey through the wilderness, the Israelites aggravated and provoked God repeatedly. First, they said they wanted to go back to Egypt and be slaves, rather than die in the wilderness. Then they demanded that God replace Moses as their leader. Then they whined about not having any meat, just manna, so God literally covered them up with quail, like 4 feet deep all over the place. Then, when Moses was on the mountain talking to God, they talked Aaron into making the golden calf, and they danced and did lewd things and fell down and worshipped it—and God sent a plague that killed 70,000 of them. He even told Moses He was going to "smoke 'em all" and make a new people for Himself starting with Moses alone (Exodus 32:10), but Moses talked Him out of that. What really irritated God was when they sent the spies into the Promised Land, the land of Canaan, and 10 of the 12 came back saying, "We're scared; we can't go in; there are giants in the land." Only Caleb and Joshua were faithful and said, "God will take care of us."

But the people still rebelled and refused to go in, and that was enough for God. He swore that the generation that came out of Egypt, every one who was 20 years old or older when they left Egypt would **not** enter the Promised Land. God said in Psalm 95: 11 and in Hebrews 3:11, "So I swore in My wrath: They shall not enter into My rest." In the KJV, along in the middle of the passage, it says, "their carcasses fell in the wilderness." God must not have been too happy to allow His people to be reduced to carcasses. Why would God swear, and make them wander in the wilderness for 40 years, 'til they all fell dead? The answer is in Hebrews 3:19, "because of their unbelief." It was because they didn't trust Him; in fact, they refused to trust him. Elsewhere in the passage, it says that Caleb and Joshua were the only ones of their generation who survived to enter the Promised Land. All the rest fell in the wilderness. Why? In the 4th chapter of Hebrews, it says that God swore He wouldn't let them rest, because they didn't trust Him.

This was almost exactly the same reaction the "lord" had in the story of the "talents" (also called "The Unfaithful Servant"). The offense was "no trust," and the solution was "outer darkness," "wailing and gnashing of teeth," and being "left to wander in the wilderness until they fell dead."

Here's my conclusion: Back at the beginning of this chapter about trust, we talked about the story of Shadrach, Meshach, and Abednego, whom you might call "faithful servants." What did they say to Nebuchadnezzar's decree? "We don't have to answer you on this matter [we don't care what you say]. If you throw us in the fire, our God, Whom we serve, is able to deliver us from your hand, O King. **But even if He doesn't,** know this, **we will not serve your gods and we will not worship the gold image you have set up**." They were faithful men, and that's what God is looking for in us: Faithfulness. Trust. Trust enough to stake your life on it. I'm gonna' trust God with my whole heart, soul, strength, and might. The Bible is just full of this. This is the primary meeting place of God and us, and Jesus is the reason we trust.

Here are some parting thoughts for this chapter:

"For God so loved the world, He gave his only Son, that whoever believes [trusts] in Him will not die, but have everlasting life" (John 3:16). God loves, we trust, and we have eternal life with Him.

"Pay attention to what I say, and trust Him who sent Me, and You have eternal life. You will never be condemned, you have passed from death to life" (John 5:24). Trust God, and have eternal life.

Ultimately, salvation and eternal life are not about love, obedience, perfection, or repentance, but rather wholehearted, gut level, no holds barred, life or death, **trust**.

THEME 5: OBEDIENCE

THE TEST OF ALL TESTS

In the 22nd Chapter of Genesis is the story of the time when God told Abraham to get his son Isaac, the "Son of God's Promise," and take him up on a mountain, and "offer him there as a burnt offering." Literally, he was told to "take him up there, put him on an altar to the Lord, cut his throat, and burn him up." The very next verse in the story says, "So Abraham got up early the next morning, got his stuff together and started out."

Before I go on, I need to tell you that for most of my life, this has been the hardest passage in the Old Testament, maybe in the whole Bible, for me to understand. There's another one in the New Testament that's almost as hard.

You already know that God liked Abraham better than your average guy, because he trusted Him. God and Abe had become friends who talked together frequently. Some years before, Abraham had interceded with the Lord about the saving of Sodom, and the Lord had acceded to his requests to not destroy the city if even 10 righteous men could be found. You might even say that Abraham was used to talking to God. So I was wondering why he didn't say something to God in response to this most difficult command? I mean, something like, "Would you please explain this to me? I'm going to do it in any event. I'd just like to know what purpose is being served by this command." Or maybe, "I'm sorry Lord, I thought this child, this 'son of promise,' was going to be the tool You were going to use to fulfill Your promises to me."

Of course, through it all, Abraham was exceptionally reverent and respectful to the Lord. It makes me think of the time when Jesus asked Peter three times, "Do you love Me?" and Peter says, "Lord, you know everything. You know I love you."

Also, Abraham was not afraid of the Lord God. He loved Him,

he trusted Him, and he expected more good things from God. I guess we'll find out for sure when we all get to heaven, but I'd bet my bottom dollar that "our Father Abraham" had no sense at all that the Lord God Almighty was a god of hellfire and brimstone, anger, judgment, and punishment—as many people today seem to believe of the "God of the Old Testament." I bet Abe thought God was a God of love, certainly to him, in any event. This was the same God who had given him a child when he was 100 years old, and his wife was 90.

The problem may be that most of us have never loved God or trusted Him as much as Abraham did. So why didn't Abraham say something to God after this? It might be because God's command was clearly a serious matter, requiring the utmost in reverence, both for God and the situation. Maybe it was because Abraham was so flabbergasted by it, though I really don't think that was it. Maybe it was because Abraham was pondering how in the world he could ever explain to Isaac (much less Isaac's momma, Sarah) how or why he could even think of doing such a thing. (Just between me and you, if it weren't so serious, it'd be actually crazy even to consider. Even today, no one wants to talk about this event, because it sounds so crazy that God would tell His friend, His best friend, Abraham, to kill his own son. I think I'd be speechless, too.)

What about all this from Isaac's viewpoint? It says in verse 5 that Isaac was "a lad," or maybe translated, "a young man," big enough to carry the load of wood that would be required for the burnt offering. What d'ya' think? Maybe 15? Big enough that if he'd known what was fixin' to happen, he might have tried to run away and save himself. I don't think so though, 'cause it says in verse 9, "When they got to the place God had told him about, Abraham built an altar, put the wood on it, and he bound Isaac his son and laid him on the altar." By this time, Isaac had to know what was happening, so he must have willingly submitted out of respect for Abraham and for God. Whew!

You know, another crazy thing about this story is what it says in Hebrews 11:17-19 about this event: "By faith [trust] Abraham, when he was tested, offered up his only son . . . concluding that God was able to raise him up, even from the dead." It's not so funny or crazy, but maybe very revealing that Isaac was Abraham's **only** son (of the promise), and Jesus is God's **only** begotten Son. Abraham's son was raised from the dead **figuratively**; Jesus was raised from the dead

literally. It's sorta' the ultimate in historical, physical, and biblical fore-shadowing. Even more to the point of this discussion, this passage from Hebrews says, "Abraham was willing to sacrifice his only son as an offering to God, because he trusted that God would raise him from the dead."

There are two other clues to what Abraham was thinking in this event about how much he trusted God. In verse 5, he tells the two young men who came with them, "Y'all wait here and keep the donkey, and me and the boy will go worship on the mountain, and we will come back to you." Then Isaac says, "Father, we've got all the stuff for the offering, the wood and the fire, but where is the lamb?" And Abraham said, "The Lord will provide the lamb for the offering" (and He did, too). Do you think Abraham knew something he wasn't letting on? Or was it just gut-level, whole-hog trust?

Now, in the very first verse of this passage, Genesis 22:1, it says, "Now it came to pass, after these things, that God tested Abraham." The test was to sacrifice Isaac, from which the big question always arises, "Why would God do that?" Yes, I know we're not supposed to question God (supposedly because it shows a lack of faith, but the God I serve is big, strong, and trustworthy enough, to stand up to the most intense degree of questioning). For the sake of argument, one I agree with, the Bible and the hymnal both say we're supposed to "trust and obey, for there's no other way, to be happy in Jesus, but to trust and obey" (from "Trust and Obey," by J. H. Sammis, 1834, public domain.)

Well, first, several places in the Bible it says, in various ways, "tribulation (testing) builds character" (for example, Romans 5:3-4), and it does. So this event may have added some character to ol' Abe. Another reason may be that God wanted to make sure that Abraham loved Him more than anything or anyone else in the world. To me, this particular test was less about how much Abraham loved his son, Isaac, and more about how much he loved the idea of what Isaac represented in terms of making Abraham the "Father of many nations." As A.W. Tozer said, in his book *The Pursuit of God*, "To the wondering patriarch He now says, in effect, 'It's all right, Abraham. I never intended that you should actually slay the lad. I only wanted to remove him from the temple of your heart that I might reign unchallenged there.'"

Maybe another reason for this event was what was mentioned earlier about foreshadowing. It really is clear in the Bible that, from the beginning, God's preferred means of reconciling Himself to men (really His only method and means) is by grace through **faith**, and this episode is but one of many examples of that message found in the Bible. Abraham gaining righteousness through **faith**, the first one ever to do that, is what makes him our (spiritual) "Father."

Toward the end of the passage, it says that Abraham called the place, "The-Lord-Will-Provide" (in Hebrew that's "Jehovah Jireh"), which means, "God will take care of us" (if we'll just trust Him). This really is the message that God has been sending us all the time, throughout history, in the Bible and out—**He'll take care of us if we'll just trust Him**. Maybe this is also part of God's purpose for devising this "test" for Abraham.

Toward the end of the passage, in verse 12, is the published reason why God tested Abraham, when it says, "And [God] said, 'Stop; don't hurt the boy, for now I know that you fear [trust and obey] God, since you have not withheld your son, your only son, from Me." So that's the reason, like Tozer might say, "to remove Isaac and the idea of you being the father of many nations, from the throne of your heart, so I can reign unchallenged there." I agree with Rev. Tozer. But you know what I think? This may have been a reassurance to God about how much Abraham feared, reverenced, trusted, and obeyed God, even though I think God already knew that. He already knew that Abraham loved, trusted, and obeyed Him more than anything or anybody else in the whole world, or even in the world to come. I really think this test was to **let Abraham know** how much he loved God, that he loved Him more than the "Promise". And when the test was over, Abraham knew. Praise God! That's trust, obey, humble, love, serve, and most of all surrender, all rolled into one.

You know, the epilogue to this story is in Hebrews 11: 17-19. It says (Tex's paraphrase), "Abraham was willing to sacrifice Isaac, because he believed that God would raise him from the dead, from whence he received him (because in his heart Abraham had already made the decision to obey)."

TEX'S THOUGHTS ON OBEDIENCE

What does it mean to be "obedient"? I think obedience has two parts—doing right and doing what God says. Generally, most people would say that "doing right" means abiding by the rules, being moral and ethical, and treating others like you'd like to be treated. Of course, all those things are "right" in a sense. But what is "right" in a behavioral sense? When you are a child, doing right means doing whatever your parent or guardian says to do: Go to bed, get up, wash your hands, eat this, eat now, don't chew with your mouth open, don't talk with your mouth full, don't backsass your momma. Pretty simple stuff; basically, do what you're supposed to. Many people directly equate their relationship with God in exactly the same way. Having a relationship with God, doing what God says, is exactly the same as the relationship a "good" child has with a "good" parent.

I submit to you that having a relationship with God is a good deal more. In fact, I submit that having a relationship with God, any relationship with God, is a qualitatively different experience from the relationship a child has with his or her parent.

Obedience is saying "yes" when God tells you something to do (in an immediate sense), for example, "If you love me you'll keep my commandments" (John 14:15), and "This is my commandment, that you love one another" (John 15:12). I cannot do right by myself. I can only do right as I surrender and trust God to work His will in me. Only as I die to myself, and let Jesus live His life in me (Luke 9:23-24) can I live up to His standard, which is, "Be ye perfect [whole, complete, entire, wanting nothing], even as your Father in heaven is perfect" (Matthew 5:48).

Philippians 2:5-8 says, in a general way, "Let this mind [attitude] be in you which was also in Christ Jesus . . . Who, being found as a man . . . humbled Himself, and became a slave, and was obedient unto death, even death on a cross." It says a lot of other stuff in there, too, but the point it makes is that Jesus was obedient unto death; and we're supposed to let Jesus' mind [attitude] be in us, particularly that part of Jesus' attitude which was obedient unto death. Try to fit that in with what it says in Luke 9:23 above about denying yourself (your sinful nature), taking up your cross daily (the cross of death to you and life from Him), and following Him.

Genesis 15:6 and Romans 4:3 say, "Abraham believed [trusted] God, and it was credited to him for righteousness." Basically, Abraham was just like us and didn't do right all the time. In fact, like us, he didn't do right a lot of the time, but God did not judge him. God didn't even say, "Trust me and do right all the time," or "Trust me and **try** to do right all the time." God didn't say anything except, "You do trust me, so I'll count that trust for righteousness." God, in His Word, says that "because Abraham believes [trusts] in Me, I'm going to count it as if he had done right all the time." This is hard to understand, but it must mean that in order to "do right" in God's eyes, to keep God's commandments, to live standing face to face with God, the main thing you have to do is trust Him.

If you genuinely, truly, completely trust Him, you **will** obey Him, on a minute-by-minute basis. That's what He wants. Even if you aren't perfect, and you're only able to really trust Him a little bit, some of the time, He still wants you, because He's looking at your heart, and He knows you're trying to trust. Like it says about what the father with the demon-possessed son said, "Yes I believe, help me in my unbelief" (Mark 9:24). I trust, but help me, Lord, when I'm scared.

In John 5: 24, Jesus says, "If you pay attention to what I say, and trust Him who sent Me, you have eternal life, you shall never be condemned, you have passed from death unto life." Now wait, where's that line about, "Oh and by the way, try to do right all the time." It's not in there. You know why, it's because God already knows that you can't do right all the time. He doesn't even want you to do right all the time, because if you did, then you could boast in what you'd done. God doesn't want that. He wants you to boast in what He's done. (Ephesians 2:8-9)

To overcome all the problems, difficulties, and insurmountable obstacles in your life, you must focus on the solution, not on the problem. If you want to walk on water, you can't look at the waves, worry about the waves, or become immersed in the awful things the waves and the water are going to do to you. You must focus on the solution, and the only solution is Jesus. You must focus on Jesus. You must immerse yourself in the Word of God, in the relationship of daily prayer and meditation with Jesus; at every turn, at every threat to your peace and stability, you must focus yourself on drawing closer to Jesus, on surrendering yourself more to Jesus, on spending more time concentrating every fiber of your being on Him. This is what obedience is all about. Surrendering your whole self to God through Jesus; focusing your whole attention on Jesus, so that in you He develops a disciple; so that you begin dying to yourself, so Jesus can live His eternal life in and through you (Luke 9:23-24).

You have to throw all your cares on Him, for He cares for you (1 Peter 5:7). You have to give up trusting yourself (none of us are very trustworthy), give all your problems to Him, and make up your mind that you're just not going to think about them anymore, that you're just going to let Jesus do whatever He wants to about them and about you, and that you're going to spend your time developing a relationship with Him. This is the essence of obedience to God.

You don't really have much choice. Nothing else works. You've already tried all the other stuff, and you're still in the same fix as before, 'cept maybe worse. Jesus is the only solution that works!

James 1:22-25

"But be ye doers of the word, and not hearers only, deceiving yourselves. For if anyone is a hearer of the word and not a doer, he is like a man observing his natural face in the mirror; for he observes himself, goes away, and immediately forgets what kind of man he was. But he who looks into the perfect law of liberty and continues in it, and is not a forgetful hearer but a doer of the work, this one will be blessed in what he does."

Wow! Did you hear that? Anybody who hears the Word but doesn't do anything about it is like a man who looks at himself in the mirror, and as soon as he turns away, he forgets what he looked like. In other words, he deceives himself into thinking that he looks like something he really isn't—into thinking he's a good Christian because he says he's a good Christian.

While this whole book is about doing what the Word says, what is James talking about in this particular passage? It's about looking into the perfect law of liberty. The perfect law of liberty is the liberty we get from surrendering our whole selves to Jesus, so He can live His eternal life in us. It's letting Him do whatever He wants to with our lives, on a minute-by-minute basis. That is true obedience. It is dying to myself, so Jesus can live His own life in me (Luke 9:23-24). The reason they call it the "perfect" law of liberty is because only Jesus is perfect, and only He can make us perfectly free, free from our sins, free from our pasts, and most of all, free from our*selves*. My friend Red Smith, who is serving a 25-year sentence in prison, says, "I thank God every day that He rescued me from myself." There's a man who knows what true freedom is all about.

Let's say, for a minute, that the man who is a hearer and not a doer, the guy who can't remember what he looks like—you know, the one who is deceiving himself into thinking he's something he's not, but he wants to change—what is he supposed to do? Well, it sounds like he is supposed to look into the "perfect law of liberty" and quit looking in the mirror at himself.

What is that again? It must be something different from the "traditional" law, the law that says, don't, don't, don't, and judges and punishes if you do. It must be something like what Paul talks about in Romans 8, when he says, "There is therefore now no condemnation to them that are in Christ Jesus . . . to them that walk not after the flesh, but after the Spirit; for what the law could not do, in that it was weak through the flesh; God, sending His own Son, in the likeness of sinful flesh, and for sin, condemned sin in the flesh; so that the law could be fulfilled in us, who walk not after the flesh, but after the Spirit." That's the "perfect law of liberty," the law that gets fulfilled in us when we die to ourselves so Jesus can live His perfect, eternal life in us, because we don't walk after the sinful nature, but after the Holy Spirit, and so fulfill the Perfect Law of Liberty. Then, we *aren't* the ones who end up looking in the mirror and wondering who in the world we are.

More to the point, true obedience lies in doing what the verse says, "Walk not after the sinful nature, but walk after the Spirit." That's obedience—not abiding by the rules, but surrendering yourself to Jesus so He can live His life in you. Because He is the only perfectly obedient one, so only He can fulfill the perfect law of liberty in you and me, by living His life in us.

A great parallel to this passage is the one in Matthew 7:24-27, where it says, "Whoever hears these sayings of Mine, and does them, I will liken him to a wise man who built his house on the rock; . . . But everyone who hears these sayings of Mine, and does not do them, will be like a foolish man who built his house on the sand." (If you do what I say, you're smart. If you don't do what I say, you're a fool.)

1 Samuel 15:22-23, KJV

"But Samuel replied [to King Saul]: 'Does the LORD delight in burnt offerings and sacrifices as much as in obeying the voice of the LORD? To obey is better than sacrifice, and to heed is better than the fat of rams. For rebellion is like the sin of witchcraft, and arrogance [stubbornness] like the evil of idolatry. Because you have rejected the word of the LORD, he has rejected you as king.'"

Animal sacrifice (at least formal religious sacrifice as in the burnt offerings in the tabernacle and then in the temple) was an effort by men to say they were sorry for their sins and to do something to prove their sincerity. In this verse, Samuel is saying (and God is saying through Samuel), that God is not one bit impressed with people saying they're sorry and still going on and being disobedient anyway. Here's a modern translation, "Being obedient is a **whole lot better** than saying you're sorry. Instead of saying you're sorry afterward, you could have (should have) done right to start with!"

What does He say next? He immediately starts talking about rebellion. Why does He do that? You think maybe it's because He (God) thinks that disobedience is the same as rebellion? Well, let's say God would be willing to cut them a little slack. Maybe one time of disobedience deserves mercy; maybe for two times, you're just being like a little kid and you just forgot. But if you keep doing it over and over, especially when God has made such a big deal out of this particular command—in this case, God told Saul to kill everybody and everything in the Amalekites' whole country, but Saul kept a bunch of the animals, and he did not kill Agag, the king of the Amalekites— then yes, God equates such disobedience with rebellion.

Then He says, "Rebellion is as the sin of witchcraft and

stubbornness is like the evil of idolatry." It sounds like God thinks 1) rebellion is consorting with evil spirits, which is any spirit besides the Holy Spirit, and 2) stubbornness, which is being disobedient over and over, is like worshipping idols and not God.

In a proverbial nutshell, God doesn't like disobedience. He's merciful, but He doesn't like stubborn, continuing disobedience, the kind where you look Him in the eye and say, "I know You don't like it; but I don't care; I'm gonna' do it anyway." God looks at your heart, and He knows if you say it that way, even if you say you're really sorry and you promise never to do it again. He knows you better than you know you. He knows if you really want to do right or if you're just saying that. The funny thing is, in this story about Samuel and Saul, as soon as Samuel said, "Because you have rejected the word of the Lord, He has also rejected you from being king," then Saul says, "I have sinned . . . please pardon my sin." I'm sooo sorry. What a bunch of phony crap. If that's the way a person is in his heart, God knows it, and He rejects it.

I don't know about you, but I have done what Saul did a thousand times. Maybe not on such a grand scale, but it's only because I'm just a wimp compared to King Saul. I've done it in my heart. I've looked God in the eye and said, "I know this is wrong, and I know You don't like it, but I'm going to do it anyway." Maybe I thought God would forgive me; maybe I didn't even care at the time whether He forgave me or not, but I was on a completely different wave length.

So how do we get ourselves away from this willful disobedience? In a word, we don't and we can't. What is it Paul says, "Who will deliver me from this wretched man that I am?" (Romans 7:24). You only get one guess—of course, it's God. So if God is so hard on willful disobedience, why would He even consider delivering such jerks as us? It's because He wants to. What is the one thing that will persuade Him to do it? Only our humble recognition that we don't have a chance except to completely surrender ourselves to Him, daily, and let Him live His eternal life in us. And to keep on surrendering and renewing our relationship with Him daily.

Matthew 21:28-32

In this passage, Jesus tells the chief priests and the elders the story of the man who had two sons. He went to the first and said, "Go to the vineyard." And the son said, "I will not." But afterward, he regretted it and went. Then the father went to the second son and said the same. That son said, "I'll go." But he didn't. Then Jesus said, "Which one of the sons did the will of his father?" They said, "The first."

Then Jesus said, "The tax collectors and harlots enter the kingdom of God before you. John [the Baptist] came teaching righteousness, and you didn't believe him; but the tax collectors and harlots believed him; and when you saw them, you still didn't relent and believe."

True obedience is to completely surrender to the will of God for you. It is to say, "I'm making a deal with You God. I'll do whatever you want me to, and You can do whatever You want to with me." This is a minute-by-minute commitment. This is getting up every morning and saying, "Okay, Lord, I'm ready. Tell me where you want me to go today. Show me the people you want me to talk to and be with today. Let me see the adventure of Your presence in my life, in my comings and goings. I do not have a plan. I do not have an agenda. I do not have a preconceived notion about how I'm supposed to look or act." It is to echo the scripture, "As the servants eye is on the hand of his Master, so is my heart stayed on You" (Psalm 123:2). As God shows me His will, I will follow.

Luke 9:23

Jesus said, "If any man would be my disciple, let him deny himself, and take up his cross daily, and follow Me. For whoever would save his life will lose it; but whoever will lose his life for My sake, will find it. For what does it profit a man if he should gain the whole world and lose his own soul?"

What does this mean, "take up his cross"? Look at Galatians 2:20, where it says, "I am crucified with Christ, nevertheless I live, yet not I, but Christ lives in me, and the life I now live in the flesh, I live by the faith of [trust in] the Son of God, who loved me and gave Himself for me." To "take up your cross" means to die to yourself so that Jesus can live His eternal life in you. Whoever is willing to die to himself daily is the one who is being obedient. Quit trying to get your way, and let Jesus live in you so He can have His way with you and with those around you. It's a daily act of surrender, humbling yourself, and giving plumb up.

Why is it so hard to be obedient to God? Why is it so hard to "deny yourself, and take up your cross daily, and follow Him"? The free enterprise, democratic, materialistic, individualistic, independent character of the culture of the United States of America in the 20th and 21st centuries is directly at odds with this passage. There is a cognitive disconnect between this passage and the way we live, think, and organize our lives. Apart from a few, minor religious societies such as the Amish and Mennonites and Orthodox Jews, we have all turned away from focusing on God. We have made a religion of focusing on ourselves. Our whole society has turned from God to money, possessions, and self-promotion of the grossest kind.

There are exceptions to every rule, but I'd say my background, my upbringing, and my social situation are pretty representative of a great cross-section of people in America—not just white, European lineage, nominally Christian, people, but many Asians and Africans (of several religions), who have come here seeking their education and fortune over the past 100 years. With most, if not all of them, as with me, there is a great conflict between the teaching of our former cultures and the religion(s) on which those cultures were based, and the present culture of America, that is based on the religion of self, possessions, and control by men, rather than submission to God. 'Scuse me, but the short version of this philosophy, this so-called religion, is "It's all about me and none about you." Yet we support this culture with all kinds of good sounding, well meaning lies about what great people we are for organizing and running our lives this way. There is a great cognitive disconnect between the "American Dream" of "self, money, and stuff" on the one hand, and "deny yourself, take up your cross, daily, and follow Me" on the other.

What do we do to reconcile this conflict? Well, we have three choices: 1) Give plumb up and follow Him, 2) Pursue education, money, power, and control, and the devil take the hindermost, or 3) keep doing what most of us have been doing our whole lives for generations, which is to give lip service to God but continue our lives pursuing good college, good job, good spouse, good house in a good part of town, good schools for our kids, good clubs, good insurance, good investments, good vacations, and good retirement, not to mention independence and control of our own lives, not being obligated to anybody else, least of all our families, parents, kids, or God.

If you're a middle-class American, from middle-class American stock, and you don't fit #3 above like a glove, I think you are either conning yourself or you're ignoring reality.

Let me tell you how I measure up to #3. I've been going to church most of my life. My parents' families have been professing Christians as far back as we've been able to trace them; some lines date as far back as the 1600s. Some were true believers, genuine trusters in Jesus; a few were pastors along the way, Catholics turned Baptists.

My paternal grandmother, Meta, trusted Jesus. She was fully involved in all the activities of her church. She took all her kids to church, all nine of them. She took care of the poor and the sick in her community. She read the Bible, studied it, and meditated on it. When I was a child, she was in her 80s, nearly blind, and every time I'd come to visit she'd get me to read the Bible to her. Her Bible was wore plumb out. It had duct tape down the back to keep it together. But she wouldn't let us get her a new one because the old one had all her notes in the margins. She was relentless in her pursuit of God; she prayed long and hard every day. Not all her kids came to God, but it wasn't for lack of her praying for them, telling them about God, and showing them what it was like to be someone who truly "denied herself, and took up her cross daily, and followed Him." Four of her sons surrendered their lives to God, one early, three later. Three became deacons, all true trustors in Jesus who raised their kids to trust God, though some fell away. They loved God with all their hearts.

That's the kind of people I came from; that's the kind of people who influenced me. My momma came from a different branch, but her family was also committed to Jesus for generations. My momma was standing beside me when I was 10 during the invitation at a church in Lubbock, Texas, and I broke down crying. She said, "What's the matter?" I said, "I don't know." She said, "I think you better go down." ("Go down" means go down the aisle and surrender yourself to Jesus.) And I did. I couldn't really tell at the beginning, but my life was changed, and God has been moving in my life ever since. I've run away over and over, but He always brings me back, closer and closer to Him—He just won't give up.

But here's the hitch. At the same time I was turning toward God, I also was being raised to get along in the American culture. I got a vision of how this combination of circumstances works out. The culture side looks like it wins, but the God side is the way of true obedience. Here's the way it was in the 1950s in the good ol' U.S.A.

From my earliest memories, I was raised with certain expectations. In the beginning, it was my parents' expectations for me, but as I grew older I imbibed their expectations and they became my own. When I started to school, I knew that I was expected to do well there, to make good grades, to be obedient, to work hard on projects, and to be respectful to my teachers and all authorities. I didn't just practice this in school; I lived it. My momma had been teaching more than 20 years when I was born, and she got her master's degree in education when I was in the first grade. So I knew what was expected of me and I generally lived up to the expectations. In fact, by the time I got saved at age 10, I really felt the "calling of God" to be a lawyer. I did well in school and graduated 4th in my high school class of 400. I finished two years of college, and then had a few interruptions, including marriage, the Army, and the Viet Nam war before I got in the "oil bidness," and I was off to the races.

From early in life, maybe junior high school, I thought I'd be a millionaire by the time I was 30. I was well on my way with a big, distinctive house, rental property for extra income, and a great job with opportunities for more money on the side. 'Course I was out of town a lot and worked long hours when I was home. Not much "focus on the family," but I was certainly living up to everyone's expectations about education, job, money and stuff. Like I was saying, I was reading and applying the principles of Napolean Hill's *Think and Grow Rich* from an early age. Hill said, "Whatever the mind of man can conceive and believe, he can achieve." I was right there. (Wait, where was God in all this? You remember, lip service.)

I even had some "extra trimmings." I was involved in political service as a teen, active in political campaigns, and I even ran for office (but didn't win). I served on many civic, church, and charitable committees. Wait, what about family? Sad to say, I hardly thought about family. 'Course even at that, I was right in the middle of almost everyone's expectations for success in our culture and society.

Back to a prior question: Where was God in all of this? Where was, "Deny myself, take up my cross daily, and follow Jesus"? You probably already got the answer—He was nowhere. The only time I turned around to talk to or listen to God was when He did something to get my attention and make me remember how little I was really in control. And He did, too. He came when I was 27, and I followed Him 'til I was 32, and then fell away for 5 years or so. I went back to my life of trying to make money, get stuff, and run my life. He came again when I was 37 when I nearly died of intestinal disorders. He resurrected me, almost from the dead, but it didn't take long 'til I was hard at it again, money and stuff, money and stuff.

Finally, about 40, I decided that God was calling me to go to law school (my words, not His), and I did it. I decided that I could really do something for other people and probably make a lot of money at the same time. Little did I know that in the process, God was leading me down the path toward Him. Pretty late in life, age 50-something, after practicing criminal defense law for 6-7 years, I finally gave up to God for the last time. At this writing, I've been going on with God about ten years, and I think He's finally got a good scald on me this time. Kinda' like Peter said when Jesus asked them if they were going to go away like the others, and Peter said, "Where would we go?"

I finally gave up at 55. I quit living the divided life. I quit trying to do my own thing while struggling to satisfy God; never "denying myself, and taking up my cross daily, and following Him." I finally decided that I'd just give plumb up, like God had been asking me to do for most of my life. It was hard to do, but I did it. Yes, I still have a job that God uses to give me money, and I am still involved in "activities" that don't look much different from before. But both my heart and my head are in a whole different place. I spend a lot more time lately seeking God's face, I'm practicing trusting Him than ever before, and I'm sharing His love, mercy, and grace. Like some old rock song says, "I guess you have to finally decide, Say yes to one and let the other one ride." Well, I did that; I have said yes to "The One." I have let the other one (myself) ride. My Bible tells me to deny myself, take up my cross (the cross of death to me and life from Jesus) every single day, and follow Him. Now, that is what obedience is all about.

Isaiah 1:18-20

"Come now, and let us reason together, says the LORD, Though your sins are like scarlet, They shall be as white as snow; Though they are red like crimson, They shall be as wool. If you are willing and obedient, You shall eat the good of the land; But if you refuse and rebel, You shall be devoured by the sword; for the mouth of the LORD has spoken."

Whew! That is stout. Where is "God is love" in that? That doesn't sound very loving. Sounds like, "If you straighten up and fly right, you'll be fine. But if you mess up, you're dead meat." Yet that's what it says, and that's what it means; there's no denying it.

But wait, is that all there is to it? Is this passage really exposing God as a mean Person? Actually it's kinda' funny. I'm over 60; I've got three grown kids and an 16-year-old. This reminds me of a parent talking to a child. He says, "Come on, let's talk. I want to explain something to you. To start with, people are all a bunch of sinners. Nobody does right all the time. Everybody messes up. Sometimes a lot. But if you listen and pay attention to what I say, you'll be okay anyway (see John 5:24). Here's the deal, if you do good, good things will happen; if you do bad, bad things will happen. If you make good decisions . . . if you make bad decisions . . ." You can almost hear Jesus saying, "He who has ears to hear, let him hear."

What are the key words in the passage? "Willing and obedient" vs. "refuse and rebel." It all comes down to attitude. Willing is about being agreeable, submissive, forgiving, and open. Obedient is about being humble, poor in spirit, conciliatory, kind, and friendly. "Refuse and rebel" is just the opposite—they're about arrogance, force, conflict, dispute, and ill will.

These are things any right-thinking parent would say to their child. I'm reminded of one time when my 3-year-old daughter, Lindsey (now 38), got out in the street a little ways in front of our house. 'Course we'd told her many times not to get in the street; it's a busy street, lots of college kids going by fast in their hot cars. This time I saw an opportunity for a special lesson. I said, "Lindsey, come here, I want to show you something." I sat down on the curb with my feet in the street, and I stood her in the street just in front of me; and I said,

"You have to be careful. If you don't watch out, and you step in the street, even accidentally, a car might come by and **hit** you and **hurt** you." As I said this, I grabbed her and swept her off her feet, and she cried; she was scared.

You probably know the rest of the story. She never got back in the street again. I guess some people might say that was mean. They might say there are better ways to teach that lesson. Maybe. But here it is, 35 years later, and I still have my daughter; grown and married, with four kids of her own, a gift of God to me. It makes me grin when I think about it.

So it looks like maybe God isn't such a mean person after all. It's like Paul says in Ephesians, "Be kind to one another, tenderhearted, forgiving one another [and good things will happen]" (Ephesians 4:32), or as it says in 1 Samuel 15:23, "Rebellion is like witchcraft, and stubbornness is like worshiping idols [and bad things will happen]." One thing more—it is true that these things will come to pass, "Because the mouth of the Lord has spoken."

Matthew 7:24-27

Jesus says, "Therefore whoever hears these sayings of Mine, and does them, I will liken him to a wise man who built his house on the rock: and the rain descended, the floods came, and the winds blew and beat on that house; and it did not fall, for it was founded on the rock.

"But everyone who hears these sayings of Mine, and does not do them, will be like a foolish man who built his house on the sand: and the rain descended, the floods came, and the winds blew and beat on that house; and it fell. And great was its fall."

Let's see, we were talking about obedience. What does this passage have to do with obedience? Well, this may not be the dictionary definition, but obedience is listening and paying attention to the instructions and doing what they tell you. Jesus also says, "If you listen, and do what I tell you [be obedient], here's what will happen: I'll think you are like a wise man who built his house on a rock." The Lord Jesus, the Incarnate God, will think you are wise, as if you had built your house on a rock.

I don't know for sure what analogy Jesus is making by talking about the house, but I always think He's talking about your life, your beliefs, the way you look at things. You may be familiar with the expression "worldview"; how you see the world and your place in it. I think that's what He's talking about when He says your "house"; it's the values and beliefs on which you base your life—in a spiritual sense, often in a natural sense, and in a social, political, emotional, mental, psychological sense—the values and beliefs on which you base your life really are your house.

What about "the rock"? Who or what is Jesus referring to by using that expression? I don't know about other translations, but in the NKJV it says, "built on the rock." It doesn't say "a" rock or "bedrock." It says "the" rock. It's just too easy isn't it? Where I come from, "the" rock is Jesus. Isn't it great? In so many words, Jesus is saying, "If you pay attention, and do what I say, I'll think you're a wise person who bases his whole life (you've built your whole house) on Me and My Words!"

It's interesting that at the end of the first half of this passage it says that the house was in a big storm, but it did not fall, because it was "founded" on "the rock." Just so you'll know, this house we're talking about is no trailer house or mobile home that'll blow over and tear up in the first strong wind. This is a real house. It isn't just parked on that rock. It's not just sitting on skids waiting to float away in the first high water. My vision is one in which they cut deep precision holes in the rock and set the pillars deep, so the house and the rock become one. That's "founded" on the rock.

If you've ever been to church much, you've probably heard the song, "The Solid Rock," by Edwin Mote, written in 1834. It goes like this:

My hope is built on nothing less
Than Jesus' blood and righteousness.
I dare not trust the sweetest frame,
But wholly lean on Jesus' Name.

Chorus
On Christ the solid Rock I stand,
All other ground is sinking sand;
All other ground is sinking sand.

When darkness seems to hide His face,
I rest on His unchanging grace.
In every high and stormy gale,
My anchor holds within the veil.

Chorus

His oath, His covenant, His blood,
Support me in the whelming flood.
When all around my soul gives way,
He then is all my Hope and Stay.

Chorus

When He shall come with trumpet sound,
Oh may I then in Him be found.
Dressed in His righteousness alone,
Faultless to stand before the throne.

On Christ the solid Rock I stand,
All other ground is sinking sand;
All other ground is sinking sand.

So build your life on the rock, the solid rock that is Jesus.

Since we've got that fixed in our minds, it's almost an afterthought to talk about building on the sand. Jesus says, "Only a fool would do that."

When my "old" kids were little, we used to go to Big Bend National Park almost every Spring break, and we'd camp near the Rio Grande River in the Cottonwood Campground on the West side of the Park. It was always great fun, great experiences, and great memories. We used to spend all day tubing down the river for miles, then get out and walk back, sunburned, wet, tired, and hungry, but happy. We'd have hot dogs and marshmallows over the fire, we'd sing a few songs, maybe even tell a ghost story, and then we'd sleep well in the fresh air.

When we'd go down the river, there were always a lot of twists and turns with a lot of big sand bars sticking out of the water, on the inside of the bends in the river, and on the outside of the bends there'd be deep, fast-flowing water.

The funny thing was, the next year we'd go down the same place, and the sand bars would be gone, or they'd be moved to the side, and the main stream would be where the sand was before. That experience reminds me of this passage about building your house on the sand.

What are the ingredients of this parable about the house on the sand? Well, I guess the "house" still means me or you and our lives, the things we base our lives on, and the things we surround ourselves with—all the things we rely on when the storm comes. If those things are founded on sand, and the sand moves or disappears every time a storm comes, then we're gonna' be living on very shaky ground; you might say a precarious existence. If whatever you trust in and rely on is moving all the time, how secure can you be? How much peace can you have? Not much.

Take money for example, (including cash, CD's, retirement accounts, securities, bonds, mutual funds, insurance, or other investments like land or cattle, or gold or silver). What do all these things have in common? They're constantly moving and changing, constantly shifting in value, going up and down in price. Even cash money is constantly losing value because of inflation. All these things are a lot like sand, since every time the wind blows, every time it rains, everything moves. It's an amazing analogy when Jesus says, "Only a fool would live in [trust in] a house that was built on the sand."

Yet that's what most of us are depending on here in America. I don't know about you, but I live on the edge. I live from paycheck to paycheck. Sometimes I hit a lick and I have some extra money, so I buy a different car, take a trip, or pay down my credit cards.

A few times I've tried to put a little money aside for a rainy day, but I've about quit doing that; it just never seems to work out. Something always happens (medical bills, car repairs, something unexpected) to use up the money I've set aside. It's almost as if God is saying, "Don't store up stuff on earth, where moth and rust corrupts and thieves break in and steal. But store up treasure in heaven, where the moths and the rust and the thieves can't get it" (Matthew 6:19-20). And here's the central line of the passage, "because where your treasure is, there is where your heart is, too!" (Tex's paraphrase)

'Course the problem is if we trust in stuff that doesn't last, then we're literally crushed when the bottom falls out. Like Black Thursday in '29, when the bottom really did fall out, and people started jumping out the windows. More recently, in Fall 2008, when the "oil bidness" fell apart, the stock market shrunk by about 50%, the economy went down, unemployment went up, and lots of people lost their jobs along with retirement funds and medical insurance. For a while, even the people who still had jobs were scared to death for fear they were going to lose them, and people were grasping for straws, hoping against hope that they wouldn't be next. I'm talking about carrying around this sick feeling in the pit of your stomach, wondering how long you could last before you were living in your car, too.

I heard a story about a national company with offices here in Houston. During the Christmas holidays in 2008, all the employees got a Christmas Card with a keycard in it and a note that said, "On January 2, 2009, when you return to our offices, if your keycard doesn't work, report to the guard shack and a security guard will escort you into the building so you can retrieve your personal belongings and vacate the premises." What a Christmas gift! What a great Christmas vacation! So if all your trust is in your job, and you lose it like that, it wouldn't take much to push you out that window, too. So who can you trust?

I hate to say it, but in spite of my declarations of trust in the Lord, I rationalize my way into trusting lots of things besides Him. I wouldn't usually call those things gods or idols that I worship, but when I reflect on the way I act in relation to those things, I'm amazed at how near I come to worshipping them. Yet those things can't do much more for me than statues carved of wood, stone, silver, or gold.

Take insurance, for example. Yes, like many folks, I spend a great deal of money every month on insurance: House insurance (fire and casualty insurance, required by the lender); car insurance (required by law), medical insurance, and life insurance. While some have even more than this, I estimate that we spend more than $2,000 per month on our various kinds of insurance.

Yet what do I think about insurance? I think it's a waste of money. I think if anything happened to any of the stuff I possess, and I lost it, that God would give me some more stuff: house, cars, furniture, clothes, jewelry. I didn't have any of that stuff before I had insurance. Insurance didn't help me get it, and insurance won't replace it, certainly not with the same kind or quality or quantity as before. When all is said and done, God is the only One who is able to take care of all the stuff I've got. What was it Job said? "The Lord gave and the Lord has taken away. Blessed be the Name of the Lord" (Job 1:21).

Over the years, we've paid more and more for medical insurance. We've had to keep raising the deductibles to keep the payments where we could stand them, so we end up paying a larger and larger proportion of the medical bills ourselves. But the real point in this case is that we keep on buying and paying for it, and trying to take care of ourselves, instead of letting God take care of us. Yes, I know that sounds stupid, to trust God with no safety net, with no visible means of support. I'm with you. My wife and I rationalize that you can't even get admitted to a hospital without insurance (unless it's an emergency), so it's almost mandatory to have an insurance card. Let's see, where is trust in God in that?

Here is another little highlight from my life. I have Crohn's disease, and as a result I can't get insurance at all, or if I can, it's 1) prohibitively expensive, 2) there's an exclusion for anything related to Crohn's (and the insurance companies can always find a way that any ailment is either a direct or indirect result of the Crohn's), and 3) the deductible is so high that you end up paying all your medical bills out of pocket, unless it is a genuine catastrophe (that you're probably going to die from anyway). So, since I don't have any insurance, I'm forced into the position of having to trust God. It's kinda' humorous for someone who so often professes to trust God, and who preaches that trusting God through Jesus is the only way to have peace on earth, or eternal life in heaven. But that's me—I have feet of clay.

At the same time, this situation has been the source of God's miraculous presence in my life. It's almost as if He was blessing me for trusting Him, even when He knows, and I know He knows, that the only reason I was trusting Him was because I had no choice. 'Course how often is it that we only come to God when we have absolutely no place else to go? So this next story is no less miraculous.

When I was 37 (also with no insurance, but back then only because I was young and dumb and didn't think I needed it and couldn't afford it anyway), I claimed that I trusted God. It must've been because I had no choice. I got really sick, so sick that I finally gave up and went to the emergency room to get some pain medicine 'cause the stomach cramps were killing me. Well, over the next 3 weeks, I got all caught up on medical care. I lost 16 pints of blood in 7 days; I had surgery to remove most of my colon; I lost 50 lbs., and I spent months recovering. That was my first episode. I don't even remember how much it cost but I never could have paid it. I guess if I'd died, my life insurance would have paid the bills. I paid a little along for years and then quit paying. I guess they just wrote it off as a bad debt. I'm ashamed to say that I haven't paid all my bills all my life but I'm doing the best I can. I did finally pay off the surgeon who operated on me and part of the hospital bill. They never even reported me to the credit bureau. The reason I know that is later I tried to buy a house and the loan went through. I've shaken my head ever since then that God allowed us to buy that house. It was just a miracle, because the hospital wasn't the only bill I didn't pay back then.

Since then, I've had amazingly good health except for a few episodes, and because I've made more money, I've been able to pay my bills pretty steadily. It's been slow sometimes and took longer than they'd have liked, but I paid them. As I look back, God has done a better job of taking care of me and my bills and my lifestyle than I would've done if I'd had insurance; even if I'd had the money to buy really good broad-based coverage.

On the second pass (when I was 58) I had a blockage in my intestines, and I don't remember much about it, but my wife said the doctors told her that if I'd waited much longer I wouldn't have made it. They spent a day or two trying to fix it with medication, and then they did a major surgical revision of my whole digestive area. I was in the hospital for 13 days. The surgical bill wasn't too bad, and I paid it pretty promptly, but the hospital bill was $44,000.

I was scared to call them and even talk about paying it. I figured they'd say something about like, "Give us both arms and one leg as collateral, and you can have them back when you've paid the bill." A few weeks after I got out of the hospital, I gutted up and called them.

This nice young lady answered the phone and I told her who I was. She pulled up my account and said, "You owe us a total of $44,000 and change. Who is your insurance company?"

Well, after I caught my breath I said, "I don't have any insurance."

She said, "Wait just a minute." I waited, and in about a minute she came back on the line and said, "Since you don't have any insurance, we are reducing the bill by 40%; so that will be $26,400; and since you've paid about $2,000 already, you owe us right at $24,000. Would you like to have a time payment plan?"

I couldn't believe my ears. I said, "Yes."

She said, "We'll give you two years to pay at $1,019.87 per month."

I asked her how much the interest was going to be and she said, "We don't charge interest."

It just happened at that particular moment that I was making pretty good money, and I was able to pay the bill on time, without missing a payment. I don't know what anyone else calls that, but I call that a bonafide miracle, hand delivered by God. I still can hardly believe that really happened the way it did. I've tried to add up how much I would've paid for insurance if I could have bought it for all those years, and I can't even figure it out, but it would've been a lot more than $1,000 per month for two years. I know a lot of people who are paying that much or more for a car they're not going to keep for many years. I'm hoping to keep my body for quite some time to come (if the Lord is willing). I have seen a miracle and it is me.

Since then, I've had another small run-in with the doctors, and I'm still paying on that. They're not near as nice—they didn't even talk about both reduction and time payment plan; it was either-or. I also didn't have near as much disposable income, so I'm still paying, and they're still calling me—but they didn't come and get me and haul me off.

I'm still able to get up and go to work, so I can pay them and everybody else. God is still giving me all my needs (and a lot of my wants) by His riches in glory in Christ Jesus (Phil. 4:19); just another every day miracle, if you ask me.

Now, back to that house on the sand. Are you going to worship (trust) God or are you going to worship (trust) money? The problem is not that we don't know which is which or which is right. The problem is the insidious nature of the beast (yes, I'm talking about the beast in the book of Revelation.) He uses all the devices at his disposal— self-righteousness, pride, our desire to control ourselves and others, our desire to look good in the eyes of the world and keep up with the Joneses. As long as we keep thinking we can take care of ourselves, that we don't need to bother God with having to take care of us, we can keep on avoiding trusting in and relying on God to save us from ourselves. But if we continue to rely on all those crutches the world provides, then we'll stay trapped by our own devices, and the devil will be more than willing to give us all the rope we need to hang ourselves.

It's kinda' like the other side of the coin from what is presented in 2 Timothy 2:24-26, KJV, where it says, "The servant of the Lord must not strive, but be gentle unto all men; apt to teach, patient, in meekness instructing those who would oppose; if peradventure [maybe] God will give them repentance to the recognition of the truth, so they can withdraw themselves from the snare of the devil, by whom they are taken captive at his will."

Did you get that? We believe these lies the devil tells us about how money and stuff will take care of us, and we're trapped by the lies and the stuff, yet we keep trying to live in that house that's sitting on the sand, waiting for the storm and the flood to come. Are you ready?

Just one more thing. I don't care, and God doesn't care, how many times He's asked you before to trust in Him, and you haven't done it. He still wants you, and He still wants you to trust in Him and have a real close relationship with Him. He's still standing there with His Hand out, waiting for you to come take His hand. It's a strange thing. What I was always taught, when I was a kid, was that if I'd go down the aisle, confess my sins before the congregation, and repent (turn around and go the other way), then God (who sent His Son to die for our sins) would accept me, save me, redeem me, and reconcile me to himself. So I did it. And I always thought it was all about me reaching up to God on His throne, and giving all the right answers.

The funny thing is, it's not that way at all. God is all around us, just like it says in the Bible. He is always available, and even when we're **way** out in the bushes, the Holy Spirit is there, steadily sending us messages about how He wants to have a relationship with us. He follows us to the bushes, and the bars, and the alleys, hoping that wherever we get the message, He'll be there to help us. In some of those other places, we're actually more likely to get it, rather than the places we usually think about when we're good about going to church.

Getting back to obedience and building on the sand as a metaphor for basing our lives on principles and practices that shift and change, we should touch on another aspect of this subject. If, as I alluded to earlier, obedience is about doing what God tells us to do, then what about the first of the Ten Commandments, "Thou shalt have no other gods before [besides] Me." It comes back to that question about whom or what do we worship or serve? Whom do we really trust? To whom do we really turn when we're in dire straits with nowhere else to turn?

Well, I'm good (or bad) about saying that ultimately I trust God—not my job, my employer, my network of friends and relatives, or my piddly bank account or credit cards. But do I really? I say that, but every time I get in a bind, I'm steadily calculating where I'm going to go to stay afloat for another few days or weeks. The funny thing is, something usually "falls out of the sky" that I was completely not expecting, so clearly that it just had to be God. It's happened over and over so often that I just can't deny that God really has delivered me from evil, destruction, or punishment when I didn't deserve it. That's God's mercy (I hope you know by now that mercy is when God loves you and takes care of you, even when you deserve to be punished).

The problem is that we all have been in that position, when to our logical mind it looks like there is a logical man-made explanation for how we got out of that trap, and we don't give the credit to God. Somebody always comes by and says, "You know that just couldn't be God; that was your boss, or your rich uncle, or just the luck of the draw." And the sad thing is we let it slide and agree by omission. We don't say, "You may think that, but I know it was God." Just so you'll know, nobody else may think a thing about it, but God didn't miss it. The true miracle is that God still loves us anyway. Some people go for years, running in the bushes, worshipping those idols of "other stuff" taking care of them, growing more and more calcified in their position of trusting something else besides God, acknowledging something else besides God as their real god (often it's ourselves). The really sad part is that we're not only worshipping idols, but we're getting more and more used to trusting in "the house on the sand"; and we're getting closer and closer to the time of "great was the fall of it." That's disobedience and the fruits (the results) of disobedience all rolled into one.

In case somebody didn't get it, trusting in something else besides God to take care of you is not only building your house on the sand (basing your life on shifting, shaky stuff), but it's also worshipping idols; serving other gods than the one true God. That's disobedience of the first order, and that's the exact definition of what Jesus was talking about when he said, "Everyone who hears My words, and does not do them is like a foolish man who built on sand." Only an idiot would do such a thing, right? I guess if you want you can join me as a "recovering" idiot—you know, like members of AA talk about being a "recovering" alcoholic." We never completely grow out of it; we have to get up every morning, turn ourselves over to God one more time, and say, "One more time Lord, I'm turning myself over to You; I'm dying to myself so You can live Your eternal life in me. I love You."

Matthew 11:25-30

"At that time Jesus said, 'I praise you, Father, Lord of heaven and earth, because you have hidden these things from the wise and prudent, and revealed them to babes (little children). Yes, Father, for this was your good pleasure. All things have been committed to me by my Father. No one knows the Son except the Father, and **no one knows the Father except the Son and those to whom the Son chooses to reveal Him.** Come to me, all you who are weary and burdened, and I will give you rest. Take my yoke upon you and learn from me, for I am gentle and lowly of heart, and you will find rest for your souls. For my yoke is easy and my burden is light."

So what do "babes" have to do with "yokes"? And why did Jesus talk about revelations, as in revelations from God and who they reach? Why burdens, yokes, humility, and rest, all in the same passage? And what do these things have to do with obedience, particularly obedience to God? I guess first it would be good to try to figure out what this passage is really saying to us, here in affluent America, in the 21st century. Let's look at the first part of the passage again with a few insertions:

"Jesus said, 'I praise you, Father, Lord of heaven and earth, because you have hidden [why?] these things [what things?] from the wise and prudent, and revealed [why now?] them to little children [babes].'" Let's look at the second bracket first. What things? I don't know for sure, but I've got two maybes: 1) "these things" may be the things Jesus just finished talking about in the previous passage, verses 20-24. He's saying how sad he is, and how sad they should be, for Chorazin, Bethsaida, and Capernaum, because they never repented and turned to God, even though they were the cities in which He did His greatest miracles and healings. He compares them to Tyre and Sidon, home of the heathen Phoenicians, and even to Sodom (you know about Sodom), saying in effect, "On judgment day it's gonna' be better for Tyre and Sidon and Sodom, than for you who think you're so high and mighty, because you'll be brought down to hell." Surely "these things" of the verses immediately prior are at least some of what Jesus is talking about that God has "hidden" from the "wise and prudent," who may well be the people of these cities. The leaders of these cities may well have heard Jesus' message and even saw the miracles He did, but they either didn't get it or didn't think they needed to listen. Maybe they're members of that same group Jesus often talked about and referred to as "having eyes they see not, and having ears they hear not, and neither to they understand" (Mark 8:18). They may be the very same guys, who were "wise and prudent" in their own eyes but foolish in God's eyes (1 Corinthians 1:20-27).

On the other hand, as I remember it, when I was a kid, my momma and my Sunday School teachers, and even our preachers, when they'd talk about this passage, they talked about "these things" being all the truths that Jesus taught, not just a portion of one chapter, but the entire wisdom that the life and teachings of Jesus embody. In this view, it's not just about the cities that ignored the teachings and the miracles of Jesus, who either didn't get or refused to listen to any of God's message. It is also about all the "wise and prudent" of humanity, the well educated, disciplined, intelligent, self-controlled, properly trained, socially acceptable, and law-abiding—just the kind of people the world wants to know. Jesus says in effect, "Thank you Father, that You wanted to hide the truth about You from those proud people. I'm glad; I agree with you!" I may be mistaken, but to me that is exactly what He's saying.

That's just the beginning because in addition to being "hidden" from the "wise and prudent," they were "revealed to babes"—who are polar opposites. How unwise and un-prudent can you get? They not only haven't learned "wisdom and prudence," but they're helpless, undisciplined, uncontrolled, and unable to figure out what's going on. Yet God, the Father, with Jesus, the Son, applauding, revealed all these things to people who don't know how to row, who can't even find the boat—babes.

To me, the best part is God's "revealing." He didn't make 'em go to college, take a pilgrimage, fast, pray, or beg for mercy. He just revealed the things of heaven to them. He picked the ones who couldn't possibly do anything to pay Him back, and He shined His Light into their hearts, simply because He wanted to. He knew they'd be genuinely glad to receive the truth and the light and the miracles of Jesus. He knew they would respond by trusting Him to take care of them. He knew they were the "fertile ground," the "good soil" that was waiting to receive the seeds of His truth (Matthew 13:23). Hallelujah!

Then Jesus says, "No one knows the Son except the Father, and no one knows the Father except the Son and those to whom the Son chooses to reveal Him." Jesus chose to "reveal" God (by instant transmission, a flash of light) to those babes. I guess the best we can hope for is to be one of the babes, and the only way to do that is to surrender our whole selves to Him, to die to our *selves* and let Him live His eternal life in us.

How's that for a message about revelation? 'Course you know what's so great about revelation? You don't have to work at it. It just sorta' comes to you, usually when you're not even looking, not even expecting it. If "babes" get revelation from Jesus, maybe that includes people besides infants, toddlers, and little children. Maybe it includes those who are cast in similar roles, who are virtually ignored by the world, who have no value. Perhaps it includes people who are poor, not just in money, but in spirit (Matthew 5:3), or people who don't quite get it or don't quite have it, mentally, emotionally, psychologically, or socially. Perhaps He's referring to those who are a lot like the next group Jesus talks about in this passage, when He says, "Come to Me, all you who labor and are heavily burdened, and I will give you rest." They sound like the same people to me, especially when it comes right on the heels of what He just said before.

You know what else 'babes' have that those other guys (the wise and prudent) don't have? The babes are listening—they're paying attention, they're actually looking for some help, they're hungry for help. Deep in their hearts, they know they've been carrying this need around with them ever since they can remember. They're ready for some help when Jesus comes up and says, "Come to Me—all you folks who are listening, you people who are paying attention, yes, you, who are tired and burdened, and sick and tired of being tired and burdened—and I will give you **rest**!" There's a lot of people out

Out o' th' Bushes

there, and you may be one of them, who don't need anything quite as bad as they need a little rest (a little relief)—from work, worry, debt, guilt, and fear. They've been looking for a little rest for a very long time. They'd do just about anything to get a little relief. So now they're standing on their tiptoes, waiting to hear what Jesus is going to say next.

Then He says, "Take My yoke upon you and learn of Me, for I am gentle and lowly of heart [humble], and you shall find rest unto your souls. For My yoke is easy and My burden is light." What do you have to do to get relief? Take Jesus' yoke. What does that mean? What is a yoke anyway? A yoke is a piece of harness that people in underdeveloped countries still use to control their oxen, mules, and donkeys. It fits around their necks and they chain the wagon or plow to the yoke so the animals can pull it. There's a "single-tree" yoke (for one cow or mule), and there's a "double-tree" yoke for two oxen or donkeys to pull together. In that case, there's a long beam that hooks the two yokes together. So if you "take Jesus' yoke" on you, you are making yourself available to do His work, to carry His load. And "learn of Me"? That's easy; it's doing the things we've been talking about in this book.

It may sound like work, but it's not so much a physical yoke as it is a spiritual yoke. Being yoked with Jesus can't be all bad though, because if you're going to help Him carry His burdens, He's also gonna' help you carry yours and help pull your load. Then He says, "My yoke is easy." Maybe it means it fits right and doesn't rub; maybe it even sorta' feels good to pull the load when everything is working right, and you're accomplishing something, and doing it together—especially when He then says, "For My yoke is easy, and My burden is light." It's almost humorous, considering I'm always thinking, "My yoke is always rubbing me the wrong way, and my burden always feels so heavy and unbearable."

Now, what does all this have to do with obedience? The yoke speaks of the work you're called to, the load you have to carry. It also speaks of the rules and the restrictions you have to work under, and the fact that you have to do it with others (at least one other), and that you're guided in your work by a usually Unseen Hand. Obedience is about your attitude to the situation in which we all find ourselves. If you're always struggling against the place and the work you're in, it's hard; you get tired and overburdened. But if you turn yourself and your work and you situation over to God through Jesus, then it just improves everything all around.

If you think, as do the wise and prudent, that you're in control, and you're gonna' make everything turn out like you want it to (by doing all the right things the right way), and you don't need any help, you may be in for a rude awakening.

On the other hand, if you're a humble babe, and you know how badly you need help, God through Jesus will reveal to you all the things you need to live a happy, fulfilled life. You'll know that taking Jesus' yoke, His Spirit, and His discipline on you (being obedient in your heart to do whatever He wants you to), is exactly what you've been waiting for and hoping for, all your life. So taking Jesus' yoke upon you, and learning about Him, may be exactly what obedience is about.

Matthew 18:1-4

"At that time the disciples came to Jesus and asked, 'Who is the greatest in the kingdom of heaven?' He called a little child and had him stand among them. And he said, 'I tell you the truth, unless you change and become like little children, you will never enter the kingdom of heaven. Therefore, whoever humbles himself like this child is the greatest in the kingdom of heaven.'"

Who is greatest? This child. Unless you get changed and become as this child, you're not going to make it to heaven. So what is it about this child, about children in general, that makes them "great" in the kingdom of heaven? What is it about children that makes them spiritually different from your average "run-of-the-mill" human?

I say it's being humble; it's humility, and not just a little bit. They haven't even thought about being better than somebody else. They have no illusions about being in control, and they are not telling others what to do. They're just glad somebody is taking care of them, especially if it's someone who loves them. They're not worrying about tomorrow, this afternoon, this evening, or even two hours from now. They're just glad to be here; they're just taking it all in with a look of wonder at the adventure they're in the middle of.

Probably the most enduring and endearing quality of children is their willingness to trust the ones they love. They do it so much it's scary. They're a lot like dogs that love and trust you even if they're mistreated, malnourished, put in danger, used, or abused. It takes a lot to turn them off. Even when they do wrong and they get punished, when they don't understand what's happening or why, they still love and trust. It's built in to their hearts and their souls.

That's what Jesus is talking about when He says, "Unless you become as a little child, you won't enter the kingdom." In other words, you just won't get it; it won't soak in, and you won't ever enjoy the fruits of knowing God. Of all the people who earnestly desire to draw near to God—who want to know the real peace, the real love, the real security of knowing Jesus, to have the Holy Spirit of the one true God inside your very own heart—it's the little children who are going to get there; it's those who are actually converted and become as little children who are going to enjoy being in God's presence, both now and later.

So what was the original question? What in the world does this have to do with obedience? Everything. Again, like the last passage, it's all about attitude. It's about living one moment at a time in the hollow of God's Hand. It's that attitude of "I'm so glad to be here, I can't wait to see what's going to happen next." It's about forsaking the rat race, the American Dream, and the long grueling trip to the top of the corporate ladder, so you can rest in God's lap. It's about changing your focus from long-term planning to moment-by-moment living. It's about waking up every morning and saying, "Okay, Lord, here I am. Where do You want me to go, what do You want me to do, today, right now?" In some crazy way, your insides change to the point where you actually start to think that it's not only more important, but it's actually more fun, more pleasurable, to talk to people about God; to share His love, mercy, and forgiveness, than it is to chase fame and fortune. When you begin to do that, you begin to enjoy the "being in heaven" that comes from "being converted and becoming like a little child." When you follow Jesus' advice in this verse, it's the most obedient thing you'll ever do.

Matthew 21:28-32

In the "Parable of the Two Sons," Jesus said, "But what do you think? A man had two sons, and he came to the first and said, 'Son, go, work today in my vineyard.' He answered and said, 'I will not,' but afterward he regretted it and went. Then he came to the second and said likewise. And he answered and said, 'I go, sir,' but he did not go. Which of the two did the will of his father?" [The Pharisees] said to Him, "The first." Jesus said to them, "Assuredly, I say to you that tax collectors and harlots enter the kingdom of God before you. For John came to you in the way of righteousness, and you did not believe him; but tax collectors and harlots believed him; and when you saw it, you [**still**] did not afterward relent and believe him."

The simple connection between this passage and obedience is this: "No matter what you **say**, what God cares about and what really matters (in the spiritual realm as in the natural realm) is what you **do**." So the Pharisees were right in their answer, but here's the twist: Jesus skips right to the meat of the discussion, which is, "You guys say all the right things and you answer all the questions correctly, but you don't do right. Not only that, but the bad people, the people you despise because they don't do right and don't have all the right answers, they are going to get into heaven before you. They believed John's preaching and turned, but you didn't believe and you didn't turn even when you saw how they were changed."

So I guess you could say, "Practice what you preach," and God will like you, but that might not be quite right either, because God looks at our hearts and He knows what's going on, even if you're real good at hiding it from everyone else. So doing right is not necessarily obedient if your heart's not in the right place. Just like the two sons, the first son said, "No, I won't go," but then he regretted it and went. His heart must have been in the right place. The second son said the right thing, but his heart must not have been right, 'cause he didn't go . . . sorta' like the Pharisees.

So obedience must be about having your heart right. And how do you do that again? You humble yourself, you surrender to Jesus, and you trust Him, and His Spirit comes into your heart. You're ol' heart just can't get any more all right than that.

John 7:17

"If anyone wills to do His will, (that is, be obedient)—he shall know concerning the doctrine. Anyone who wants to do His will can test this teaching and know whether it's from God or whether he's making it up." (*The Message*).

"If any man desires to do His will (God's pleasure), he will know (have the needed illumination to recognize, and can tell for himself) whether the teaching [is from God]" (Amplified).

"Anyone who wants to do the will of God will know whether My teaching is from God or is merely my own" (NLT).

"Wills to do His will" means "desires to be obedient." What do you get if you desire to be obedient to God? You know whether peoples' doctrines are true, right, from God. If you really desire to be obedient, you receive discernment. You will "know (have the needed illumination [light] to recognize, and can tell for yourself) whether the teaching is from God." This is a simple little principle, but it is a great fruit of the Spirit to have discernment about other people and their preaching, teaching, and doctrines. I like Mr. Peterson's version, "You'll know if they're making it up." What a great gift it is if you can hear someone teach and know whether they're making it up, or whether it's God's truth. Praise the Lord! What a great reason to be obedient. What a great fruit of the Spirit!

Romans 6:16

"Don't you know that to whoever you present [surrender] yourselves to obey, you are that one's slaves, whether to sin [of the devil] leading to death, or of obedience [to God] leading to righteousness?"

This is getting down to the nitty gritty of obedience and the hard-core central issues. To put it in West Texas English, "Don't you get it? If you surrender to sin, you get enslaved by the devil, and it leads to death." Like it says in 2 Timothy 2:25-26, "Maybe God will give them repentance to the recognition of the truth; so they can withdraw themselves from the snare of the devil, by whom they are taken captive at his will." If you surrender yourself to sin, you become entrapped in the snare (the net) of the devil, and you're taken captive (enslaved) to do his will. Like one of those big nets in the jungle they use to catch tigers, where they step on a trigger under a flat rock, and it springs the trap and the net swoops them up into the air. You're caught.

"But, if you surrender to [be obedient to] God, it leads to righteousness which is life." You get to choose. If you choose to be obedient to God, He'll keep you safe from the devil. Something about like this: "Obedience to God leads to eternal life through Jesus Christ our Lord." Or maybe you remember this verse, in Romans 6:23, "The wages of sin is death, but the gift of God is eternal life through Jesus Christ our Lord." I love that verse. If you sin, you get what you deserve (wages), which is death, but if you choose God, you get His gift of eternal life through Jesus (because of what He's done for us). If we surrender ourselves to God instead of to the devil, we get a gift of forgiveness. Thank God!

Let me run that by you one more time: If you obey, surrender to, run with, fill your life with, sin and the devil and his demons and demon-filled people, you get death—but if you obey, surrender to, fill your life with God, Jesus and the Holy Spirit, and run with people who are filled with the Spirit, you get eternal life, starting right now.

Sin = slavery to the devil = death
Obedience = slavery to God = eternal life
Obedience = Eternal Life
Which would you rather have?

Romans 8:1-4

"Therefore, [there is] now no condemnation [no adjudging guilty of wrong] for those who are in Christ Jesus, who live [and] walk not after the dictates of the flesh, but after the dictates of the Spirit. For the law of the Spirit of life [which is] in Christ Jesus [the law of our new being] has freed me from the law of sin and of death. For God has done what the Law could not do, [its power] being weakened by the flesh [the entire nature of man without the Holy Spirit]. Sending His own Son in the guise of sinful flesh and as an offering for sin, [God] condemned sin in the flesh [subdued, overcame, deprived it of its power over all who accept that sacrifice], So that the righteous and just requirement of the Law might be fully met in us who live and move not in the ways of the flesh but in the ways of the Spirit [our lives governed not by the standards and according to the dictates of the flesh, but controlled by the Holy Spirit]" (Amplified).

This passage rolls the whole battle between good and evil up in a nutshell. It contains all the historical, philosophical, legal, and spiritual elements of what God has been doing on earth since the beginning. God created us to have communion with Him, which means friendship. When we (through Adam and Eve) chose not to obey God's instructions, we withdrew ourselves from that relationship. In an effort to mend the relationship, God made a covenant with Abraham, a covenant based on trust, but the people refused to abide by the terms of the covenant. Then he made a covenant with the people through Moses, "The Ten Commandments," but the people either would not, or could not, live up to the conditions of that covenant either. Then, even in the Old Testament, God began to tell the people about His desire to change them from the inside out. In Ezekiel 36:26, He said, "I'm going to take away your hearts of stone and give you hearts of flesh." In Isaiah, He began to talk about the Messiah, the Christ, who would come to rule and reign as the suffering Savior, but the people just didn't get it. So He sent His own Son, Jesus, to show the people how much He (God) loved them. He showed them what love was all about. He laid down His life for the flock, and then He arose and ascended into Heaven, after which He sent His own personal Spirit, the Holy Spirit of God, to live in our hearts and to change our hearts from stone to flesh.

When it says, "The law was weak through the flesh" (Romans 8:3), it means that we cannot possibly live up to the requirements of the law in our own nature, our own sinful nature, our own selfish nature. Yet this is what we have been steadily trying to do since shortly after we first came to earth. We just can't obey because our flesh is sinful and weak. Even though we want to obey, we want to do right, we just can't get it done, because our flesh is weak. Our natural fleshly, worldly nature is weak. That's the "law of sin and death."

But on the other hand, when it says, "The law of the Spirit of life in Christ Jesus, has made me free from the law of sin and death," it means that the Spirit of Life, the Spirit of Jesus Christ, the Holy Spirit of God, **is able** to obey God because He is God. When we surrender our natural selves; when we die to our natural selves and live a new life with Jesus, His Spirit overcomes the law of sin and death that is operating in us and makes it possible to live up to God's requirements. He does it; we don't.

"There is therefore now no condemnation to them that are in Christ Jesus" means that I don't have to feel guilty for anything I have done in the past or that I am going to do in the future, because Jesus died and shed His blood on the cross, and when we accept the gifts He gave us, we die with Him and He begins to live His eternal life in us. I don't have to feel guilty about anything, because Jesus took care of all of that. No one can shake my confidence or my trust in Him. Hallelujah! If He's fixed everything, and He doesn't care, then I don't need, want, or have to care, either.

If you have accepted God's gift through Jesus Christ, you have His Holy Spirit residing in your own personal heart, there's nothing anyone (even the devil) can do or say to take that away.

What does it mean if you have the Holy Spirit in your heart, mind, body, and soul? It means that you "walk not after the flesh, but after the Spirit." You behave differently; you begin to feel differently in your heart. You begin to have that knowing, that trusting, that absolute conviction that God is taking care of you, and you really don't have to worry about anything anymore. You have the first inkling that you are able to live up to God's standards for your life, because God now is doing it in you, and it is no longer you doing it at all.

Sometimes you even find yourself feeling things toward other people (like love, mercy, and forgiveness) that you never felt before. You find yourself doing good things that you never would have considered doing before. You have this secret knowing in your heart that you really are changed, like the Bible says will happen when you really start to trust in God. You start to realize that a real-live genuine miracle is taking place in your very own heart. You have this strange notion that you actually are beginning to "bear fruit" like it says is supposed to happen when you surrender to and trust in Jesus—fruit like love, joy, peace, patience, kindness, goodness, faithfulness, gentleness and self-control (Galatians 5:20), and that other kind of fruit, such as "going into all the world and making disciples" (Matthew 28:19). You start saying the right things without really trying, and people start coming up asking questions about Jesus and His life, and you even have some vague notion of what to say. Wow! This brings to mind that line about, "Take no thought beforehand for what you shall speak, for it is not you that speak, but the Holy Ghost!" (Mark 13:9-11). Where you used to be worried sick (I'm talking about sorta' nauseated) that you weren't going to say the right thing for the Lord, now you feel this sense of anticipation beforehand because you know you're fixin' to get the chance to hear what God is going to say to someone **through you** about Jesus. Hallelujah!

It's not all of a sudden, it sorta' comes on you slow, when you're not expecting it. You see these little signs of the Holy Spirit moving in your heart, doing things in your life, and making things happen that you never thought possible. That is what obedience is about; it's when God does it **in you**! It's when the Spirit of life in Christ Jesus begins to **set you free** from the law of sin and death, and you can feel it, see it, and know that it's happening in your very own personal heart, soul, and body.

Galatians 6:7-8

"Don't be deceived, God is not mocked (scorned, belittled, made light of), for whatever you sow (plant), that shall you also reap (harvest); for if you sow unto the flesh (your sinful nature); you will reap corruption . . . if you sow unto the Spirit (the Holy Spirit of God), you will reap of the Spirit life everlasting" (Amplified).

If you read the doctrines and the sacred writings of the Hindus and the Buddhists, you'll learn about karma. I know there's more to it than this, but in a Western philosophical way, karma is about sowing and reaping, which is to say that it is truth. It's truth that almost anyone can understand if they've lived long enough to observe the way things happen on the earth. It's truth on a natural level, it's truth on a spiritual level, and the Bible is full of it. We've touched on a few passages, like the one about "grape seeds grow grapes," and "thorn seeds bear thorns," and how you will know a tree by its fruit" (Luke 6:44).

Do you know it says that if you give to others, God will give to you? "Give and it shall be given unto you, pressed down, shaken together, and running over, shall the Lord pour into your lap" (Luke 6:38). It's not necessarily that others will give you something back but

God will. It's just another aspect of "reaping what you sow," which is a spiritual law set up by God. The Golden Rule says, "Do unto others as you would have them do to you," and then Jesus adds, "for this is the law and the prophets" (Matthew 7:12). That means this is the short version of all that is taught in the Law (the Torah of the Old Testament) and the Prophets (people like Isaiah, Jeremiah, Ezekiel, Daniel, and those guys). If you want good things to happen, do, say, and give good things. If you do, say, and give bad things, what do you think is going to happen?

This passage is just a confirmation of the one above, Romans 8:1-4. It's like the story about the old Indian chief who was teaching his young braves how to live. He said, "Each day, in my heart, there are two wolves fighting; a white wolf who fights for good, and a black wolf who fights for evil." One of the young braves said, "Great chief, which wolf is going to win?" The answer came, "The one that I feed the most."

The fight is still between the **flesh** (the spirit of sin and death) and the **Spirit** (of life in Jesus). If we plant (feed) our sinful nature, we will reap (harvest) from our sinful nature death. If we plant (feed) ourselves with the Spirit of life, we will harvest eternal life.

Obedience is about feeding the white wolf every day. It is about planting seeds of the Spirit of life in Christ Jesus, every day. It is about surrendering yourself, denying yourself, dying to yourself (your sinful nature) every day, and living to Jesus. That is what obedience is about: knowing that every day, you **do** "reap what you sow."

Philippians 2:5-8

"Let this same attitude and purpose and [humble] mind be in you which was in Christ Jesus: [Let Him be your example in humility:] Who, although being essentially one with God and in the form of God, possessing the fullness of the attributes which make God, did not think this equality with God was a thing to be eagerly grasped or retained, but stripped Himself [of all privileges and rightful dignity], so as to assume the guise of a servant [slave], in that He became like men and was born a human being. And after He had appeared in human form, He abased and humbled Himself [still further] and carried His obedience to the extreme of death, even the death of the cross!" (Amplified)

"Think of yourselves the way Christ Jesus thought of himself. He had equal status with God but didn't think so much of himself that he had to cling to the advantages of that status no matter what. Not at all. When the time came, he set aside the privileges of deity and took on the status of a slave, became human! Having become human, he stayed human. It was an incredibly humbling process. He didn't claim special privileges. Instead, he lived a selfless, obedient life and then died a selfless, obedient death—and the worst kind of death at that—a crucifixion" (*The Message*)

It's about attitude, all over again. That's what this verse is about, and what this "life in Jesus" is about: "Let this attitude be in you (and me) that was also in Christ Jesus." What is "this attitude"? This attitude is being humble; it all comes back to humility. Jesus knew He was (and is) God. He didn't think it was necessary to "lord it over" everybody. He was secure enough in Who He is that He was willing (and able) to lay all His divinity down, all the power and authority, creativity, superiority, and holiness, and come down to earth and be born as a little baby. Some days, I think that the willingness to be born as a little baby—to go through the humiliation of learning to talk, walk, and control your bodily functions, and to grow up in a little house in a little village far away from the capital of a very little country—would almost be as bad as dying on the cross. Thirty years of obscurity after being the Lord of the universe would be a little frustrating.

It's funny, but when Jesus was brought back up before Pilate, after being whipped almost to death, Pilate says to Him, "Don't you know I have the power to crucify You, and power to release You?" If Jesus hadn't been hurting so badly from the beating, He would almost have had to laugh at the very idea of Pilate having power over Him. But He did let Pilate know who was really in control when He said, "You could have no power at all against Me unless it had been given you from above" (John 19:11).

So Jesus truly exemplified the humility that Paul is talking about in Philippians 2:5-8. He knew who He was, and He knew what it was to surrender Himself to God and to the duty to which God had called Him. He was humble enough to be obedient, even unto death, even unto death on a cross. He was obedient even though he knew exactly what was fixin' to happen to Him. When He prayed in the Garden, "Oh My Father, if it is possible, let this cup pass from Me; but not My will, but Your will be done" (Matthew 26:39). That's obedience.

So Paul says, "Let that attitude; let that kind of obedience be in you." Of course, the obedience is not just in saying the right words but in doing the right thing. The right thing is in surrendering to God's will—even if that means surrendering to the troops of the Sanhedrin, to the Chief Priests and Elders, and the Pharisees and the Sadducees, to the beatings, mockings, and the crown of thorns—and doing it with the right attitude, in obedient surrender; like it says in Isaiah 53:7, "He was led as a Lamb to the slaughter . . . and He opened not His mouth."

I honestly don't know what you and I are going to have to go through in our lives, particularly in our lives as servants and disciples of Jesus Christ. Someone has said, "The fields of the harvest of the believers in Jesus are watered with the blood of the martyrs." Undoubtedly, this is a true statement. I don't know if you or I are going to be a martyr or if we're only going to have to put up with a little ridicule, or if we will have to endure prison because of our faith, like Paul and Silas, and many brothers and sisters before us have done. I don't know if any of us will be torn limb from limb by wild animals, as were many Christians in Rome, but I pray that we will be able to stand against the devil and be obedient, even unto to death, as those saints were, and as Jesus was.

The only way we will be able to stand is if we are totally surrendered to Jesus so that His Holy Spirit so fills us that it is He who is doing the standing, the enduring, and the obeying, 'cause I'm pretty certain that we can't possibly do things like that under our own power. Thank God we don't have to do something like that by ourselves, without Him being right there with us and within us.

In Hebrews 5:5-9, it says, "So also Christ did not glorify Himself to become High Priest, but it was He who said to Him: 'You are My Son, Today I have begotten You.' . . . Who, in the days of His flesh, when He had offered up prayers and supplications, with vehement cries and tears to Him who was able to save Him from death, and was heard because of His godly fear, though He was a Son, yet He learned obedience by the things which He suffered. And having been perfected, He became the author of eternal salvation to all who obey Him."

I have not yet fully understood what this passage is talking about, but clearly it is concerned with the previous passage from Philippians, and it says several of the same things as in that passage. In addition, it says a few other things that would do us good to consider. It says that when Jesus was praying in the Garden, he did it with "vehement cries and tears": 1) to Him who was able to save Him from death, 2) He was heard by God because of His godly fear, and 3) He learned obedience by the things which He suffered.

Like I said, I don't fully understand the implications of this passage, but it certainly has to do with the obedience that Jesus exhibited in His Passion, and it calls on us to have that same obedience that was in Christ Jesus. Maybe we won't have to suffer the same things He suffered, but maybe we can learn that same obedience from the things we have to suffer in serving our Lord.

At the end it says, "And having been perfected, He became the author of eternal salvation to all who obey Him." The main thing we are called to do by these passages is to **obey Him**. That is definitely what obedience is all about.

THEME 6: SERVICE

JOHN BROWN'S BODY

By Stephen Vincent Benet

Sometimes there comes a crack in Time itself.
Sometimes the earth is torn by something blind.
Sometimes an image that has stood so long
It seems implanted as the polar star
Is moved against an unfathomed force
That suddenly will not have it any more.
Call it the mores, call it God or Fate,
Call it Mansoul or economic law,
That force exists and moves.
And when it moves
It will employ a hard and actual stone
to batter into bits an actual wall
And change the actual scheme of things.

John Brown
Was such a stone—unreasoning as the stone,
Destructive as the stone, and, if you like,
Heroic and devoted as such a stone.
He had no gift for life, no gift to bring
Life but his body and a cutting edge,
But he knew how to die.
And yardstick law
Gave him six weeks to burn that hoarded knowledge
In one swift fire whose sparks fell like coals
On every State in the Union.

Listen now,
Listen, the bearded lips are speaking now,
There are no more guerilla-raids to plan,

Tex Tonroy

There are no more hard questions to be solved
Of right and wrong, no need to beg for peace,
Here is the peace unbegged, here is the end,
Here in the insolence of the sun cast off,
Here is the voice already fixed with night.

Samuel

JOHN BROWN'S SPEECH

I have, may it please the Court, a few words to say.

In the first place I deny everything but what I have all along admitted: of a design on my part to free slaves . . .

Had I interfered in the matter which I admit, and which I admit has been fairly proved . . . had I so interfered in behalf of the rich, the powerful, the intelligent, or the so-called great . . . and suffered and sacrificed, what I have in this interference, it would have been all right. Every man in this Court would have deemed it an act worthy of reward rather than punishment.

I see a book kissed that I suppose to be the Bible, or at least the New Testament, which teaches me that all things whatsoever I would that men should do unto me, I should do even so to them. It teaches me further to remember them that are in bonds as bound with them. I endeavored to act up to that instruction. I say I am yet too young to understand that God is any respecter of Persons.

I believe that to have interfered as I have done, as I have always freely admitted I have done in behalf of His despised poor, I did not wrong, but right. Now if it is deemed necessary that I should forfeit my life for the furtherance of the ends of justice and mingle my blood further with the blood of my children and with the blood of millions in this slave country whose rights are disregarded by wicked, cruel and unjust enactments, I say, let it be done.

Let me say one word further. I feel entirely satisfied with the treatment I have received on my trial. Considering all the circumstances, it has been more generous than I expected. But I feel no consciousness of guilt. I have stated from the first what was my intention and what was not. I never had any design against the liberty of any person, nor any disposition to commit treason or incite slaves to rebel or make any general insurrection. I never encouraged any man to do so but always discouraged any idea of that kind.

Let me say also, in regard to the statements made by some of those connected with me, I hear it has been stated by some of them that I have *induced them to join with me. But the contrary is true. I do not say this to injure them, but as regretting their weakness. Not one but joined me of his own accord, and the greater part at their own expense. A number of them I never saw, and never had a word of conversation with, till the day they came to me, and that was for the purpose I have stated.*

Now I have done.

The voice ceased. There was a deep, brief pause.
The judge pronounced the formal words of death . . .
He left one last written message:

"I, John Brown, am now quite certain that the crimes of this guilty land: will never be purged away: but with Blood. I had as I now think; vainly flattered myself that without very much bloodshed; it might be done." (*John Brown's Body,* Stephen Vincent Benét, 1927, © 2010, Robert Dean Frelow, Pomona NY. Used by permission)

TEX'S THOUGHTS ON SERVICE

Romans 12:1-2

"I beseech you therefore, brethren, by the mercies of God, that you present your bodies a living sacrifice, holy, acceptable to God, which is your reasonable service. And do not be conformed to this world, but be transformed by the renewing of your mind, that you may prove what is that good and acceptable and perfect will of God."

If we're talking about "presenting our bodies as a living sacrifice," which is our "reasonable" and some say "spiritual" service, aren't we talking about talking to others about God? About telling what we have seen and heard? (Acts 4:18-20) About revealing the Spirit that is in our hearts? About demonstrating what God does through people who love Him (hopefully that's us)?

When we serve in the natural (traditional) sense of doing something for or giving something to others, shouldn't we be prepared to "give an answer for the hope that is in us"? (1 Peter 3:15) Also, isn't that our unique opportunity and one of our primary duties in beginning the process of making disciples, to spread the Gospel (the Good News) of Jesus Christ (Matthew 9:31)?

For lack of a better expression, I'm going to define "spiritual service" first as *connecting* with the brothers and sisters God has picked out before the foundations of the earth to be His, and then as *making disciples* of those He has called. Depending on where you are on the continuum—moving from knowing a disciple, to being a disciple, to making disciples, to teaching disciples—will determine where you pick up in this discussion. I'm praying that God will help us all to see where we truly are, and He'll help us all to start moving up the continuum from being consumers of God's blessings to being sharers of God's blessings, to being "teachers" of sharers. Like it says in 2

Timothy 2:2, "The things you've heard from me in the presence of many witnesses, commit these things to faithful men, who will be able to teach others also." If we're claiming to be trusters in Jesus, then that's what we're supposed to being doing, or at least learning to do. That is: making disciples.

Serving: Our Mission

Our mission then, if we choose to accept it, is to move from being consumers of God's blessings to being servants and sharers of God's love and His blessings. In short, make disciples, baptize, and teach, knowing that He's with us and He has all authority (Matthew 28:18). Another way to say it is know a disciple, be a disciple, make a disciple, and teach disciples . . . for Jesus (per 2 Timothy 2:2 above).

What does it mean to serve? People serve in the military or as a waiter; they provide service, such as phone service, garbage service, lawn service, or auto service. As Christians we're supposed to provide spiritual service. Jesus says, "You know the rulers of the Gentiles lord it over them, and those who are great exercise authority over them. But it will not be so among you; but whoever desires to become great among you, let him be your servant. And whoever desires to be first among you, let him be your slave, just as the Son of Man did not come to be served, but to serve, and to give His life a ransom for many (Matthew 20:25-28)."

A modern day translation might be, "Be like Me. Be ready to be humble. Be ready to serve. Be ready to give your life." If you hang around with Jesus much at all, you keep hearing this message, "Be humble. Don't just **play** like a servant (slave), don't just **act** like a servant (slave), but **be** a servant (slave) in your heart. Be willing to surrender yourself, to give your life a ransom for others (whether by living or by dying). Be willing to 'stand in the gap'."

I am reminded of a verse from the "Battle Hymn of the Republic,"

"In the beauty of the lilies,
    Christ was born across the sea,
With a glory in His bosom
    that transfigures you and me,
As He died to make men holy,

let us die to make men free,
While God is marching on."

Most people now-a-days sing, "let us 'live' to make men free."
Maybe they gave up the thought of dying for freedom, but not John
Brown. How does "dying so they may live" or "living so they may
be free" fit in with the numerous admonitions in the Bible about
"spiritual service"?

"Regular" service, doing good deeds, is central to God's design
and plan for us, as His children and as members of Jesus' Body, to do
as it says in James, "I will show you my faith by my works. . . . Was
not Abraham justified by works when he offered Isaac his son on the
altar? Do you see that faith was working together with his works
and by works faith was made perfect? And the Scripture was fulfilled
which says, 'Abraham believed [trusted] God and it was accounted to
him for righteousness,' and he was called the 'Friend of God'. You see
then, that a man is justified by works, and not by faith only" (James
2:18, 21-23).

It's necessary to remember that the only works that matter are
those that arise from our surrender to the Spirit to use us in finding
and in doing the works, it is nevertheless true that works (service) are
central to God's design and plan for us (His people) on this earth.

I've spent the last 15 years or so working and teaching youth and
adults in a local church, and I've learned a great deal about service.
I've seen a lot of service and I've even participated in some of it. In
the process, I've learned something. Sometimes, when you do a good
work, especially for someone you don't know, who can't do anything
for you, they might ask, "Why did you do that for me?" The right
answer is, "God did it" or "Jesus told me to do it." And then they say,
"Who is this Jesus" or "What do you mean?" What are you going to
say? Are you going to be ready to give an answer for the hope you have
in your heart (1 Peter 3:15)? Or maybe you don't say anything, and they
still get the message; stranger things have happened.

What about ol' John Brown? Clearly he made a reasoned decision
to give his life for others. God must have been in it, moving him
inexorably to that untenable position where he could choose nothing
else. In any case, he did it. He did choose; he did the act required. His

faith in the one true God was confirmed by his act. He presented his body, first as a living sacrifice (Romans 12:1) and then as a martyr.

Sometimes we get confused thinking that the highest calling of Christians is to render physical service, such as: feed the hungry, give drink to the thirsty, house the stranger, clothe the naked, nurse the sick, and visit the prisoners (Matthew 25:35-40). We do a lot of those things in accomplishing the task of providing spiritual service, which is all about making disciples, witnessing to what God has done in our lives, and letting the mind (attitude) of Jesus be in us. In so doing, we also become willing to humble ourselves, we become servants (slaves) for others, and we commit to being obedient unto death. In all of this, we are all about giving an answer of the reason for the hope we have within us, in a gentle, respectful way.

In sum, true Christian or spiritual service is about "denying ourselves, taking up our cross daily (the cross of death to us), letting Jesus live His life in us, and following Him." (Luke 9:23). If we want to be Jesus' disciples, this is the mission that we do with joy.

John 13:1-17

This passage talks about how at the beginning of the Passover supper, which became our "Lord's Supper," Jesus washed the disciples' feet, after which, he said, "You call me Teacher and Lord, and you say well, for so I am. If I then, your Lord and Teacher, have washed your feet, you also ought to wash one another's feet. For I have given you an example that you should do as I have done to you. Most assuredly, I say to you, a servant is not greater than his master; nor is he who is sent greater that he who sent him. If you know these things, blessed are you if you do them" (John 13:13-17).

In some way that we do not fully understand, this foot-washing ceremony is a symbol of the service that Jesus expects us to render to others. At least one aspect that we should consider is that if Jesus, the Lord of all creation, was willing to get down on his knees and wash the feet of the disciples, then we ought to be willing to do similarly humble acts of service for others. Many Christians throughout history, even to this very day, have been willing and have done such selfless acts. Consider Mother Teresa and the members of her order, who spend their days and nights digging in the trash behind fancy restaurants in

Calcutta so they'd have food to feed the dying people to whom they ministered as their lifelong calling.

Tertullian, the 3rd century bishop of the church said, "The blood of the Martyrs waters the seed of the church." Someone has said there have been as many martyrs in the 20th century as in any century before. In the service of humanity, in the service of the church, in the service of the poor, the sick, and the prisoners, many of God's servants have given their lives, often accepting oppression, false imprisonments, and assassinations, such as the countless sacrifices during the Holocaust. Most martyrs remain nameless in history, but a few live on in the hearts of their people, such as Dietrich Bonhoeffer, the German priest who was executed a week before Hitler's reign of terror ended; Oscar Romero, the Archbishop of El Salvador; and Janani Luwum, Anglican bishop of Uganda, who was executed by Idi Amin on February 16, 1977. The blood of this wonderful bishop eventually became the seed of a new church in Uganda, one with spiritual power and fidelity matched by none. Surely these examples are some of what Jesus was talking about when He said that we should serve as He served.

As we move along the "Way" of Jesus, from being a spectator to being a disciple, we reach a point where we realize that we have already crossed over from watching what others are doing, to "being like Jesus," and we don't even know exactly when it happened. When we were standing over there watching, we said to ourselves, "I can't imagine that anyone would actually do **that** for God." And now we're standing over here saying, "I don't know if God would want me to do that, but if He does, I'm ready." That's what He's talking about when He talks about serving, service, or being a servant.

It's kinda' like what Paul "Bear" Bryant, the football coach, said about commitment: "There's three levels of commitment. The first level is, 'I'll try.' The second level is, 'I'll do my very best.' The third level is, 'I'll do whatever it takes.'"

I always used to think that "whatever it takes" meant that you're willing to do anything the situation requires in order to win. Of course, Bear Bryant was talking about winning at all costs; or at least that's the reasonable assumption. He was probably trying to emphasize the idea that you're supposed to put out the extra effort it takes to be better on any given day than your opponent.

In the situation we've been discussing, however, of serving Jesus and serving others by letting Him live His life through us, "whatever it takes" has a whole new meaning. Then it starts to mean something more—surrendering more, giving up more of yourself, sacrificing more of your time or your energy or your money, or whatever Jesus asks of you—simply because you want to please Him, simply because you want to be more like Him, simply because "it is no longer I, but Christ, who lives in me" (Galatians 2:20). That's spiritual service, 'cause it quits being about your plans and your design for your life, and it starts being about God's design and His plans for your life.

Romans 12:1

"I beg of you brothers, that you present yourselves as a living sacrifice; holy, and acceptable unto God, which is your reasonable service."

Reasonable service is to present our bodies as living sacrifices. What does this mean? Some of the translations say "reasonable service of worship." I guess I, and most people I know, equate "worship" with singing songs to God, praising God with music and adoration, which means telling God how much we love Him and telling others about His attributes. Sometimes prayer is worship, or certainly worship is all interwoven with prayer and vice versa.

In olden times, when the Levites served in the temple at Jerusalem, everything they did was considered worship, from the services of cleansing, to the services of sacrificing animals, to the services of praying for the people; all was considered service and worship. How does that relate to what we do today, in our "worship services"? Occasionally, in some churches in America, God is truly, fully, and profoundly worshipped, and the people are truly served in services of baptism, prayer, and anointing. Lives are touched and lives are changed when the worship service is more than 15 minutes of singing, 15 minutes of preaching, and a warm goodbye.

Sometimes there may be more "service of worship" to God out there in the world than in the "houses of worship." God may be more pleased and more touched (more worshipped) by the services that are performed on behalf of the tired, the poor, the huddled masses yearning to be free, the hungry, the thirsty, the sick, and the prisoners. You know, Jesus said, "If you've done it to the least of these, My brothers and sisters, you have done it to Me" (Matthew 25:45).

At His premier appearance in the synagogue in Nazareth, taking the passage from Isaiah, Jesus also said, "The Spirit of the Lord is on Me, because He has anointed Me to preach good news to the poor. He has sent Me to proclaim freedom for the prisoners and recovery of sight for the blind, release to the oppressed, to proclaim the year of the Lord's favor" (Luke 4:18).

It sounds to me like God's Spirit anointed Jesus to be a priest to people in all the ways mentioned in this verse. Likewise, when we trust Jesus, His Spirit comes to dwell in our hearts, and we become His priests for the people with whom God puts us. Not just the ordained pastors, elders and clergy, but all of us. Like Peter says in his first letter, "But you are a chosen people, a royal priesthood, a holy nation, a people belonging to God, that you may declare the praises of Him who called you out of the darkness into His marvelous light" (1 Peter 2:9). That's us—priests, pastors, shepherds. Like Jesus. Anointed to serve the people, and in the process God is worshipped, 'cause we "declare the praises of Him who called us out of the darkness into His marvelous light." (1 Peter 2:9) Hallelujah! That's service; that's worship!

Psalm 100:1

"Make a joyful noise unto the Lord. Serve the Lord with gladness."

Some versions say "worship" the Lord with gladness. I'd agree with worshipping with gladness, but I think God likes it when we **serve** Him with gladness as well. What does this mean?

It sounds to me like serving the Lord with gladness means, "And whatever you do, do all to the glory of God" (Colossians 3:17). If you have that attitude, then your least act of service becomes an act of worship, and the attitude you should have in doing a service, or in being a servant, to others or to God, is one of gladness, like, "I'm just glad I get to be here," "I'm just glad God let me get up this morning," "I'm just glad God gave me a little vision so I could see how and whom I should serve."

Matthew 4:19, Fishing for Men

If serving means, at least in part, to become a disciple of Jesus Christ, and if being a disciple of Jesus means surrendering ourselves to Him, dying to ourselves, living to and for Jesus, and following Him, what does it mean when He says, "Follow Me, and I will make you fishers of men?" (Matthew 4:19) and "Pray the Lord of the harvest, that He will send laborers" (Matthew 9:38)?

I like that analogy of "fishers of men" because the guys He was talking to made their living as fishermen and knew all about fishing. They knew about the weather that was best for catching fish, about the spots in the lake that were best, the time of day that was best, and what kind of nets were best to catch the most fish with the least amount of work. They knew about working hard all night and catching nothing, and about getting up early the next morning to try again when their hands were blistered and bleeding and their backs were nearly broken from tugging on the nets.

To these men, Jesus walks up and says, "Follow Me, and I'll make you fishers of men." Knowing only what the "fishing" part of that invitation meant, they abandoned their nets, got up right then, and fell in behind Him. This is truly astounding. There must have been something about this man that they just couldn't resist. Was it that they sensed He was calling them to a higher form of service than providing fish for their families and community?

If we're talking about "spiritual service" as in Romans 12:1-2, aren't we talking about talking to others about God—about revealing the Spirit that is in our hearts, about demonstrating what God does through people who love Him? About telling others what we have seen and heard (about Jesus)? (Acts 4:18-20)

1 Peter 3:15, Give an Answer

When we serve in the traditional (human) sense of doing something or giving something, shouldn't we be prepared to "give an answer for the hope that is in us" for why we believe, why we trust, why we serve? Isn't that our unique opportunity and our primary duty in starting the process of making disciples, to tell the Gospel, the good news of Jesus?

When I was a kid, I was fascinated by that expression, "fishers of men." There is a long tradition in the church I went to of "catching men for the Lord." Sometimes it's also called witnessing, sharing the Gospel, the Roman Road, or evangelism. In those days, after "gettin' saved," witnessing was one of the most, if not **the** most important thing you had to do to be a good Christian. Witnessing was put forth as the best "evidence" of whether are not you are a good Christian—more than attending church, more than giving money, more than caring for the sick, visiting the prisoners, or feeding the hungry, and even more than being "good" (that is: abiding by all the commandments). This didn't just mean "tell what you've seen and heard" (Acts 4:18-20) or "give a reason for the hope that's in you" (1 Peter 3:15). It was much more than that—it was hard-core, Bible-thumpin', cold-turkey, in-your-face, insistent, make up your mind right now, kind of witnessing. It was the kind of approach that included questions like, "If you die tonight, do you know for sure that you're going to heaven? Do you know Jesus as your Savior? Do you remember when you were saved? We're all a bunch of sinners—are you born again?"

As it turns out, most Christians, even genuine "born-again" believers, don't adhere to this kind of witnessing tradition. You probably can't imagine the guilt associated with this practice. It's crushing. Whenever you're with your church family, you feel constantly ashamed because you don't ask each person you meet one of those "bottom line" questions. 'Course you don't feel too bad, because most of them aren't doing that well at it either.

You know why? Maybe it's 'cause we're gutless chickens. It is the hardest work in town to ask someone you never saw before if they have a personal relationship with the eternal God. It's hard for you, it's hard for them, and it's hard for any innocent bystanders. Or maybe it's not lack of courage—maybe it's a kinda' sub-conscious recognition of how hard it is to do anything for God when you're operating solely in your own power without input from God by His Holy Spirit.

Some would say the problem is "method" or "procedure," and if you just use the right one, and you do it over and over, like a trained pig, eventually you get to the place you can do it with some proficiency. I've heard stories about people like that, and I believe they've actually offered the "plan of salvation" to more than 25,000 individual people, or so they say. Whew! They must have done it with the Holy Spirit moving in their hearts or they just couldn't have done it at all.

I have desired in my heart to be like that. I have longed to talk to everyone I see about God, but I guess I'm just not strong enough (or maybe surrendered enough). The best I've been able to do is talk to 'em about something non-threatening and pray silently that God will move. Sometimes He does, and we get around to talking about Him. Then it's a miracle!

Matthew 28:19, Sharing the Gospel

In Acts 2:37; after Peter had made his first sermon on the first Day of Pentecost after Jesus' ascension, it says, "Now when they heard this, they were cut to the heart, and said to Peter and the rest of the apostles, 'Men and brethren, what shall we do?'

As it turns out, as I was in the middle of writing this very passage, in this very book, when just such a miracle happened. It was so clear, so evident, that God woke me up in the middle of the night, at 3:00 am in fact, to write it down. **Here's the story:** Whenever we can on Friday nights, it's our habit to go to the Barnes & Noble bookstore in our community. We usually meet some friends, Harold and Betty, their two grown daughters, Laura and Suzanne, and their families. Darrell is married to Laura and they have two children, Luke and Katie. Katie is about 5 and she is adopted; she's from Kunming, China, and she's been here since she was 8½ months old. It turns out that all these folks claim the name of Jesus. Maybe we met by accident, but I don't much believe in coincidences, so it might just be God. Darrell is studying to be a pastor.

About four years ago, he went to Kunming for the first time to adopt and take custody of Katie. He loved Kunming and vowed to return. Darrell has been back at least once before, and returned again just a few weeks ago. While there, he became acquainted with a local Christian man who was a professor at a university there. During this visit of about two weeks, he had the opportunity to talk to and share with a number of students who were studying English. He even went to some parties with them in the evenings where they showed videos about Jesus and the Gospel. On one occasion, while waiting for the video to begin, he was talking to a young woman, call her Kim, and they were discussing what she liked to do in her spare time. Kim said, "I enjoy reading English and American classic literature, *Jane Eyre, Pride and Prejudice,* and others. I hope to be a writer someday."

Then she asked Darrell what he likes to read, and he said, "I like to read the Bible and other books about the Bible. Do you know about the Bible?" She confirmed she did.

"Are you a Christian?" she asked.

He said, "Yes, I am."

She said, "I think it would be good to be a Christian."

Darrell almost fell out of his chair, but he said, "Let's go back here in the back of the room and talk." For a few minutes, he shared some passages from the Bible, including the Gospel contained in John 3:16 and other verses.

Kim responded with, "What do I need to do to be a Christian?" Darrell told her, and she prayed to receive Jesus right then and there.

What a miracle! No one could possibly deny the presence of God in that conversation. Certainly the Holy Spirit was moving in Kim's heart. It seems just as clear that God used Darrell to supply several things as well: 1) He was willing to be there, 2) He was willing to engage in this open conversation (so open because the Holy Spirit had prepared the way), and 3) He was ready, willing and able to share the Gospel. Wow!

Darrell also told of others he talked to during his stay in Kunming, including some who wanted to argue the finer points of religion (also atheism). In one such discussion, he won his point about why people should believe in God, and confounded his opponent, but he lost the match, which was to persuade that person to be converted. Darrell left those occasions knowing that only God is in control of the results.

What is the point of this story? It's this: God wants us to be ready to share the Gospel, and to be able to lead someone to make a commitment to Jesus, not just say nice words and pray that they get it by osmosis.

Matthew 28:18-20, Making Disciples: Show 'Em!

What does it say in Matthew 28:19? "Go therefore, and teach [make disciples of] all nations." This means "make disciples" in the sense of "show 'em what to do to grow up in the faith," but it also means make disciples in the sense of "do the things necessary to bring them into the family, the household, of God." In other words, "Show 'em what they need to do to get in." That's what Darrell was doing in sharing the Gospel with Kim and in leading her to pray the prayer of salvation.

That's what I've been trying to get around to in this chapter. It's not enough to be a "good Christian," to do "good works" for the glory of God, and pray. We also have to be ready, willing and able to share the message of God's love and mercy through Jesus and tell 'em what they need to say and do (and think and understand) to be converted and have a relationship with God through Jesus Christ.

That is a part of what "spiritual service" means in this day and age. If we're not doing it, we're not living up to God's expectations for us. If we know what to say should the occasion arise, and we are willing to say it, then God, Jesus and the Holy Spirit, will use us as His disciples to 1) tell 'em the Gospel, 2) teach 'em what to do and say, and 3) help 'em to keep on doing it.

Darrell raised another point that should be addressed. In that university community in Kunming (a city of 6 million people), there are a number of Chinese Christian students who volunteer to "mentor" (read "disciple") their fellow students. In the early stages, it's just doing little things like giving them Bibles, getting them involved in prayer and Bible study groups, and helping them to continue coming to the small group meetings in homes. In more advanced situations, it's teaching them and showing them the tools they need to make disciples, too. The things we usually think about when we use the word discipleship are activities that are no less an important part of what we're calling "spiritual service" than evangelism. They are the "keeping on doing it" part of discipleship.

So if you're gonna' share the Gospel, the Good News of Jesus, the Evangel of the Lord, what are you going to say? There are a lot of truly committed Christians who just don't know what to say, even if God "sets it up" for them like He did for Darrell in Kunming.

Some think people need to understand a few things before they pray to receive Jesus, e.g., all have sinned, and because of sin they're separated from God (Romans 3:23), and the wages of sin is death, but the gift of God is eternal life through Jesus Christ our Lord (Romans 6:23).

Others emphasize the following: 1) God created us to have

fellowship with Him and enjoy His presence forever, but 2) because of Adam's rejection of God's plan for him (and us through Adam) we are all infected with a "sin nature," 3) the only way to be delivered from that sin nature is to "die to our sinful selfish nature so that Jesus can come to live His eternal, redemption life in us, and 4) this eternal life begins today, right here, right now, and continues forever.

The thing people are most desperately seeking is mercy, and the best thing you can do is to talk to them about how much God loves them. They already know what worthless sinners they are, and how ashamed they are, and how guilty they feel. They just want a little mercy and a little relief.

It is important to note that everyone does not have to use the same words as you or me to come to Jesus. Different groups of people use different words, but they all can be effective through the Holy Spirit. God looks at our hearts. As Oswald Chambers said, "Let God be as original with other people as He is with you."

William "Bill" Fay is the man I referred to earlier who has personally shared the Gospel with more than 25,000 individual people (that was some time before 1999; heaven knows how many people he's shared with by now, 2015). He wrote a book called *Share Jesus Without Fear*. Certainly this is not the only method for learning to share the Gospel, but it is one method, and we can use it to discuss the issues involved it with other methods. His method uses five "Share Jesus" questions, seven scriptures, and five "commitment" questions. The great thing about this method is that it gets us all to thinking about what we can say, and how we can be prepared for the many different responses you get when you talk to people about Jesus.

John 5:24, Short and to the Point

Off and on during my Christian life, I've thought there was just something wrong with this "canned pitch" way of talking to people about Jesus. I'm really a John 5:24 kinda' guy, where Jesus said, "If you'll pay attention to what I say, and trust Him who sent Me, you have eternal life; you will never be condemned; you have passed from death unto life." It's short and straight to the point. Jesus didn't manipulate people. He told them how it is and how they were and then let them decide. Each encounter was 'tailor made' for that particular person.

Consider Saul of Tarsus, Nathaniel, the rich young ruler, or Nicodemus, and consider how individually Jesus treated each of them. You just have to be open. If you really want to talk to someone about God, He'll fix it so you have a chance to do it. You don't need a canned pitch but we must be prepared to "give an answer, a reason for the hope that is in us" (1 Peter 3:15), and knowing the basic points of the Gospel is very important in sharing with others.

The Miracle Method

I have an alternative method for sharing Jesus. I'll call it the "Miracle Method," because it is not about what I do or say as much as it is about surrendering and letting God move by His Spirit. It's kind of the opposite of that line, "God helps those who help themselves," which really isn't true. What is true is, "God helps those who get out of the way and let Him help them." The "Miracle Method" is this: Everyone has problems. Some are easy to cover up, and some people are good at covering them up, but sometimes when your problems are really bad, you get desperate. You have to have help, sooner rather than later. It doesn't matter who caused it; sometimes you, sometimes others, sometimes some natural catastrophe puts you in an untenable position. **Then** what are you going to do? Have I got a deal for you! You can turn to God. He can help you. He can and will deliver you! What do you have to do to get Him to help you? All you have to do; all you **can** do is accept His help. And how do you accept it? You trust him. You say, "Oh Lord, I need help. I can't help myself. I have nowhere else to turn. So I'm going to turn to You. I'm going to trust You to take care of me. Since I've been doing such a pitiful job of running my life for myself, I'm going to surrender and let You run it. I'm going to accept Your promise from John 3:16 and believe (trust) in You." And you'll be amazed. God will really take you at your word and start helping you and changing you, and you'll never be the same again.

Acts 2:38, Repent and Be Baptized

Now what about all those places in the Bible where it says you have to confess and repent of your sins before you can (or will) be saved? John the Baptist and Peter said as much. What did they mean? Repent means to turn away from your sin (from your sinful, selfish nature) and turn to God. Being baptized means that you want to make, and **you make** an announcement to the world that you have trusted Jesus and turned from the darkness to the light. Baptism is a symbol of what has already happened in your heart. When you have that change of heart, God sends His Holy Spirit to live in your own private heart, to lead, guide, comfort and help you to follow Him.

How Can You Tell if People Are Christians?

Some days I think we need to make that commitment to trust in to Jesus every day. It would clear up any doubts we have about who is running our lives and what we're doing here.

Whatever you may think about all the issues presented in this section, talking to others about Jesus and about how to have a saving relationship with Jesus is an integral part of being a disciple. If we're not at some stage in the process of being and making disciples, then we're not living up to the standard of service taught by Jesus and the apostles in the Bible.

How can you tell if people are Christians? There are several things:

1. They love one another.
2. They trust God through thick and thin.
3. They seek God's will, and His Power, and His direction in their lives.
4. They bear fruit:
   a. Fruit of the Spirit
   b. Fruit of more disciples
5. They pray.
6. They tell what they've seen and heard about what God is doing in their lives and in the lives of others (they just can't help it).
7. They are ready to give a reason for the hope that is in them.
8. They make disciples.
9. They gather themselves together regularly.

2 Timothy 2:2, The Discipleship Verse

All these things go together; they're woven together to bring honor and glory to God. Like Paul said to Timothy, "And the things you have heard from me before many witnesses, the same teach to faithful men, who shall be able to teach others also" (2 Timothy 2:2). Paul is writing and talking about four generations of discipleship, 1) Paul, 2) Timothy, 3) faithful people, and 4) others. Our job or duty, if we choose to accept it, is to willingly put ourselves in this continuum, and then move, grow, develop, and progress in it for the rest of our natural lives. This is clearest and most concise description of what a Christian is and what a Christian does that I've ever encountered. This is part of what being a servant of Jesus is about. As it says, "Paul planted, Apollos watered, but God gives the increase" (1 Corinthians 3:6).

How do you do evangelism on a "grand" scale and still be able to speak to people on an individual basis, and still draw each individual into a discipleship relationship? We're not talking about tallying up numbers here; we're making disciples for Jesus Christ, the Son of the Living God!

On the other hand, or more to the point, individual witnessing is all about relationship. How does that fit in with evangelism campaigns or "made to order," "pre-packaged," "canned" pitches about the Gospel? How do those things fit in with "making disciples" as opposed to "getting people saved"? In the end, everyone who "comes to the knowledge of the Son of God" (Ephesians 4:13) and who becomes a disciple of Jesus to such an extent that he or she "makes disciples," has two characteristics in common: 1) They have been touched in their hearts by the Spirit of the Living God, and 2) they have a close, personal relationship with another disciple of Jesus; a person who is their teacher, mentor, guide, brother or sister in the Lord; someone who not only **tells** them the who, what, where, when, how, and why of having a relationship with God through Jesus in the Holy Spirit, but **shows** them how it's done in the situations and circumstances of life—trials, tribulations, mountains, valleys, victories, and defeats.

Paul and Timothy had a relationship like I'm talking about, and Paul had a similar relationship with several other brothers and sisters that are mentioned in the Bible: Barnabas, Silas, Luke, even John Mark.

Jesus had 12 disciples (apostles) who are named in the Bible, but he had a special relationship with three: Peter, James, and John. He took only these three along with Him on special events, like the Transfiguration and in the Garden. He shared special confidences with them. The other guys got the message of the Way of Jesus, but these three, Peter, James, and John, really got it. Without going into detail, I'm convinced this is the way God has designed humans to learn and become what He wants them to be (in the natural realm, too, but especially in the spiritual realm).

God's Primary Tools: Relationships and Demonstration

Relationships and demonstration are the primary tools God uses to teach us, mold us, and guide us into understanding the really important things about life. 'Course the main one is the "parent/child" relationship. When you're born, your momma is your first exposure to training, which is a lot less "book learnin'" and a lot more demonstration—you know "monkey-see, monkey-do." As we all know, the impact of what your momma (or your dad) tells you is a lot greater and more intense than whatever anyone else tells you. It's like magic how much better and longer you remember parental correction and discipline than any other kind. You know why? It's because subconsciously you know that they love you, and no matter how mad they get or how mad they make you, you know they mean it when they say they're doin' it for your own good.

God's like that, which is the reason we call Him our heavenly Father. 'Course, since He's the source of all things, effectively He is both our heavenly Father and Mother rolled into one. There's a lot of stuff in the Bible about how the ones He loves he chastens (corrects and disciplines), for example Proverbs 13:24. It even says any son who the Father doesn't correct isn't really a son. (Hebrews 12:8 KJV). What's so neat about our God is that He's personal—He wants to have a personal relationship with us like an earthly father or mother, but more so.

There are many other discipleship relationships on the earth within God's plan, and they all have one primary characteristic: they seek to instill, implant, and incorporate the parent's values, standards, and beliefs into the child. Biological children have a head start, since they got the genes from their parents goin' in, which means they're more likely to see things the same way. But the training matters, too, which is why adopted children sometimes "get" the package and the message more than biological kids. In the spiritual realm, 'we're all adopted, because our true parent is the one true God, and Jesus is the firstborn among many brothers and sisters, as it says in Romans 8:29.

All who seek to serve God and others must do it by letting the Spirit use us to help Him instill the characteristics of Jesus in others. That's spiritual service. I've had only a few relationships like that in my time walking with the Lord, but those few have been the most memorable of my life. I may be wrong about this, because God knows about a lot I've missed, but at least to me, those relationships have done more for the advancement of the kingdom of God and Jesus on this earth than all of the rest of my religious and spiritual activity put together.

In Philemon verse 6, Paul says, "[I pray] that the sharing of your faith will promote in you full understanding of every good thing we have in Christ Jesus." Did you get that? Talking to others about Jesus, telling them the Gospel, (sharing your faith) will help **you** understand all the great things that **you** have in Jesus (not to mention what it'll do for others). I've often thought and said that we all learn more by teaching than we do by just listening. I guarantee you I do. If I'm going to teach someone else, I have to actually think about what I'm saying, and I have to pray that God will make it soak in on me so He can use me to let it flow out to others. Since people are paying attention, you better have your facts straight.

One reason we are so resistant to sharing the Gospel is because we're not used to it. We may never have heard anyone do it, much less done it ourselves. Yet how are we ever going to bear fruit in the biblical sense of making disciples if we don't talk to others about Jesus? Talking to people about Jesus is simple but not easy. Getting started is kinda' the hardest part, but the more you do it the easier it gets. And it's not enough to just tell them about Jesus, God's love, Jesus' death and resurrection, our need to be saved, or their need for Jesus, but we also have to ask them to make a decision, for themselves, about Jesus. We can talk about sweetness and light, heaven and hell, and good works and philosophy, but we've missed the boat if we don't ask others to make a commitment to Jesus. Does anyone tell them what it really means to be saved? They need to know what God can and will do with their problems—their guilt, fear, anger, shame, sadness, and depression if they'll just surrender their lives to Him.

Sharing Jesus: A Group Project

'Course, some people think that sharing Jesus is a group project. "The Walk to Emmaus" is sorta' like that. A team of about 50 people get together and invite 36 men or women to review the basics of Christianity over a three-day weekend. It's supposed to be about training Christian leaders, and presumably all those participating are committed Christians who want to learn more about their faith and service in the church. Funny thing is, they may be committed to service in the church, but they may never have actually made a personal commitment to Jesus Christ as their Lord and Savior. So they go on the Walk to Emmaus, ostensibly for a different reason, and they wind up getting saved in an eternal, life-changing way. Praise the Lord!

Certainly, personal evangelism is a team or partnership project, like Jesus sending out the disciples "two-by-two," and like Paul taking Barnabas or Silas or others with him on his missionary journeys.

Tell a Story, Maybe Your Story

One good way to get started talking to others about Jesus is tell them a story. A good example of such a story is about Colonel William Barrett Travis, when he was the commander of the garrison at San Antonio de Bexar, historically and affectionately known as The Alamo.

It was March 1, 1836. There were 182 Texian fighting men inside the walls of the Alamo, and about 2,400 Mexican soldiers outside it, within the town of San Antonio. They had been under siege for about a month and things were getting desperate. Travis had already written his final letter to the Texas Congress at Washington on the Brazos, asking for reinforcements but knowing already that they had no reinforcements to send.

Travis called all of them out into the plaza of the old mission. They even brought Jim Bowie out on his cot 'cause he was too sick to walk. Travis pulled out his sword and drew a long straight line in the sand, then turned and addressed the troops. "We've been waiting and hoping for reinforcements, but probably there won't be any. We hear the Mexicans are gonna' attack at daybreak, and it'll be a miracle if we come out alive. If you want to leave, there's the door. You might make it out through the cattle pens in the middle of the night. But if you want to stay and fight, cross the line."

Well, they all kinda' stood there a minute, looking at Travis, making a furtive glance up and down the line to see if anyone was moving. Then Bowie motioned to his cot bearers and said, "Move me over there," and they did. Slowly, one by one, others started to move, and then in groups of four and seven and ten, 'til at the last the ones in the back and they'd all crossed the line. It was a solemn moment. No hurrahs. No hand shaking or back slapping, just the deep acceptance of the fact that they were all committed. Like Travis said in his last letter, "God and Texas, victory or death."

"Crossing the line" is about commitment, and it's the kind of commitment God is looking for in us. It's a gut level willingness to sacrifice all for Jesus—the kind of commitment He made for you and me. Even better, maybe you could tell them how you came to the point of surrendering you own personal self to Jesus; certainly that must be a story about commitment.

I guess the next question is, dear reader, "Are you ready to make that kind of commitment?" If you are, then pray this prayer with me: "Dear Lord, I'm a sinner. I know you sent Jesus to save me. I accept Your gift of salvation. I trust that You have saved me and that You'll keep me. I give my whole life to You, so you can do whatever You want to with me. In Jesus' name, amen.

Me and Lindsey, My Baby

As I mentioned earlier, Lindsey is my daughter. Now she's 38, tall, 5'9", with brown hair and hazel eyes. She's a beautiful young woman who must've gotten her looks from her momma. As of this writing (2015), she has four children, Leah is 4, Hope is 2, and Joshua and Caleb are both 9 months.

When Lindsey was a little girl, she was bright, attentive, loving, and friendly. Even as a small child, she had love in her heart that she shared with everyone. I'm sure I'm not a bit prejudiced when I say that she was, and is, my favorite person in the whole world. 'Course I say that about a few other people in my life, too!

When Lindsey was about 6, we were sitting at the dining table while her momma was cooking supper. We were talking about God and Jesus. I asked her if she understood John 3:16, and she said she did. I asked her if she understood about sin. She said, "That's when you do something bad."

"Do you know that you do things bad?"

"Yes."

"Do you know that God sent Jesus to die for you to save you from the bad things you do."

"Yes."

"Do you want to accept Jesus as your personal Savior so you can live with Him for the rest of your life, and then go to heaven?"

"Yes."

"Okay, let's pray. You pray after me." And we prayed the sinner's prayer.

I guess some would say that Lindsey didn't really know what was going on, that it was just words. I don't know. I was there and it seemed to me like the Holy Spirit was there. We both cried. I think maybe her momma was standing in the kitchen crying, too.

I don't know for sure if anything happened, but I have heard Lindsey say many times that she never has been afraid of dying, 'cause she knows God is taking care of her.

After that, we meant to have her go down the aisle to the front of the church and get accepted as a full-fledged member. I don't think we did it though because soon after that we moved to Colorado, and though we went to church, we didn't really find a home. We finally moved back to Texas, but by that time our family was wandering in the bushes . . . and we stayed there a long time.

After Lindsey graduated from high school, she went on to college at Sam Houston State in Huntsville, where she lived with her brother, Andy. During that whole time, from age 12 to 22, maybe 10 years, as far as I know she hardly ever went to church or thought much about God. It's sad to say that neither did the rest of us; a pretty hard time was had by all. This is why I say our family was wandering in the bushes for a long time.

When she graduated from college, she moved to Houston where

she got a job at a TV station. It was low pay and long hours, but it had high potential in the distant future. Well, she liked it in the beginning, but it was high on stress and low on encouragement. She worked 30 hours a week at $8.00 per hour, which meant she was still living with her momma, which was a stretch. So she got a job in the oil bidness, which paid a lot more money, and soon she got her own house and a new car, and she was "runnin' in high cotton," as they used to say.

'Course that's the problem with money; it makes you think you don't need God, that you've got everything under control, that you're bullet proof. Because of that, you are also able to do things you know you shouldn't do, but you do them anyway because they're there, because everybody's doing them, and because you get a buzz. The problem is, you reap what you sow, what goes around comes around, and the things you do will find you out. In the end, you get caught.

One day Lindsey was at Macy's buying a dress for a party. She picked the dress out and paid for it, but on the way out, she picked out a pair of shoes and left the store without paying for them. They must've caught her on the security cameras, because a security guard stopped her outside the store, took her to an office, and called the cops. Pretty soon, a police officer came to arrest her and take her downtown. He was doing an inventory on her purse when he found a little pill called "extasy," and what started out as a little shoplifting case quickly evolved into a felony drug case.

Why did she do it? Like Flip Wilson used to say on TV, "The debil made me do it." There's a verse in the Bible that talks about that same thing. It says people need to recognize the truth about themselves and God, "that they may come to their senses and escape the snare [net or trap] of the devil, having been taken captive by him to do his will" (2 Timothy 2:26). Maybe that's what happened. Sometime long before, she had let the devil take her captive, and she couldn't do anything else. From her standpoint, she thought it would be a buzz; she didn't think she'd get caught. She was way past the point of caring if it was wrong.

Well, it was all downhill from there—the back seat of a police car, handcuffed, the long, long trip downtown. She tried to call me but didn't get me. She got hold of her mom, and we got the ball rolling to get her bonded out. She was booked into the county jail about 4:00 pm, and we were hoping for release about 8:00.

Finally, about 1:00 am, Lindsey came out of the jail and sat down in my car. The first thing she said to me was, "I know God did this." She told me how, while she was waiting in the holding cell, there were two other girls with her, older, in their 30s, who were singing "Amazing Grace." Must've been a sign, ya' think? As we drove home, she told me the revelations she'd had while she was waiting, about feeling scared, guilty, nauseated, worried, and ashamed, but down deep glad that this phase of her life was over—but still wantin' some drugs to settle her down.

The end result was that she pled guilty to possession of drugs and they dismissed the shoplifting charge. She was sentenced to 3 years deferred adjudication with probation, which involved monthly meetings with the probation officer and monthly urine tests to check for drug use. She attended 90 AA meetings in 90 days, then weekly. She did 100 hours of community service, working in a "Salvation Army style" thrift and clothing store.

At first, we'd get together on Saturday mornings to talk, just Lindsey and me. Mostly we'd talk about what had been happening since last week. Some days were hard, but she was gradually, slowly coming to life.

We slowly began to talk more about God. After a while, we invited Waymon, a Christian brother, to join us, and we got to talkin' about Jesus more and more, about how He was changing our lives. We had a few other people join us, off and on, and sometimes we met at each other's homes but mostly at Denny's. Occasionally, we'd have Bible studies, but usually we'd end up telling stories about what God was doing with our lives.

We're still doing it. She's gotten married, had the babies mentioned above, but we still meet early on Saturday mornings, but now we're meeting at Lindsey and Wes's house, because of all the kids. Wes is a true believer, a true truster in Jesus, and he is thoroughly involved in discipleship on a regular basis. Since Lindsey and I began our discipleship journey, much has happened. She reads Oswald Chambers' *My Utmost for His Highest*, and she has a quiet time most every day. She has become involved in Bible Study Fellowship, a non-denominational Bible study group that does in-depth Bible study each week. Lindsey was a discussion group leader for several years, and she calls me often to discuss the verses and topics in their lessons. God uses BSF in a mighty way to touch our lives. Lindsey introduced Wes to BSF, and he has been actively involved as well.

Somewhere along the way, Lindsey also became involved in Walk to Emmaus, the interdenominational organization to train Christian leaders mentioned earlier. A great tool for discipleship, it's built around weekend retreats to learn emotionally what we know mentally about Jesus. Lindsey spent 3 years on the Board of Directors of the local Walk to Emmaus community, and she has worked on several weekend retreats in many different capacities.

Before all the kids, she was doing this at the same time she and Wes were involved in a local church, leading small groups, teaching, and keeping the faith. They have both been involved in Kairos, a ministry to men and women in prison. They have a full life in ministry for the Lord. Wow! Praise the Lord! Hallelujah! All this from a start just getting together to talk about what Jesus is doing in our lives.

Amazing grace and mercy! This *is* the life that is in Jesus Christ. This short story is a central part of my own discipleship training and experience. The things God has done in Lindsey's and my life, and in the lives of others, are truly amazing. To think that it started with a relationship that grew from a seed that was planted in a holding cell in Harris County Jail in Houston. Praise God from whom all blessings flow!

This is an example of "one-on-one" mentoring, like the relationship between Paul and Timothy. One-on-one discipleship is a key building block in God's plan for building the body of Christ. It's a good illustration of **"know a disciple, be a disciple, make disciples, teach disciples" for Jesus.** Even more than evangelical, door-to-door, street-corner witnessing, this pattern of building a relationship with one other person is the basic starting point for "making disciples" as described in Matthew 28:18-20.

More than great evangelical crusades, where thousands of people respond to the call and then fall through the cracks in the discipleship process; the one-on-one method of discipleship has on it the seal of the Holy Spirit of Jesus. This is the service that Jesus is calling us to as members of His Body. This is not just for clergy, preachers, or church staff, but it's for all of us. It's also not to be done just at the church, or just at the cell group meetings once a week, but in our homes with our children, at work with our co-workers, those with whom we serve in a civic or charitable way, and those with whom we socialize. This relationship of discipling has grown into a "family" where the members are discipling and being discipled. God has developed it as a center for growth of other ministries in the body, in Lindsey, in Wes, in me, and in unknown others who have been touched by God.

So how does this relate to service and serving? We serve best when we best do the will of the Father and of our Lord Jesus. As it says in the Great Commission, "Go, make disciples, baptize 'em, teach 'em,"—that's service. As Jesus says in John, "A new commandment I give you, that you love one another. By this shall all men know you are my disciples, if you have love one for another" (John 13:34). The relationship created and developed in these teacher-student, mentor-mentee, father-son, mother-daughter style relationships are the epitome of "love one another," and they're evidence of discipleship at the same time. That's service to God and to the brothers and sisters in the body.

Through such relationships come the stories that best demonstrate the presence of God's Holy Spirit in our lives. Like Peter and John said, "We can't help but tell what we've seen and heard" (Acts 4:18-20). That's the gift of moment-by-moment surrender and obedience that God gives us and others as we get to tell what we've seen and heard. Praise the Lord! How better can we serve? Aren't those stories a central part of what Jesus is talking about when He says, "Follow me, and I will make you fishers of men"?

Hebrews 10:24-25

"Let us think of ways to motivate one another to acts of love and good works. And let us not neglect our meeting together, as some people do, but encourage one another, especially now that the day of his return is drawing near." (NLT)

Another aspect of service is "meeting together" from this verse, which is worded "gathering ourselves together" in the KJV. When I was a kid in the 50s (yes, I know, I'm old), we went to church pretty much every time the doors were open—Sunday morning for Sunday School and church, Sunday evening for "training union" and worship service, Wednesday night supper, prayer meeting, and choir practice, Thursday night visiting, and lots of Saturdays, parties, and picnics with the youth and other members of the church. We went to church or a church activity almost every day of the week. Oh, don't get me wrong. We were fully involved in school stuff, too, often with some of the same people. Just about everybody we knew went to some church and had most of the same kinds of activities. Even kids who didn't usually go to church went in the summers so they could play on teams in the church softball league to keep sharp for school.

We all had a sense of God's presence in our lives and in our community. We heard a lot of preaching, we studied the Bible, and we even talked about religious and spiritual things quite a bit. None of this, however, is quite the same as what's going on in my life now.

Luke 24:13-35, Walk to Emmaus

In the last ten years, I've become involved in an experience that has had a profound effect on my life. Oh, I still go to church, and I'm still involved in similar activities related to my church, but this is different. About 12 years ago, I went on a weekend retreat called "Walk to Emmaus," which is an ecumenical program that is concerned primarily with "developing Christian leaders" (their term). I really think it's about "developing practicing Christians."

One guy I know said it like this: "Emmaus is about experiencing emotionally what you already knew intellectually." I'd say it's about feeling the presence of God through the Holy Spirit as opposed to just understanding something about Him with your mind. Remember that line earlier about God seeing what's going on in your heart? This is about God touching and moving your heart, not just your mind.

One thing they emphasize in Emmaus is "Reunion Groups," which are weekly small group meetings of 5-6 people. They have a discussion about how they're doing in living their lives as Christians. At least that's the published purpose, but in practice, it's about each of us telling stories about what God is doing in our lives and what He's saying to us as we live and move from day to day. These are truly amazing experiences that are even better than church. God touches our hearts every time, and the Spirit is moving every time. This is a qualitatively different experience from most of the activities that we used to do (and still do) in church. This is more like the way it was in the early days of the Church, at Jerusalem, like it says in Acts:

"All the believers devoted themselves to the apostles' teaching, and to fellowship, and to sharing in meals (including the Lord's Supper), and to prayer. . . . They worshiped together at the Temple each day, met in homes for the Lord's Supper, and shared their meals with great joy and generosity, all the while praising God and enjoying the goodwill of all the people. And each day the Lord added to their fellowship those who were being saved. (Acts 2:42, 46-47, NLT).

We're sharing our hearts and our souls with each other and with God, through His Holy Spirit. It's like the Spirit in me is speaking to the Spirit in you. You just never saw or felt anything like it. Whether they know it or not, somehow or other, this experience is very much an act of service, for everyone who is involved in it. Let me tell you, being an instrument of God that He can use to touch other peoples' lives is an act of service in any context. If you're not already involved in a group like this (whether it's Emmaus or another), please find some Christian brothers or sisters and sign up today. It'll change your life, but you'll never know how much until you try it. This is the real version of "gathering yourselves together." (like in Hebrews 10:24-25)

Uncle Snooks

My daddy's brother and favorite person—probably even counting my momma, my sister, and me—was Uncle Snooks. He was five years older than my daddy but they were bosom buddies. With a little slack for the difference in their ages, they grew up together. After they were grown, they spent some time apart, but during my life, my daddy respected, followed, confided in, and depended on my Uncle Snooks more than any other person. But that's another story.

My Uncle Snooks' real name was Francis Bartholomew Tonroy. Now you know why they called him "Snooks." Yes, I know it's kinda' weird but that's him. He was the spiritual patriarch of our family and a deacon in our church. He was involved in every aspect of the church—business, personal, teaching, hiring, and money, but especially the spiritual.

Almost every Sunday after church, we went to Uncle Snooks and Aunt Cleo's house for Sunday dinner. They had five kids who were almost like my brothers and sisters. On Saturday mornings, I'd go with my daddy out to Uncle Snooks' feed store to visit. In the winter,

I'd stand by the big gas heater or climb on the big sacks of feed and listen to my daddy and Uncle Snooks talk. It's amazing all the things a little kid can hear when he's listening.

Uncle Snooks was usually a quiet man, and unlike most of the people in my daddy's family, he didn't talk real loud. Most of my uncles, 5 of them, enjoyed arguing just for entertainment. They'd stand almost toe-to-toe and talk to each other at the top of their lungs for hours at a time. They enjoyed picking the most inane subject to argue about, like one time when I was about 6 or 7, I heard Uncle Rink and Uncle Morris argue for more than two hours about whether the word before "delinquent" was "julevine" or "juvenile."

Snooks didn't say much, but when he said something, people listened. Actually, I don't know about other people, but I listened. He wore big thick glasses, and he didn't have a reputation for being a manly man; he was more of the studious type. But he was the one on whom my daddy always depended when he was in "a tight." One time my daddy went to a convention in Amarillo and got drunk. On the way home, he was arrested for driving while intoxicated in his brand-new Packard automobile. He got arrested in Plainview, about 50 miles from home, and sure enough, Uncle Snooks was there in the morning to bail him out and drive him home. A lot of people depended on Uncle Snooks like that. Whenever any of his brothers couldn't figure out what to do about some problem they were having, they'd go to Snooks for advice.

On Thursday evenings, we went "visiting" for the church, the purpose of which was to invite people back to church after they had come to visit our church the first time. Uncle Snooks would follow the usual practice and tell people he was from our church, and that he'd come to tell them how we were happy they'd visited us, and how we'd be glad if they'd come back and join us as members; but he had a bigger purpose. After he got through with the formalities, he'd talk to them about Jesus. I don't remember exactly what he said every time, but I do remember that you could tell God was there by His Spirit, and that everyone in the room knew it, too.

Usually, Uncle Snooks would just ask them if they knew Jesus, a simple question but with a lot of weight behind it. 'Course in Lubbock, Texas, in the 1950s, almost everybody knew what he was talking about. Hardly anybody would even try to get by with saying, "I go to the so-n-so church," or "I got baptized when I was a kid," or even "My daddy was a preacher." If they said something like that, as a means of putting him off, Snooks would just say, "Yes, but do you do you know Jesus as your Lord and Savior?" (in other words, let's get right to the point).

Then he'd tell them about what Jesus had done in his life, all the ways Jesus had helped him and his family. Depending on who he was talking to, he'd tell different stories about what it meant when he said, "Jesus can fix whatever is wrong with you." It was really crazy. People would start talking to him and telling him what was wrong with them, and lots of times they started crying while they were telling it—about sicknesses they'd had for years and couldn't get over, or kids who'd gone crazy and gotten in trouble with the law and gone to prison, or about feuds in their families where they hadn't talked to their sisters and brothers for years and years.

Sometimes Uncle Snooks would tell them what to do; other times, he'd say he didn't know what to do, but he'd always say, "Let's pray." Always, before the end of the conversation, he'd also say, if the occasion called for it, "Would you like to be saved?" If they said yes, he'd lead them down the "Roman Road," which meant telling them about verses in Romans like, "All have sinned and come short of the glory of God" (Romans 3:23), "The wages of sin is death, but the gift of God is eternal life through Jesus Christ our Lord" (Romans 6:23), "For God so loved the world, He gave his only begotten Son, that whoever believes in Him, will not perish but have eternal life" (John 3:16), and "If you will confess with your mouth the Lord Jesus, and believe in your heart that God raised Him from the dead; you will be saved. For with the heart man believes unto righteousness, and with the mouth confession is made to salvation" (Romans 10:9-11). After each verse, he'd ask them if they understood, and they'd have a little discussion, and maybe he'd explain it to them a little.

At the end he'd say, "Would you like to ask Jesus to come into your heart?" Sometimes they would say they weren't ready, and if so, he wouldn't push them much. At the most he might way, "Well, you never know what might happen, so don't wait too long."

Lots of times, they'd say yes, and he'd lead them in a short prayer for salvation: "Dear Lord, I know I'm a sinner. I know You died to save me from my sins. Please come into my heart. I give You my life to do what You want to with it. In Jesus' name, amen."

Then we'd go. Usually as we're going out the door, he'd say something like, "Our church is down off the corner of Main and College Ave. We'd sure like to have you come."

I don't know about y'all, but to me what Uncle Snooks did was an act of service to God and to men, an act of service with eternal consequences.

Brother Homer

During the time I knew Homer Duncan, he was the pastor and minister of the Gospel at Grace Bible Church in Lubbock, Texas. For his day job, he ran a little Christian publishing company called the Missionary Crusader, which printed all kinds of pamphlets about Christianity in a number of different languages and sent them all over the world. He was particularly interested in ministering to the people of India, where he went every summer to teach young preachers in Christian seminaries. He'd stay there two or three months and then come back to publishing and pastoring.

Brother Homer was the nearest thing to an apostle that I ever personally knew. He knew what "planting churches" was all about. He had a wisdom and a way of sharing the Gospel that made me think of Paul, Peter, and John. There was a sense of absolute surrender to Jesus and a profound sense of peace about him whenever you were in his presence. I remember how I first became acquainted with him. It was during one of my "on-fire-for-the-Lord" spells, when I was 27 years old, driving down Avenue H in Lubbock, and I saw the sign, "Missionary Crusader" and pulled in to see what it was.

Inside, there was an old man sitting at an old wooden desk with books and papers stacked all over the place, right in the front room of the office. We introduced ourselves and he invited me to sit down—no appointment, no invitation, just come in and sit down and we'll talk. It must've been a divine appointment. He kinda' told me all about it, and I got the message loud and clear. God was telling me to pay attention, and I was thinking, "How can I become a part of this?" When it was time to go, he said, "We have a little prayer meeting on Tuesday afternoons here. We'd be glad to have you come."

I made it a point to come to those prayer meetings; I hardly ever missed. It was just me and four or five old men, but I didn't feel out of place. I thought it was a great gift of God that He'd let me be there in His presence with all those men of God. I kept up with Brother Homer for several years, going to prayer meetings, buying and distributing books, and giving money. I even tried to go to India with Brother Homer one time but for some reason I didn't get to. Finally, I moved away from Lubbock, and sorta' lost touch, but I'd always went by when I was in town. A few years later, Brother Homer died. His son and some other people still ran the publishing house, but it was sorta' fading, too.

He may be gone but he's not forgotten. I think the thing about Brother Homer that touched me most, and carried me on with the Lord, was how he'd explain Biblical things in ways that were so easy to understand and remember, so I could tell them to other people when the right time came. Things like "secular humanism," and how the "the gospel will be preached unto all the nations before the end can come," and the difference between "judgment" and "discernment." I believe that Homer Duncan was one of those people who best exemplifies what it means to "deny yourself, and take up your cross daily, and follow Me." If we're talking about serving, Homer Duncan qualifies as a servant of Jesus and men.

Loyde Castle

An ordained preacher and my brother in Jesus, ever since Loyde Castle got saved, he has stayed "on fire for Jesus" in his own way. He never had a big church, and lots of the time he hasn't had any church at all, but he has never gone back on his commitment to follow Jesus. Loyde Castle is responsible for me being ordained as a minister in the body of Christ, which happened at the Grace Chapel near Lubbock, Texas, where Loyde Castle was the pastor at the time.

Loyde has always been called by God to minister to the physical and spiritual needs of children and youth. He's run bus programs to bring kids to Sunday School and church, and he's started homes for unwed mothers and also children's homes to take care of orphans or kids who'd run away from home (or the parents had run away from their kids). He collects money to take care of other preachers who are struggling to start churches in poor areas. He's always had a fulltime job as a carpenter and builder, but he still makes time for another fulltime job as a minister to God and the people.

Loyde and I have a similar understanding about what it means to serve Jesus and others. We have supported each other through thick and thin in our struggles to serve Jesus. Very likely many of our problems have been self-induced but we have persevered in supporting each other. Now we're both involved in Emmaus and Kairos (though in different parts of the state), and we're both still praying for and trying to serve prisoners and their families.

You know that line in Proverbs about "there is a friend who is closer than a brother"? That's Loyde Castle and me. Thank God that He has put people like Loyde Castle in my life. Loyde is one of God's lights to my path and one of His joys to my heart. When I think about service, I think about God sending Loyde Castle my way.

James 5:13-20, Praying is Service

"Is anyone among you in trouble? Let them pray. Is anyone happy? Let them sing songs of praise. Is anyone among you sick? Let them call the elders of the church to pray over them and anoint them with oil in the name of the Lord. And the prayer offered in faith will make the sick person well; the Lord will raise them up. If they have sinned, they will be forgiven. Therefore confess your sins to each other and pray for each other so that you may be healed. The prayer of a righteous person is powerful and effective.

"Elijah was a human being, even as we are. He prayed earnestly that it would not rain, and it did not rain on the land for three and a half years. Again he prayed, and the heavens gave rain, and the earth produced its crops.

"My brothers and sisters, if one of you should wander from the truth and someone should bring that person back; remember this: Whoever turns a sinner from the error of their way will save them from death and cover over a multitude of sins."

What does this passage mean if we're talking about service? This passage is about several things that people do who believe in, trust in, and surrender to Jesus. These things are not exactly things that they're supposed to do, as a duty, but things they do because it's in their hearts and it has to come out (it's part of their spiritual nature). Down in his heart, James was a serious truster in Jesus, and because he had personally experienced these events, he knew what he was talkin' about. His observations in this passage really are practices we ought to keep, because they really are part of what it means to serve and to be a servant, both to God and others.

So first, if you are in trouble, pray. I'm sure you already know that every prayer is an act of faith, an act of trust in God. It's a service to God to ask for His help; even when you're saying, "Help! Please! Right Now! I've tried everything else and nothing is working! I'm so desperate, this is such a big problem, a big trouble, such an emergency, such a life and death matter, I'm actually praying, begging, for help. And You God are the only One who is remotely capable of helping me. The monsters are fixin' to get me, and You're the only One who can get my fat out of the fire." God likes it when you recognize that He can help you, and you're willing to prove it by asking for His help.

Then, when you're happy (like when God answers your particular prayer and gets you out of trouble for the 43rd time this week), sing praises! Hallelujah! By the way, that word means praise God, and it's the only word that translates the same in all languages. In Hebrew, *Jah* or *Yah* is God, which is where we get JHWH or YHWH, which means "to be" and is considered God's name. See Exodus 3:14, where God's name is translated "I am that I am," which is pronounced Yahweh with vowels added (there are no vowels in Hebrew). Some translations use Jehovah instead of Yahweh. "Hallelu" means praise, so put together it means praise God.

The next line is almost the same: "If you're sick, call the elders to pray." I always think it'll work just as well if you pray as if you ask someone else to pray, 'cause God is listening to little ol' you just as much (maybe more) than He's listening to the elders, because the same Spirit that's in them is in you. But so what, if you're a little scared that you need some extra fire power, "Call on the elders to pray for you and anoint you with oil in the name of the Lord." You will get well; you can write it down in your book. Sometimes you get well right away; you begin to feel it within a few minutes. Other times it takes more time. Maybe you have to sleep it off for a while. Sometimes it takes months, or even years, to fully heal, but not often. Usually you'll begin to notice the change within a few days. God is in full control.

He is arranging everything to be perfect for you and for Him and for the other people involved as well (not only your physical health, but your mental, emotional, and spiritual health as well). It's not just remarkable how this happens; it's positively miraculous. I have several things wrong with me that have been going on in my body for years, but I still feel as good as I've ever felt. Sometimes it's like Paul's "thorn in the flesh" when I really despair of the condition like he did, but most of the time it's a minor inconvenience that helps me remember to be thankful for all the multitude of good things that are going on in my life. I believe that my lifespan in not shortened because God is extremely merciful and His grace truly is sufficient (2 Corinthians 12:9). I don't have to worry because He really does give me the peace that passes all understanding. Philippians 4:6-7 says, "Don't worry about anything; but giving thanks for what you have, tell God what you need; and the peace that passes all understanding will guard your heart and your mind, through Jesus Christ our Lord." Just so you'll know, if you ever had any doubt, this verse works every time—not the verse, but Our Lord; because you're truly rendering a "service of worship" to God when you trust in Him in this way.

So pray for yourself and pray for others. Call the elders, get in a big circle, everybody hold hands, and pray. Wow! How much God likes to see people pray. Or put the prayee in the middle and let everybody get around them and lay hands on them (maybe in multiple layers where there's circles of people laying hands on the backs of the people in front) so that they can feel the touch of God in their hearts and in their bodies. You just can't imagine the way the Spirit moves in you, inside and out, when a bunch of people get together and get down and pray!

Another big benefit of praying is that you feel God's presence when you pray. You feel it when you pray by yourself, but to me you feel His presence even more when you pray out loud in the company of others. I don't know about you, but honest to goodness, one of my favorite things on the face of this earth is to feel God's presence!

About the oil, I guess there are some Christians who have been anointing people with oil for a long time, since Jesus' day, but where I came from, I never heard of anyone anointing someone with oil except in the Bible. We baptized with water, we had the Lord's Supper with wafers and grape juice, and we ordained people with the laying on of hands. We also prayed for people without laying on of hands, mostly just holding hands, but without oil. Until a few years ago, I was completely without experience about oil, which goes to show you what I know.

Oil is a symbol of the Holy Spirit, of God's blessing being poured out on the king, or on one whom God had chosen to be king, like Samuel did to David. I guess back then oil was a symbol of the cleansing and the perfume of anointing (that's about the Holy Spirit as well).

Long ago they took a pitcher of oil and poured it over the head of the anointed one so that, according to one passage in the Bible, in ran down all over the person, on his beard and his robe. It was a physical, savory sensation as well as a spiritual one. In Psalm 133, it says that unity is "like the precious oil upon the head, running down the beard, the beard of Aaron, running down to the edge of his garments."

'Course now-a-days, people just get a little vial, like for perfume, fill it with oil, and get a drop on their finger and dab it on the forehead in the form of a cross. It seems to have the same sensation in a way, almost like the presence of the Holy Spirit in physical form. It'd almost be worth getting sick so you could get someone to anoint you with oil, the best part of which would be that you'd be healed.

Do you like that line that comes next? "And the prayer of faith will make the sick person well." Can you believe that? What is this "prayer of faith"? I hear a lot of people discussing whether people can pray for other people in the name of Jesus and the people they pray for can actually be healed. I've heard of a lot of people who have been declared terminally ill by the doctors, who have gone home to arrange their affairs and prepare to die, but over a period of time they started to get better, and then went on to live healthy, productive lives for many more years.

My momma was one. When she was 80 years old, she had some blood tests that indicated she had cancer, and her stomach was swelling, so they did exploratory surgery. The doctor came out of the operating room and said, "Her abdomen is full of lymph nodes of cancer. She can't live more than a few months. We'll give her some chemotherapy, but we don't expect it to help much, if any."

Well, she got up and went home from the hospital. She took the chemo treatments. She didn't like them much, but she only got really sick (nauseated) one time out of a long course of treatment, and her hair didn't even fall out. She lived several more happy years, getting up every day and going about her business. She eventually died when she was 91, but it wasn't because of cancer, just old age. I don't know why it turned out that way but I do know that she trusted God to take care of her. I don't even know if she prayed about it much, maybe some about not getting nauseous, but not about the disease. She knew God was going to let her live as long as it suited Him, and she was happy about that.

Like I said earlier, when we trust God He takes care of us, and when we pray He answers us. If we don't worry about the answers we have peace in our hearts and in our lives. 'Course nobody ever said there wouldn't be any suffering or sacrifice. Nobody ever said we'd understand everything or that we'd be able to explain everything because we won't and we can't.

Back to that "prayer of faith," it definitely sounds like the person doing the praying has some special ability, some special anointing from God, or he is a "righteous" man, so his prayers will be powerful and effective (just like it says later in this very passage). I used to read that line, "The fervent effectual prayer of a righteous man availeth much" (KJV) and I'd think, "Must be a really holy guy." Like Elijah, mentioned in verses 17-18, who prayed that it wouldn't rain, and it didn't rain for 3-1/2 years. Well, Elijah was a righteous man, a holy man, a prophet, and he prayed for many truly wondrous miracles. He also trained Elisha, who also prayed for people and they were healed, including one lady's son who came back from the dead (2 Kings 4:32-35). What I want to know is, what did Elijah and Elisha have that any regular old, normal, believer (truster) in Jesus doesn't have?"

The answer is **nothing**. In the Old Testament, God picked out certain people and "anointed them with His Spirit," such as kings, prophets, and priests. Elijah was one of those people, but in those days not everybody was anointed. Most people, if they wanted to find out what God said, what He wanted, or what He was going to do, had to ask one of the people who were anointed with God's Spirit. Today, since Jesus came to the earth, made the final sacrifice to reconcile us to God, rose from the dead, ascended into heaven, and sent His Spirit to be with us and to be in us, we have the same anointing that Elijah had. If we surrender ourselves to Jesus, and line ourselves up with Him and His teachings and His Spirit, we have the same direct line to God that Elijah had. It's not just that we **can** have what Elijah had, we **do** have what Elijah had. All we have to do to fully realize God's power in us is to do what Jesus says in Luke 9:23, "Deny yourself, and take up your cross daily, and follow Me." It's not easy but it's simple. It takes daily surrender and daily dying to yourself, but the results are just incomparable. You get to know the one true God for your very own self. No intermediaries; just direct contact with God through His Spirit present inside of your heart, soul, mind, and body, every minute, every second. Just like Elijah.

So if we're talking about service, what does that mean? It means that we really are God's lights in the world. It means that we really are the "salt of the earth," whereby it is flavored, "cured," saved from corruption. All we've got to do is surrender to Him and let His Spirit use us to fulfill His purposes in the world.

Who is a "righteous" person? A righteous person is one who has Jesus' righteousness in him because he has surrendered his whole self to Jesus. Not my righteousness but His righteousness is the only thing that is going to save me, the only thing that is going to make me holy, as God is holy. So if you want to have prayer that is powerful and effective, what do you have to do? You have to surrender; not just once, but every single day, every hour, every minute. Most of the time we're too busy to do that; to think about that, to even consider that. But if you try to do it, and you keep on trying, eventually it gets to be a habit; you enter a zone where you're in constant contact with the Spirit that is in you, and you begin to "pray without ceasing," you begin to "rejoice evermore," you begin to "give thanks in all things," because that really is "the will of God in Christ Jesus for you" (1 Thessalonians 5:16-18). That's where "righteous" comes from, and that's what it takes to be a servant in the biblical sense—it's all about God; "Christ in you, the hope of glory". (Colossians 1:27)

So the righteous person is not some preacher, prophet, priest, or king, but rather **you** and every person who has the Spirit of God residing in his or her heart. So if **you** pray over them and anoint them with oil, they will be delivered, healed, or made whole, because **you** are one of those special people whom God has anointed to do His will, to fulfill His purposes on this earth. "**You** are chosen, you are a royal priest, a holy person, His own special person . . ." (paraphrase,1 Peter 2:9)

The part about "the prayer of faith" is a prayer that is spoken by a person who has God's Spirit dwelling in her; it's not something she has to "work up"; it's something that is already happening in her heart, soul, and spirit because of the presence of God's Spirit in her. It's one of those "rivers of living water" that flows out of her because she trusts in Jesus as a condition of her very being; it's not just a momentary act of her will. I'm 66 years old, and I'm just now beginning to get that concept.

What does an apple tree do during the process of bearing fruit? It sits there and waits, but while it's sitting there it takes in the ingredients it uses to make fruit—water, nutrients from the soil, sun and rain from the sky. Then one day, when the time is right, it puts out leaves and begins to develop this chlorophyll that is its food, it puts out buds and blossoms and bees come along and help with the pollination, and in due time, while the tree is still waiting, the blossoms turn into little, tiny apples. Eventually, the apples grow big and ripen and get ready to be picked and eaten.

But here's the version that we would envision if we were comparing most of us to an apple tree. The apple tree gets up every morning and starts worrying about how it is going to bear fruit. It knows there must be fruit down in there somewhere, so it grunts, pushes, strains, gets tired and frustrated, and develops ulcers waiting for something to happen. It grunts and pushes, expecting I guess, for the apples to just pop out of the ends of the branches. One day no apples; the next day **pop**, and there are the fully developed, fully ripened apples. It just doesn't work that way, does it? As I said earlier, in Spanish, wait and hope are the same word, *esperar*, and sometimes I think trust could be a part of those same active verbs. While we're waiting and hoping, we're also trusting that God is going to bring it to pass, because there's not a way in the world that we're ever going to push hard enough or grunt hard enough to make those apples pop out on our tree. We're got to trust that God, by His Spirit, is going to use what He's put in us to fulfill His purposes in the world. That's the service of trust, and **that** is the same action verb we need to have when we pray, *which is down deep knowing that God is going to bring it to pass.*

Did you see that one sentence in this passage, "And if they've sinned, they'll be forgiven"? It comes right after, "The prayer offered in faith will make the sick person well, and the Lord will lift them up. *And if they have sinned, they will be forgiven.*" It doesn't even say you have to pray for their sins to be forgiven. It's almost as if the sins are what made them sick, and if you heal the sickness you take away the sins as well. What I think is that the Lord has been looking at their hearts again, and He knows what is really wrong with them. He knows that the sickness is only a symptom of what is really wrong with them, which is the sin, and he knows they can never be really well until they're healed from the sickness inside which is caused by the sin—and the only way to be healed is to be forgiven, to be redeemed. So even though you may only be praying for healing of the physical condition, God will take your small, almost unknowing prayer, and fully heal; He will fully provide for all their needs by His riches in glory in Christ Jesus (Philippians 4:19). Wow!

How is praying a service to God and to others? First, it's evidence of our trust in God's Presence in us and for us. Second, it's a gift of God to us, and a gift from us to others (and back to God). Third, it's evidence of God's righteousness dwelling in us and flowing out of us. Fourth, it's the channel by which the Spirit heals the whole person, not just one limited disease.

Right after this it says, "So confess your sins to each other and pray for each other so you can be healed." Another version, *The Message*, says, "Make this your common practice: Confess your sins to each other and pray for each other so that you can live together whole and healed." The Amplified Bible says, "Confess to one another therefore your faults (your slips, your false steps, your offenses, your sins) and pray (also) for one another, that you may be healed and restored (to a spiritual tone of mind and heart). I'm involved in a small prayer group at my church that meets on Tuesday evenings at 6:30 to pray. We pray for 30 minutes, but we don't plan to pray and we don't talk about praying; we just pray. Mostly we pray out loud so we can all hear but of course it's okay to pray to yourself while you listen to others praying. Sometimes we use the "Korean method" (our words not theirs) where everybody prays out loud at the same time. We heard that's the way they do it sometimes in Korea, except with them it's maybe 10,000 people praying out loud at the same time, but you get the idea. Usually we do that when there are so many prayer requests we can't get around to all of them in 30 minutes. Talk about a "joyful noise unto the Lord"! Usually, in our little prayer group of 7 to 15 people, we loosely follow the "ACTS" model for prayer: Adoration,

Confession, Thanksgiving, and Supplication, or using other words, Worshiping, Confessing, Thanksgiving, and Asking.

We worship by singing a song of praise, like "O Come Let Us Adore Him, for He Alone is Worthy" to the tune of "O Come All Ye Faithful" or "Jesus Loves Me", or "Spirit Song" to get us in tune with the Spirit; then we quote scriptures and phrases that honor God and bring glory to Him, like "for the Lord is good, His mercy is everlasting and His truth endures to all generations!" (Psalm 100:6)

We need to confess out loud to other people. Whoever said, "Confession is good for the soul," is exactly right. Genuine confession, which includes desperately true sorrow and recognition of the wrongs committed against God and others, is the best cleansing you'll ever know. When you confess and accept God's forgiveness, you really are set free from the burden of sin and guilt. (See James 4:8-10) Until you experience it, you really don't realize how good it feels, what a relief it is.

Notice in this verse it says, "Confess your sins to each other and pray for each other, so you may be **healed**." Notice it does not say so you may be **forgiven**. Forgiveness is a good thing and absolutely necessary, but it is just the first step in the grand design God has for you. He does forgive, but in addition He also heals, and ultimately He makes you whole.

Matthew 5:48 says, "Be perfect, even as your Father in heaven is perfect." The word that's translated "perfect" in English comes from the Greek and is the root word for our word "integer," which means a "whole" number. So "perfect" should really be "whole, entire, lacking nothing."

Even in our worldly, fleshly society, even where we are too proud to actually admit to the sins we're hiding behind closed doors, I believe there is a place for confessing the sins we're hiding in our hearts, the ones we're desperately afraid our friends, neighbors, and fellow church-members are going to find out.

As mentioned earlier, in our Emmaus community, we have what we call Reunion Groups. Officially, I think they're supposed to be "accountability" groups, which in my view means that the members of the group are supposed to share their successes, failures, and struggles as they grow and learn how to be disciples of Jesus Christ. Usually, these are small groups, only four or five people, almost always segregated by gender, so there may be some genuine, vulnerable, truthful sharing of what is really going on in their lives. The reason for keeping the groups small is because few if any of us are ready to share what is really going on with anyone we're not intimately acquainted with. This trusting atmosphere comes slowly, but when it comes, the members are more and more willing to share what's really going on deep down in the bottom of their hearts and lives, stuff they wouldn't even tell their own biological brothers or sisters. That only comes with that no holds barred, gut level trust. When somebody gets really desperate for relief from the depression they get from hiding their worst secrets, they are then able to confess and be cleansed by God's Holy Spirit. Then is when you can "confess your sins to one another and be healed"—in other words, be made whole!

The prayer of a righteous person is powerful and effective. *Who is righteous? It's anyone who has surrendered to Jesus and let His Spirit come to dwell in their heart. No one else is righteous in God's eyes.* If you want to have a powerful and effective prayer life, surrender your whole self to Jesus, deny yourself, take up your cross daily (that means "die to yourself" so Jesus can live His eternal life in you), and follow Him (Luke 9:23). That's the **only** way to have a powerful effective prayer life.

I just figured out what James is talking about in his little short story about Elijah, who had a powerful effective prayer life. Even though he was a human being, like we are, he was "righteous in God's eyes" because he was totally surrendered to God. He denied himself, so God's eternal Spirit lived in him, and when he prayed, stuff happened in response to his prayers. When you truly surrender to God, you understand and discern God's will so well that you get lined up with God and you're able to be obedient to pray for what God wants to have happen—and then it happens. I heard a pastor say that when you're praying and you're really in tune with God, He begins to tell you what He wants you to pray for, and when you pray for what God wants, those things happen.

In the last few verses of this passage, James says, (Tex's paraphrase), "If one of the brothers or sisters gets off in the bushes (**way** off), someone should go get them and bring them back."

The image I have is of losing the family dog, and everybody in the family is out looking for him, going up and down the streets hollering,

"Dawg, Dawg, Come Dawg! Here Dawgy, Dawgy!" Everyone is going down the alleys, looking over the fences to see if he was trapped in somebody's backyard, asking the kids, "Have you seen our dog? You know, big, brown with long hair and ears, 'bout this tall." Then other kids start helping you try to find him, and all the time you're hunting, you're saying a silent prayer, "Please Lord, don't let anything bad happen to our dog. Don't let him get run over, or let somebody steal him and take him off somewhere; and please Lord, don't let anybody poison him."

Well, just when it's getting dark, and you're fixin' to have to go in to supper, and you don't know what you're going to do, you turn a corner and there he is. He's happy to see you and you're really happy to see him, but because he doesn't even know he was lost, he wants to play. You want him to go home, but he's not ready, so when you try to grab him he runs away. Then you have to coax him back. You know, you turn around and act like you're gonna' leave him, and walk real slow, and finally he gets the message and beats you back to the house.

That's just what we're supposed to do for our wayward brothers and sisters. The only difference is dogs don't usually drink or take drugs or all those other things humans use to block their pain or escape their troubles. So bringing them back, rescuing them from the error of their ways, requires greater commitment to God and to them. But when you get to be there to see them turn, it's worth all the trouble. Then you begin to realize what a blessing it is to be a servant of God and others. This is what service is all about. Talk about "save them from death, and cover a multitude of sins." Praise the Lord!

2 Timothy 2:24-26

"God's servant must not be argumentative, but a gentle listener and a teacher who keeps his cool, working firmly but patiently with those who refuse to obey. You never know how or when God might sober them up with a change of heart and a turning to the truth, enabling them to escape the Devil's trap, where they are caught and held captive, forced to run his errands" (*The Message*).

"Serve" is something servants do; it's almost like that's the definition of serve. So how is "God's servant" different from your average, generic servant? It's mainly a difference of attitude. I think that regular servants were pretty humble, especially in the days of the first century. The Greek word translated "servant" in the KJV Bible is *doulos* and it means "slave." Slaves then were usually a good deal more humble and subservient than what we usually think of as servants today. I mean today even servants have rights, expectations of proper treatment, and standards. "God's servants," however, must have an attitude of more humility and more willingness to suffer for God and others than just any old servant. Like Paul says in Philippians 2:5-8, "Let this mind [this attitude] be in you that was also in Christ Jesus; . . . Who, being found as a man, humbled himself and became a slave, and was obedient unto death, even death on a cross." That is what they're talking about when they say "God's servant is patient"; it means "willing to suffer." In other words, being like Jesus, the best example of a "servant of the Lord."

Every version of this passage, whether Greek, English, or Spanish, says that one of the characteristics of a servant of the Lord is patience. The Greek word *hypomeno,* which is translated in modern versions of the Bible as patient, really means "patient of injury." The Amplified version calls it "patient and forbearing and willing to suffer." It is a first cousin to another Greek word, *hypomone,* translated as "patience," which really means "suffers long" (like it's translated in the KJV). It really means that you're willing to keep on putting up with them while you're waiting for them to turn. You suffer with them and for them as you wait, hoping and trusting that God is going to give them repentance so they can see the light and get out of the trap that the devil has them in, doing his will.

Back when I was a criminal defense attorney, pretty often I'd have these single mommas with their wayward sons come to my office. Sometimes it was just the momma, because the son was back in jail, charged with another offense while he was out on bail for a previous charge. Here she was, asking me to help her make bail so the kid can get back out again. One lady I remember had already borrowed money from her employer to make the first bail, and now she was going to borrow more money to pay me and for another bail. She must have been a trusted servant of her employer or they wouldn't have continued to loan her money. She said, "I know he's in trouble, but really down in his heart, he's a good boy, and I just have to try to help him. I can't help it." I thought about telling her she should take the money and use it to help someone whom it would help. It wouldn't have mattered though because she was going to keep on trying to help her son. Even though she knew, better than anyone else, that he didn't deserve it, that he'd be back in trouble again, sooner rather than later, she still kept on trying to help him, because she knew that God would take care of her while she was trying to do it, even if it didn't work. That's what love is about. Maybe we could think up better ways to help, but we couldn't possibly deny that the lady's heart was in exactly the right place about wanting to help her son for as long as it took, for as long as she lived. That's what love is about; that's what having a "servant's heart" is all about. Clearly that is "love suffering long."

Like Paul says in 1 Corinthians 13:7, the "love" chapter, "You put up with them, you believe the best for them, and trust God to deliver them; you keep on hoping something good is going to happen; and you endure (there's that "put up with them" again) for as long as it takes." That's the way God has been treating you (and me). Can you do any less for your brothers and sisters in and out of the body of Jesus? That is what it means to be a servant.

John 15:1-8

"I am the Real Vine and my Father is the Farmer. He cuts off every branch of me that doesn't bear grapes. And every branch that is grape-bearing he prunes back so it will bear even more. You are already pruned back by the message I have spoken. Live in me. Make your home in me just as I do in you. In the same way that a branch can't bear grapes by itself but only by being joined to the vine, you can't bear fruit unless you are joined with me. I am the Vine, you are the branches. When you're joined with me and I with you, the relationship is intimate and organic, the harvest is sure to be abundant. Separated, you can't produce a thing. Anyone who separates from me is deadwood, gathered up and thrown on the bonfire. But if you make yourselves at home with me and my words are at home in you, you can be sure that whatever you ask will be listened to and acted upon. *This is how my Father shows who he is—when you produce grapes, when you mature as my disciples*" (*The Message*).

Jesus said, "I am the Vine and my Father is the Gardener, and y'all are the branches." The fruit represents the people who come because

God used us as instruments of His love, mercy, and grace. The fruit also refers to the tender loving care that flows out of people who know Jesus to all those scared, worried, hopeless people out there in the world. So you *are* the salt and the light (Matthew 5:13-14), a planter planting the seeds of the Word (Mark 4:14), and fruit is what flows out of a servant who is not above his Master (Matthew 10:24) and who is willing to forgo the pleasure of "lording it over" 'em (Mark 10:42-43).

In this passage it says God does two things: 1) To the fruitless branches, He cuts them off and throws them in the fire, and 2) to the fruitful branches, He cleans and trims and prunes them, over and over, so they'll bear more and more fruit. 'Course God does a lot more. He put the Vine there to start with, He sent His Son to earth to make a connection with us, and He sent the Holy Spirit to nourish, comfort, guide, and teach us. God created us all to have a relationship with Him and to worship Him and enjoy Him forever. He created the world as a garden for us to live in and to enjoy. It kinda' reminds me of the bumper stickers that say, "God is my Co-pilot." Sorry, but God is nobody's co-pilot. He's the Pilot, and the Plane, and the Sky, and the Wind beneath our wings. He's the Sun, and the Sky, and the Clouds and the Rain, and the Seed. How Great is our God!

For purposes of the story, Jesus is the Vine. Of course, He also is much more—He's God; the Holy Spirit, and when He was present in the flesh, He was the conduit, the channel, for God's blessings. After He ascended, He sent the Comforter to live in our hearts, maintaining the connection between us and God while we're still here on the earth. In His role as the Vine, Jesus is giving us the food, nutrients, and genetic material we need to bear fruit that has a very close resemblance to Him, to Jesus.

"You are the branches. When you're joined with me and I with you, the relationship is intimate and organic, and the harvest is sure to be abundant" (*The Message*). A funny picture comes to mind. You meet someone on the street, he says, "What do you do for a living?" "I'm a branch." "What do you mean, a branch? Really, what do you do?" "I bear fruit." "What kind of fruit do you bear?" "Different kinds, whatever kind God puts in me."

Actually, it's a great way to serve. I mean if we're called to serve, what more could you want than to bear fruit? If bearing fruit is the best sign of your relationship with God, what more could you possibly want? Fruit makes it evident that you love God; it's the proof. It's almost like that line about what would happen if you were indicted for the crime of being a Christian—would there be enough evidence to convict you? Would there be enough fruit? Or would you be one of those branches that's going to be torn off and thrown into the fire?

This brings us to the central point of this passage. In the KJV Bible, Jesus says, "Abide in Me, and I in you. As the branch cannot bear fruit of itself, except it abide in the vine, no more can ye, except ye abide in Me." What does abide really mean? The Greek word *meno* is the word translated as abide and means "to continue firm and constant in." In the various English versions of the Bible, it is translated remain, dwell, live in, make your home in, be at home in, be vitally united, and joined. In Spanish, it's translated "to stay permanently." *The Message* seems to express it best by saying, "Live in Me. Make your home in Me just as I do in you. But if you make yourselves at home with me and my words are at home in you, you can be sure that whatever you ask will be listened to and acted upon."

The key to being a servant of the Lord lies in "making your home in Him, as He does in you." It's about staying fully, permanently, intimately, firmly and constantly, vitally united, joined to Jesus. It's like this is what we do; we are branches that are fully involved in being connected to Jesus. Maybe this is what David was talking about when he said, in the 23rd Psalm, "Surely goodness and mercy will follow me, all the days of my life, and I will dwell in the house of the Lord, forever." Hallelujah!

Did you get the answer at the end about what happens if you "dwell in the house of the Lord forever"? You live in a constant, permanent, intimate relationship with God, Jesus, and the Holy Spirit. You get to bear the fruit Jesus puts in you, and you get to feel the Holy Spirit flowing in and through you. Some days you even get to feel and see the fruit, to experience what it feels like to have the Holy Spirit of Jesus touching you inside and out. You get to see God move in other peoples' lives, right before your very eyes. It's the kind of servanthood that people are literally willing to die for because they are so immersed in what God is doing in their lives, like the martyrs that were mentioned earlier in this section. It's like that verse in Luke 10:24, where Jesus says, "For I tell you that many prophets and kings have longed to see what you see, and have not seen it, and to hear what you hear, and have not heard it." [and to feel what you have felt!] What great proof that we are Jesus' disciples!

"Herein is My Father glorified, that you bear much fruit; for by doing so you show that you are My disciples" (John 15:8). It's the proof of the pudding when God is glorified. How could we do more to show, to demonstrate, that we are His disciples, that we are servants of the Lord?

1 Peter 3:15-16

"Always be prepared to give an answer to everyone who asks you to give a reason for the hope that you have. But do this with gentleness and respect" (NIV).

This is Peter talking, you know, Simon Peter, the one about whom Jesus said, "Upon this rock will I build My church" (Matthew 16:18), which is interesting because Peter's name means rock. 'Course it could have been that Jesus was talking about what Peter said just before that. Jesus had asked, "But whom do you say that I am?" Peter answered and said, "You are the Christ, the Son of the Living God" (v. 16). Jesus said, "You didn't learn this from men; it was revealed to you by God" (v. 17), and then He said, "Upon this rock will I build My church." Same guy, big mouth Peter, but you know why Peter was one of the "big three" disciples, along with James and John? It's because he had God's Spirit growing in his heart, and God had been looking at his heart for a long time. As it says in the Spanish Bible, "He treasured the things of God in his heart."

So Peter was writing in his own letter to the churches. Actually some historians and Bible scholars think it was Mark who actually did the writing, in Peter 1 and 2, as well as in the Gospel of Mark. (They go even further to say that most of what is in the Gospel of Mark came out of Peter's mouth, and Mark was just the scribe there, too.) So Peter, clearly a sold-out serious truster in Jesus, said, "Be ready to give a reason for the hope that is in you [about Jesus]." (1 Peter 3:15).

Peter and John are the same guys who said to the Sanhedrin, the High Priests and the Elders of the Temple of Jerusalem, in Acts 4:20, "We can't help but tell the things that we have seen and heard." They had seen and heard a lot. They'd seen Jesus after He rose from the dead. They'd seen the flaming tongues of fire coming in on a mighty wind and lighting on them (Acts 2:3). They'd seen Jesus go up on top of the mountain, and fly off into the air, out of sight (Acts 1:9). They'd heard and felt and seen themselves speaking in other tongues at Pentecost so people from many nations could understand the Gospel (Acts 2:4). They'd felt the presence of the Holy Spirit of the Lord God Almighty in their own private hearts. They just couldn't help it. The stories they'd seen and heard and felt were just busting to get out of them. It was flowing out of them like rivers of living water, just like in John 7:38, and just like in that verse it was because they trusted Jesus.

I really don't know what other people think this sentence means, "Be ready to give a reason for the hope that is in you," but I think it means to be ready to tell them why you trust in Jesus. Tell them two things, 1) What happened to you to make you trust in Jesus (when you first trusted in Jesus), and 2) What any person needs to do to have an eternal personal relationship with Jesus. Lots of times those two things are all mixed up together and can't be separated or distinguished one from the other. Sometimes you really need to be able to quote them chapter and verse about how God feels about us, what He did to provide a way for us to have a relationship with Him, and what a person needs to believe in their heart and say with their mouth in order to be saved, to be born again, to be converted, to turn from the darkness to the Light.

As discussed earlier in this section of the book, some folks actually go out and witness about their faith. They have the guts or the gall to actually ask people if they're saved. I discussed that there is at least some dispute on this point among the members of the body of Christ. At this point, in discussing this verse, I'd like to leave aside any dispute, and put the emphasis on "being ready to give a reason for the hope that is in you" (for why you trust Jesus).

First, I think we all ought to think about the subject. Why do you believe? Why do you trust in Jesus? Have you ever sat down and written down, in 25 words or less, or maybe 200 words or less, why you trust in Jesus? If you haven't, maybe it would be an act of obedience and service to Jesus, the one who loved you enough to go through the pain and torture of beatings and a crucifixion for us. Write down why, as it might be a big step in the direction of being able to respond to someone who questioned you about your faith. Depending on how serious you are about following Jesus, you might even take the paper you wrote, stand in front of the mirror, and read it out loud to yourself, just for practice; just in case somebody stumbled up to you and said, "Would you please give me your reason(s) for why you trust in Jesus?"

Maybe I'm dreaming, but if we'd do those few little things of 1) thinking about what you'd say, 2) writing it down, and 3) practicing it in front of the mirror, you would actually be a whole lot more *ready* to give and answer for the hope that is in you, for why you trust Jesus. You might even understand better, just for yourself, why you trust Him. You might even begin to trust Him more just because you were willing to be obedient to get ready to do it. It only took me about 30 years to get ready to do that, and all the time I was thinking, and even sometimes telling people that I actually trusted Jesus. Sometimes maybe I really did. More than 30 years. I was probably closer to being able to give a reason when I was 10 years old than I was when I was 20, 30, or 40. About the time I reached 50, I started to really get the bug about telling people what I had seen and heard about Jesus; about giving them a reason for the hope that is in me. If God still wants me, at 66, to tell 'em about Him, then I just can't help it. I'm going to tell them, and whatever age you are, you can do it, too.

So how do you do it? I mean how is it supposed to look? I don't know. It looks different every time I do it. Sometimes it's a story about something that happened to me. Sometimes it's about something I read or saw. Sometimes it starts with a Bible verse. But every time it happens (with any good in it) it is an unplanned event. It's the craziest thing you ever saw. The Holy Spirit just sorta' enters the conversation and starts talking. I hear myself saying things that I've never said just that way before. I hear the other person saying things that sound like they were pre-written for this particular discussion—things that don't even require an answer, things that even I can respond favorably to.

All I can say about sharing your faith is what it says in the passage in Peter, "Do this with gentleness and respect." Approach people with meekness (humility) and the utmost courtesy, humbly and respectfully. If you have that Spirit in your heart, especially humility and respect, you can hardly miss. They may not be converted that minute, but the seeds certainly will have been planted. If you have that attitude in your heart, people can just feel it, and God can and will use you for His purposes. What more could you want? What more can we do to be servants for the Living God? Praise the Lord!

Mark 8:35-37

"For whoever wants to save his life will lose it, but whoever loses his life for me and for the gospel will save it. What good is it for a man to gain the whole world, yet forfeit his soul? Or what can a man give in exchange for his soul?"

"No one can be a true servant of God without knowing the principle of death and the principle of resurrection. Even the Lord Jesus Himself served on that basis. You will find in Matthew 3 that, before His public ministry ever began, our Lord was baptized. He was baptized not because He had any sin, or anything that needed cleansing. No, we know the meaning of baptism: it is a figure of death and resurrection. The ministry of the Lord did not begin until He was on that ground. After He had been baptized and had voluntarily taken the ground of death and resurrection, the Holy Spirit came upon Him, and then He ministered.

"What does this teach us? Our Lord was a sinless man. None but He has trodden this earth and known no sin. Yet as man He had a separate personality from His Father. Now we must tread very carefully when we touch our Lord, but remember His words, "I seek not mine own will, but the will of him that sent me." What does this mean? It certainly does not mean that the Lord had no will of His own. He had a will, as His own words show. As Son of Man, He had a will, but He did not do His will; He came to do the will of the Father. The point is that thing in Him which is in distinction from the Father is the human soul, which He assumed when He was "found in fashion as a man." Being a perfect man, our Lord had a soul, and of course a body, just as you and I have a soul and a body, and it was possible for Him to act from the soul, that is, from Himself.

"You remember that immediately after the Lord's baptism, and before His public ministry began, Satan came and tempted Him three times: 1) to satisfy His essential needs by turning stones to bread, 2) to secure immediate respect for His ministry by appearing miraculously in the temple court, and 3) to assume without delay the world dominion destined for Him. You might be inclined to wonder why he tempted Him to do such strange things. He might rather, you feel, have tempted Him to sin in a more thoroughgoing way, but he only said: "If thou are the Son of God, command that these stones become bread." What did it mean? The implication was this: "If You are the Son of God, You must do something to prove it. Here is a challenge. Some will certainly raise a question as to whether Your claim is real or not. Why do You not settle the matter finally now by coming out and proving it?"

"The whole subtle object of Satan was to get the Lord to act for Himself, that is, from the soul, and by the stand He took, the Lord Jesus absolutely repudiated such action. Later He defines it as His basic life-principle. I like the word in Greek: "The Son can do nothing out from himself" (John 5:19). Watchman Nee wrote, "That total denial of the soul-life was to govern all His ministry."

The soul is the seat of control in your life. The center of the struggle in our lives, our spiritual lives, is the struggle for control. We all, by virtue of our human nature, want to control. We want to control ourselves, our lives, our kids, our future, our careers, etc. We are in a life-and-death struggle for control. We glamorize this struggle, trying to make it look like it is a good thing to control. We call it self-discipline, self-respect, and independence, as opposed to being dependent on others or on God.

"God wants control of our lives, and He designed us for Him to have control of our lives. The whole crux of this struggle lies in our will. Are we willing to surrender our soul, our will, our control to Him? We are not robots. We get to choose. Are we going to deny our selves (our natural soul power), take up our cross (the cross of death to our soul), and follow Jesus, or not? We cannot serve two masters; it's God or ourselves. We will love the one, and despise the other (Matthew 6:24).

This brings us back, squarely, to the original question: What does it mean to serve? What does it mean to be a servant? After all this beating around the bush, after all the time we've all spent running into the bushes, running away from God—we get to decide, we have to decide, who we're gonna' serve. Are we gonna' serve ourselves, the devil, money and stuff, or are we gonna' serve God? Not to decide means that we'll keep on doing what we've been doing all along, which is being in bondage to ourselves, trapped by the devil to do his will.

In the end, it all comes back to the beginning of this section about service and serving. To serve really is to obey God's plan for your life. Like Paul says in Romans 12:1-2, "I beg you therefore, brothers and sisters, by God's mercy, that you present your bodies as a living sacrifice, holy, acceptable to God, which is your reasonable service. And do not be conformed to this world, but be transformed by the renewing of your mind, that you may prove [know] what is the good and acceptable and perfect will of God." Present your body as a living sacrifice—that is your reasonable service to God. It's the least you can do. That is what service is all about.

Luke 4:14-21

"Jesus returned to Galilee in the power of the Spirit, and news about him spread through the whole countryside. He was teaching in their synagogues, and everyone praised him. He went to Nazareth, where he had been brought up, and on the Sabbath day he went into the synagogue, as was his custom. He stood up to read, and the scroll of the prophet Isaiah was handed to him. Unrolling it, he found the place where it is written:

> "The Spirit of the Lord is on me, because he has anointed me to proclaim good news to the poor. He has sent me to proclaim freedom for the prisoners and recovery of sight for the blind, to set the oppressed free, to proclaim the year of the Lord's favor."
>
> "Then he rolled up the scroll, gave it back to the attendant and sat down. The eyes of everyone in the synagogue were fastened on him. He began by saying to them, 'Today this scripture is fulfilled in your hearing.'" (NIV)

First let me say that this story is about our Lord and Savior Jesus Christ, the Son of the Living God. At the beginning of his ministry, he spent 40 days in the wilderness, fasting and then being tempted by the devil. Immediately after that is where this passage comes in the Gospel of Luke. When He returned to Galilee, he returned from the wilderness, "in the Power of the Spirit." He spent a little time in the neighboring villages teaching, and then he went back to his hometown, Nazareth, where he had spent the first 30 years of his life as a child and then a carpenter. So this occasion was His 'coming out' statement before the hometown crowd.

He said, "God's Spirit is on Me. He has anointed Me." You remember about anointed; that's the evidence of gift of the Holy Spirit usually given to kings and judges, prophets and priests, not usually to lowly carpenters with no education, no ordination, and no special treatment from the High Priest or the Pharisees or Sadducees. Pretty as you please, though, Jesus gets up and says, "I'm anointed by the Spirit of the Lord. This verse from Isaiah is talking about Me."

Later in the story, it goes on to say that the people got so mad over what He said that they tried to throw him off a cliff, but He got away from them (Luke 4:29).

There are three things to say about this passage. First, in this passage from the New Testament, a passage from the Old Testament, from the prophet Isaiah, is directly quoted. That happens frequently in the Bible, and most of the time no one makes a point of it, so it kinda' slips through unnoticed. But Paul the apostle made a habit of pointing out how often passages from the Old Testament were fulfilled by things that happened in the New Testament, particularly things that Jesus did, and things that happened to Jesus, and Paul usually named the specific person and book that he was talking about. The fulfillment of prophecies was one of Paul's best evidences of the truths that were spoken about Jesus and by Jesus.

The second thing that deserves mention about this passage is what Jesus said about the passage after He got through reading it. He said, "This passage is fulfilled in your hearing." In other words, "This passage is talking about Me. I am the Anointed One. God sent me. God's Spirit is in me." Even though He was telling the truth, the neighbors in his hometown thought, "Well, what an arrogant, blasphemous thing to say! We ought to kill him for that." But Jesus didn't care, because He came, "In the Power of the Spirit."

Now what I'm fixin' to say is liable to make some people think I'm crazier, more arrogant, and just as blasphemous as those Nazarene people thought Jesus was. One day, a number of years ago, during a period when the Lord was really moving in my life, one of the times when I was not runnin' in the bushes, but instead doing my best to get as close to Jesus as I could get, I believe that God said to me, "Since you trust in Jesus, and His Spirit, My Spirit is in you, you too are anointed to proclaim good news to the poor, to proclaim freedom for the prisoners and recovery of sight for the blind, to set the oppressed free, to proclaim the year of the Lord's favor."

When He said that to my spirit, for the first time I understood that God intends to use all of us in that way, if we "give plumb up" daily and follow Him. I actually got the message of what God's purpose is for our lives. By surrendering to Jesus, the power of the Holy Spirit is upon us, and we are anointed in the same way, and those verses are fulfilled in us, just like they were fulfilled in Jesus in His ministry on this earth. In fact, in John 14:12, Jesus says, "Whoever believes in Me will do the works I have been doing, and they will do even greater things than these, because I am going to the Father." It was positively an amazing revelation. It was in there all the time, but I just wasn't paying attention.

That was when I was 27-28 years old, about 38 years ago. For a while after that, I was very close to Jesus, and He was using me to touch others for God. It was one of the best times of my life. Since then, I've drifted back to the bushes (the wilderness) two or three times, but when I was about 50, I had a jubilee year, when Jesus and His Spirit came on me again, and thank God, I've been close to Him ever since. So it's not just Jesus who is anointed to proclaim the Good News, it's me and you, too! All we have to do to get the anointing is to deny ourselves, take up our cross daily, and follow Him. In short, surrender to Him daily and follow Him.

This is not just for ordained clergy, preachers, evangelists, popes, and priests, but it's for all of us who surrender to Jesus as Lord of their lives. 1 Peter 2:9 says, "But you are a chosen people, a royal priesthood, a holy nation, God's special possession, that you may declare the praises of him who called you out of darkness into his marvelous light." That's you and me! That verse has "anointed" written all over it. In the KJV, for "God's special possession," it says "His peculiar people." You bet—that's me, and I'm glad to be here.

The third thing that deserves mention about this passage is

what it says about freedom. In the Isaiah version, it says a few words differently than the report in Luke. It says:

> "The Spirit of the Sovereign LORD is on me,
> because the LORD has anointed me
> to proclaim good news to the poor.
> He has sent me to bind up the brokenhearted,
> to proclaim freedom for the captives
> and release from darkness for the prisoners,
> to proclaim the year of the LORD's favor."

In Luke it says, "to proclaim freedom for the prisoners, to set the oppressed free."

In each version, it mentions prisoners twice—captives and prisoners, and prisoners and the oppressed. In both passages it says five things, and both times, two out of five are about prisoners.

Because I've read these verses a number of times, and because I've visited people in prisons and jails, I've thought it is interesting that Jesus' ministry should be so focused on prisoners, captives, and the oppressed. It's no accident that God uses prisons and jails to get peoples' attention and draw them to Himself. These verses also may not be talking solely about prisons with bars, but may also be talking about prisons on the outside of the bars—prisons of drugs, alcohol, depression, sexual oppression, or many other things. God uses all of these situations to get peoples' attention and draw them to Himself.

We're involved in a program called "Kairos Prison Ministry." We have a team of men who go into prisons and present weekend programs about the basic principles of Christianity. We have arrangements with the officials of various prisons (each team serves one prison) whereby we present weekend programs two weekends per year, usually once in the Spring and once in the Fall. In between times we go into the prison the 2nd Saturday of each month for "Prayer and Share" groups with the "Brothers in White" who have previously been through a Kairos Weekend. Sometimes as many as 70 or 80 men are in attendance on those Saturdays. The weekends serve 42 "pilgrims." During the weekend, we present talks about Christianity, sing songs, pray together, and discuss what we're learning while doing entertaining stuff like posters and skits. One of the best parts for the Brothers in White is the food, since on these weekends they get food they hardly ever get any other time—sliced beef, fried chicken, pizza, fresh fruits and vegetables (always in short supply in prison), and plenty of tasty desserts. We hand out dozens of cookies to each pilgrim during the weekend, and we also give a dozen cookies to each person in the prison, including staff, correctional officers, and every single prisoner, whether they're involved in the Kairos weekend or not—even those on death row get a bag of cookies. We hand out about 3,300 dozen cookies each weekend.

During these weekends, we get to develop close personal relationships with the Brothers in White. We hear many, many times from the brothers that this is the first time they ever experienced unconditional love. Forgiveness is a big focus during the weekend, and for many of the brothers, it is the first time they have ever had the opportunity to forgive and be forgiven; many are even brought to the point of forgiving themselves, by the grace of God. Many of the brothers are reconciled to their friends and family, and some are even reconciled to their enemies. Lives are changed by the power of the Holy Spirit who is always moving in our midst.

Great times are had by all, every single time. I always say, "This is the best Kairos weekend I've ever been to." I've been to more than 30 weekends, and the funny thing is, the last one really is always the best. Each time, I see new things, and I experience the presence of God in new ways. I hear new stories I can take back to my church about all the ways the Holy Spirit is moving in our lives, in our hearts, and in our relationships.

The thing that is so amazing about the experience of prison ministry is how open the brothers are to the message of the Gospel of Jesus. In Luke 5:31, Jesus says, "The healthy don't need a doctor, but the sick; I came not to call the righteous, but sinners to repentance." Someone paraphrased it like this, "I came not to save those who think they're righteous, but those who know they're sinners." The good thing about guys in prison is they know they're sinners; they've been having to think about that for years. They're ready for a little relief, so they're receptive to the message of the Gospel.

Many on the outside think they're good people, have good lives, good jobs, good family, good education, and never hurt anyone on purpose. Even if they have some skeleton in their closet, they're good at covering it up. They'd never do anything like what got those prisoners in prison. Basically good people, which also means it's hard to save people who think they're righteous.

Another group on the outside are the captives of the darkness, those who are blind, either literally or figuratively, but many of them still don't know it. Still others who have been sick and tired for a long time are ready for a little relief, and they are open and vulnerable because they are desperate for a little relief—almost as much as the Brothers in White. Those people are the ones who have decided they're going to get help, even if it requires humbling themselves, admitting their problems, and going to AA meetings, or seeking help from some other way.

Prison ministry has had a profound effect on my ministry for Jesus. It has changed it, broadened it, deepened it, and made me able to reach out to people in all walks of my life. It has helped me to understand the real problems that are caused by sin, and what I can do to help people to be delivered from their sins by sharing Jesus and His love, mercy, and grace. It's positively amazing how God has used prison ministry to change my life. I recommend it highly. Try it, and you'll be amazed, too.

So what does prison ministry have to do with service and serving? Funny thing is, every time we go to the prison, the Brothers in White are telling us how much they appreciate us coming to see them and how glad they are to get to talk to us, especially to talk about God. Whenever they say that, I'm thinking, "This is doing me more good than it is you. I just love to come here because we get to see the Spirit of the Living God move!" There's nothing I'd rather do than experience the presence of God by His Holy Spirit; it happens every time.

So what is going on here that makes going to prison a service to God and to man? First, it's about "presenting your body as a living sacrifice, which is your reasonable service of worship." Just showing up at the prison is an act of service to man, and an act of "service and worship" to God.

Second, going anywhere to worship God and talk about God and pray for yourself and others is an act of service and worship.

Third, back to our original verse, "To proclaim freedom to the prisoners." Being an inmate means being locked in 24/7 in a real prison with bars, heavy slammin' gates, and high fences with razor wire on top and guard towers with armed guards ready to shoot. Our job as servants, as disciples of Jesus, is to go in there and tell them about Him, so they can experience the freedom and deliverance that comes from knowing Jesus. They can know for their own personal selves, what it means to have the "peace that passes all understanding" (Philippians 4:7). They can know and experience the words of the "Servant Song" where it says, "Brother let me be your servant, let me be as Christ to you, Pray that I may have the grace to let you be my servant too" (Kairos Songbook). Ya' think that's service?

"Captives" are different from "prisoners." Captives are people who have been captured. They're the same people Paul is talking about in 2 Timothy 2:26, where is says, "maybe God will give them repentance so they can withdraw themselves from the snare of the devil, by whom they are taken captive to do his will." Maybe it's people like the prodigal son, who knew the Lord (his Father) but got off in the bushes (Luke 15). Or like the seed that fell in the thorny soil, where "the cares of this world and the deceitfulness of riches choked out the Word" (Matthew 13:32). Maybe our assignment, if we choose to accept it, is to do what is says in James 5:19-20, "When a brother or sister strays from the truth, you go get them and bring them back; and you save them from death and you cover a multitude of sins." Is that what "preach liberty to the captives" is about? Is that what it means to "serve"?

Fourth, what does it mean when it says "to set at liberty those who are oppressed"? Again, "oppressed" is a different condition than prisoner or captive. If you're oppressed, you're a captive all right, but you're dealing with inner demons, like fear, depression, pride, alcohol, or some other addiction or bondage. Oppressed is being pressed, depressed, repressed, and suppressed—there's lots of pressure in all those "presses." Jesus is the only one Who can deliver you, and the only way you can enjoy that deliverance, the freedom from oppression, is by surrendering to Jesus and trusting Him to deliver you and keep you safe. Then you can enjoy the peace and rest He offers. The thing is, they are only going to get the message and continue practicin' it if some sister or brother in Christ tells them and then continues to show them how it works, for as long as it takes. That's what love and service are all about.

Matthew 25, Prison Ministry

In Matthew 25:31-46: at the Last Judgment, speaking of Our Lord Jesus, it says, "Then the King will say to those on His right hand, 'Come, you blessed of My Father, inherit the kingdom prepared for you from the foundation of the world...I was in prison and you came to Me.' "Then the righteous will answer Him, saying, 'Lord, . . . when did we see You sick, or in prison, and come to You?' And the King will answer and say to them, 'Assuredly, I say to you, inasmuch as you did it to one of the least of these My brethren, you did it to Me.'

Back to going to prisons and visitin' prisoners, I started doing it a little a long time ago when I'd go to the county jail with the Gideons (they're the guys that leave those Bibles in motel rooms, at the schools, and with the members of the military, speaking of service). We'd talk to them about Jesus, play a little guitar, and sing a few songs. That was maybe 35 years ago, but honestly, it didn't seem like much came of it, and it wasn't a high point in my life as a disciple of Jesus. I didn't learn much, and I was way too dumb to teach anybody anything. I don't remember a single time of really talking to anyone personally about Jesus. The only thing I remember that was positive was they listened to what we said about Jesus. A little plantin' maybe but no harvestin'. God only knows if there was any increase. 'Course I take a little comfort from that verse that says, "The Word of God will not return void, but will accomplish the purpose for which it was sent" (Isaiah 55:11).

Then came the eight years I spent practicing criminal defense law, during which I spent a good deal of time talking to people in jails and prisons, but not usually about God. A few times, God would send me a message that He was still there, paying attention, and taking care of me and mine, even when I wasn't paying attention. I didn't make any concerted effort to share God, Jesus, the Holy Spirit, or His mercy and grace, but I got to see a lot about what life can be like without Him. Once a lady came up to me as I was leaving a courtroom and said, "I've been watching you, and God told me I should ask you to represent me on this case I've got." That was a first. I ended up representing her, and the district attorney ended up dismissing the case against her. It was a victory for her and for me, but mostly for God, because we got to share a lot with each other about Him during that case.

About the same time I quit practicing criminal defense law, I had the opportunity to go on a Kairos weekend for the first time in 2001. Since then, I've been on about 30 Kairos weekends, so many I've lost count. I've learned a lot from Kairos. I've learned that when Christian brothers and sisters band together to work for the Lord, the Holy Spirit moves in a mighty way, both in our hearts and in the hearts of those we minister to, and also on the outside, in the free world, touching people and places and things we don't even expect. It is truly a miracle.

God really is in the middle of us, when 2 or 3, or 50-60, are gathered in His name and for His purpose. I've learned that it's easier to surrender to Jesus and His will for our lives when we do it together.

I've noticed that one of the most astounding characteristics of the Kairos people in this situation is their willingness to not think more highly of themselves than they ought to think (Romans 12:3), to associate with humble people, and not to think they're smarter than anyone else.

In the NKJV, for Romans 12:9-21, there's a subtitle "Behave like a Christian." It sounds like, "If you're going to claim to be a Christian, then act like it." It's amazing how well the members of Kairos teams fulfill the conditions presented in those verses. The team members don't have a personal agenda—they're not trying to run the show and tell everyone else what to do, and they are genuinely concerned for the welfare of the other people on the team (and the brothers or sisters we minister to). There are many different jobs to be done on a Kairos weekend—from team leader to cooks, and from guys doing the talks to guys who are members of the "table families." Maybe there are exceptions, but almost every person on the team is willing to serve in any way they're asked, and they are willing to do it with the best attitude. This is a perfect example of all the ways we can "act like a Christian" as found in Romans 12. I am genuinely blessed to be a member.

The motto of Kairos is "Listen, Listen, Love, Love." Probably more than anything else known to human beings is the need for unconditional love, and the easiest and best way to show unconditional love is to listen. What I'm talking about is really focused, genuine listening, with no agenda, not just waiting for them to stop so you can tell them something, but just listening with genuine concern in your heart is the best love you can give. And many of the brothers and sisters in prison have never had anyone really listen to them. (Of course, lots of folks in the outside world are in the same predicament.) There are a few underlying meanings to "Listen, Listen, Love, Love" as well. While we're definitely interested in sharing the Gospel of Jesus with the Brothers in White, we're not trying to cram it down their throats. We tell them about Jesus, but we tell them in no uncertain terms that they don't have to make any decision, or do anything about it, unless they choose to. The proof of the pudding is that we practice what we preach, about letting them decide for themselves, or not decide at all if they don't feel led to do so. I recently had a revelation from God about why we say it twice, as in "Listen, Listen, Love, Love." It's because we listen to God and we listen to the brothers; we love God and we love the brothers. It's amazing what happens when we do what the motto suggests.

One of the central themes of a Kairos weekend is forgiveness, which is something we talk a lot about. We have three separate talks about forgiveness leading up to a forgiveness ceremony in which everyone (brothers and team members alike) writes down all the people they need to forgive (usually beginning with themselves). Then we pray over our lists, and nail them to a cross, and burn those lists up. It's a great way to start the deliverance from unforgiveness that we all need in our lives.

At the end of the Kairos weekend, on Sunday afternoon, before we pack our stuff and leave the prison, we have what we call "The Closing." At the closing, the brothers who have been our guests on the weekend have the opportunity to get up and answer three questions: 1) In what condition did you arrive here? 2) What did you find here? 3) What are you taking away with you? These closing questions are supposed to be short, but often they last a long time, because everyone gets the chance to say their piece. Many of them cry, along with most of us in the audience. Many have true conversions during the weekend that they announce at the closing. Not a few have made definite commitments to forgive people who are present and had great reconciliations right there in front of God and everybody. Hallelujah! Praise the Lord! The Holy Spirit is alive and well, and moving in every one of those closing ceremonies.

Though you may find this hard to believe, this is just a small part of all the things that happen on a Kairos weekend. As always happens when the Spirit of the Lord is present, lives are changed; almost every life there is changed, and for the better every time. Thank God in heaven for the way His purposes are fulfilled through the ministry of Kairos in the prisons of the U.S. and the world. This ministry truly is an act of God on an ongoing basis. It truly is an act of service in which people really do surrender to God, and He really does use them to touch and change other peoples' lives. "Out of their innermost beings flow rivers of living water." (John 7:38-39) This really is one of the things it means to "serve."

To me, one of the most amazing things about Kairos is the effect it has had on my growth in discipleship in the outside world. God has used Kairos to grow me up in the Lord in a way that I never would have imagined possible before I became involved in this ministry. I've learned more about what I really believe as a disciple of Jesus. Like it says in Philemon verse 6, "I pray that your sharing of the faith will make you understand every blessing we have in Christ." (Tex's paraphrase) I've learned more about what I should be doing to be a disciple of Jesus. I have been able to share Jesus in new and effective ways that I never ever thought of before I became involved in Kairos. I have become committed to Jesus in a way I never was committed before—real true commitment, real true surrender, and real willingness to die to my sinful self in ways that I didn't even understand before I became involved in this ministry. God really has used Kairos to change my life in a multitude of ways that I'm only just beginning to understand, grasp, and share. Thank God for the Kairos Prison Ministry, and for all the brothers and sisters who are involved in it. I have even begun to see what being a member of the body of Christ is really about. Praise the Lord from whom all blessings flow! Speaking of serving, because of Kairos, I am becoming a servant of Jesus and others in ways that I didn't even know existed before I became involved in Kairos. It must be God; it must be service.

CONCLUSION

IT'S ALL ABOUT SURRENDER

In thinking about how to draw this book together, I've had a vision that these six 'themes' are facets of God's personality; that in reality, spiritual reality, they are a part of an all encompassing tapestry of God's creation. I've also had a vision that all these 'themes' are just different expressions of God, Jesus and the Holy Spirit; different manifestations of Him in our hearts and lives.

'Course the underlying key to all aspects of our relationship with Jesus is our surrender to Him. So how does each of the 'Great Themes' express surrender in our lives? How does our surrender express itself in each of the 'Great Themes'? When I started this book, I thought surrender should be categorized under 'Humble', because the essence of humility is surrender; such as in Philippians 2:5, 8; where it says, "Let this mind (this attitude) be in you, which was also in Christ Jesus, Who, being found as a man, humbled himself, and became a slave, and was obedient unto death, even death on a cross." It was a surrender for Jesus, Who IS GOD, to even become a man; and when He found Himself in the body of a man, (as if that weren't enough), He surrendered Himself and became a slave; and even more, He surrendered Himself in being obedient to die for us; and if that weren't enough, to die the worst, most tortuous kind of death, on a cross." (So how can anyone imagine that this was an unplanned, random event?)

So when you get down to really thinking through all the ways Jesus was willing to demonstrate surrender before and during His life on this earth; it really does become clear that humility really is the essence of surrender; and surrender is the fullest expression of humility. But surrender is not just about being humble. We surrender equally in love, thanksgiving, trust, obedience and service. The conclusion is that **surrender is the underlying truth** of all six of these 'Great Themes'.

We started out talking about 'accepting the commission that Jesus gave us before He ascended into heaven' of 'making disciples, baptizing them, teaching them' ; of knowing a disciple, being a disciple, and making a disciples' for Jesus; of moving up the continuum of grace and righteousness to getting right up next to God; to truly drawing near to Him; close enough so we can really enjoy His Presence all the time, which is the purpose for which He created us.

Now we've come full circle in figuring out the who, what, where, when, why and how, of fulfilling the Great Commission of Jesus to us, right here on this earth, right now in the 21st Century. If you want to fulfill the Great Commission, how do you do it? You surrender your whole *self* to God, Jesus Christ and the Holy Spirit, in humble recognition that you don't have a chance, except to let Him do whatever He wants to with your life. You focus your whole *self* on figuring out ways to surrender your *self*, to deny your *self*, to die to your natural *self*, so God can live His eternal life in you. That is the full answer. Nothing more need be said.

But since I'm given to verbosity; I've got just a little more to say. LOL! It seems good, after all this time, to focus a little attention on how surrender is accomplished in each of the realms of the six Great Themes.

Love and Surrender

What is it about love that calls out to us about surrender? Well, just to hit the high points, because God loved us so much, He gave (surrendered) His only begotten Son to come down here to the earth, and become a slave, and die on a cross.

Not to fight and kill to win, but to surrender and die to win. 'Greater love hath no man than this, that he will *lay down his life* for his friends.' Of course you already know that living the truth is even harder than dying for the truth. Like it says in the Love Chapter of 1 Corinthians 13, "Love suffers long . . . love will hardly even notice when others do it wrong . . . love excuses all things, puts up with all kinds of crap, believes the best about the loved one, . . . endures all things; just like the 'mind of Christ' 'the attitude of Jesus' in Philippians 2:5. That's love; never jealous or boastful or proud or rude; always willing to surrender to others and to God.

Tex Tonroy

Humility and Surrender

As we've said before, but it bears repeating one more time; the Beatitudes are all **about humility**; which is all **about surrender**. (It's the 'mind (attitude) of Jesus'): Matt 5:3-12

1. Blessed are the poor in spirit: for theirs is the kingdom of heaven.
2. Blessed are they that mourn: for they shall be comforted.
3. Blessed are the meek (humble): for they shall inherit the earth.
4. Blessed are they which do hunger and thirst after righteousness: for they shall be filled.
5. Blessed are the merciful: for they shall obtain mercy.
6. Blessed are the pure in heart: for they shall see God.
7. Blessed are the peacemakers: for they shall be called the children of God.
8. Blessed are they which are persecuted for righteousness' sake: for theirs is the kingdom of heaven.
9. Blessed are ye, when men shall revile you, and persecute you, and shall say all manner of evil against you falsely, for my sake.
10. Rejoice, and be exceeding glad: for great is your reward in heaven: for so persecuted they the prophets which were before you.

This whole idea of surrender and humility being the same thing is perfectly expressed in "The Prayer of St. Francis":

"Lord, make me an instrument of your peace;
where there is hatred, let me sow love;
where there is injury, pardon;
where there is doubt, faith;
where there is despair, hope;
where there is darkness, light; and
where there is sadness, joy.
O Divine Master, grant that I may not so much
seek to be consoled as to console;

to be understood as to understand;
to be loved, as to love.
For it is in giving that we receive,
it is in pardoning that we are pardoned, and
it is in dying that we are born to eternal life.
Amen."

This is truly the 'Mind of Jesus', the attitude of surrender. And please remember that Jesus did not just 'say' these words for His disciples to follow; He demonstrated them, on the face of this earth. He was willing to suffer and sacrifice for us; to be merciful; to be reviled, and cursed, and persecuted for righteousness sake.

Thanksgiving and Surrender

". . . give thanks in all things", no matter what happens. (that sounds like "as your life goes along, from now til the end, give thanks; ups and downs, good and bad, happy or sad, light or dark, easy or hard. Sounds like "give thanks all the time" to me.

What I want to know is: how in the world can we 'give thanks all the time' in every event; irrespective of its apparent goodness or badness relative to our lives? The short answer is, there is only one way. And that one way is that we don't really focus our lives, our emotional 'center', on the outcome of events in our lives, because we're focused on something else. The only way we can do that is if we are focused on God, on His Presence, on His LIFE in our lives. *We can only do that when we truly surrender our selves, deny our selves, die to our selves, and focus our entire attention on Jesus and what He wants.* When we do that we begin to be able to fulfill Jesus' expectations for us, to fulfill His prayer in John 17; to become one with Him and the Father and with each other as He is one with the Father. *Complete surrender* is the only state of being in which we can experience what this passage says about Rejoicing and Praying and Being Thankful, ALL THE TIME. That's what Jesus wants for us, just like He said in John 17. So we can't give up. We've got to keep on keeping on asking and seeking and knocking. *(and surrendering and trusting and rejoicing and praying and giving thanks)*

Trust and Surrender

Trust. Surrender. As we've said before, real surrender comes from trusting your whole self to God. You can't get any relief, or rest, without trust. Funniest thing, you can't get any surrender without trust. Without trust you always have to keep watching your back, and defending yourself, and making sure all the doors are locked, and never ever letting your guard down for fear someone is going to step on you (not just your toes, but you!). But when you really trust God, when you know down in the bottom of your heart that He is always there to protect you, that He'll never leave you nor forsake you nor abandon you; THEN you can relax, then you can rest, then you can get a little relief. When you finally give up trying to take care of yourself, THEN God steps in to take care of you. Trust and Surrender, just different aspects of the very same attitude.

Obedience and Surrender

Obey. Obedience. Surrender. To overcome all the problems, the difficulties, the insurmountable obstacles in your life, you must focus on the solution, not on the problem; and the only solution is Jesus. You must focus on Jesus. You must immerse yourself in the Word of God, in the relationship of daily prayer and meditation with Jesus; at every turn, at every threat to your peace and stability you must focus yourself on drawing closer to Jesus, on surrendering yourself more to Jesus, on spending more time concentrating every fiber of your being on Him. THIS IS WHAT OBEDIENCE IS ALL ABOUT.

You don't really have much choice. Nothing else works. You've already tried all the other stuff and you're still in the same fix as before, 'cept maybe worse. Jesus is the only solution that works.

True obedience is to completely surrender to the will of God for you. To say, "I'm making a deal with You Lord. I'll do whatever you want me to, and You can do whatever You want to with me." This is a minute by minute commitment. This is getting up every morning and saying, "OK Lord, I'm ready. Tell me where you want me to go today. Show me the people you want me to talk to today. Let me see the adventure of Your Presence in my life, in my comings and goings. I do not have a plan. I do not have an agenda. I do not have a preconceived notion about how I'm supposed to look or act. "As the servants eye is on the hand of his Master, so is my heart stayed on You." (Psalm 123:2) As God shows me His will, I will follow.

True obedience lies in doing what the verse says, "Walk not after the sinful nature, but walk after the Spirit." (Romans 8:1-4) That's obedience.

Obedience is saying 'yes' when God tells you something to do (in an immediate sense). "If you love me you'll keep my commandments; and this is my commandment, that you love one another." I cannot do right by myself. I can only do right as I surrender and trust God to work His will in me. Only as I die to myself, and let Jesus live His life in me, can I live up to His standard, which is, "Be ye perfect (whole, entire, lacking nothing), even as your Father in heaven is perfect."

So how do we get ourselves away from this willful disobedience? We don't; we can't. What is it Paul says? "Who will deliver me from this wretched man that I am?" (Romans 7:23-25) You only get one guess. God. And if God is so hard on willful disobedience, why would He even consider delivering such jerks as us? Because He wants to. And what will persuade Him to do it? Nothing except our accepting His gift, completely surrendering ourselves to Him, daily, and letting Him live His eternal life in us. That is the only way we'll ever achieve obedience that will satisfy God.

Whoever is willing to die to himself (surrender) daily is the one who is being obedient. Quit trying to get your way, and let Jesus live in you so He can have His way with you and with those around you. It's a daily act of surrender; of humbling yourself; of giving plumb up.

Paul says in Romans 6:16, "Don't you know that to whoever you present [surrender] yourselves to obey, you are that one's slaves, whether to sin [of the devil] leading to death, or of obedience [to God] leading to righteousness. "Don't you get it? If you surrender to sin, you get enslaved by the devil, and it leads to death." "But, if you surrender to [be obedient to] God, it leads to righteousness which is life." You get to choose.

So obedience must be about having your heart right. And how do you do that again? You humble yourself, you surrender to Jesus, and you trust Him, and His Spirit comes into your heart. Your ole heart just can't get any more all right than that.

It's not all of a sudden; but it sorta comes on you slow, when you're not expecting it; you see these little signs of the Holy Spirit moving in your heart, doing things in your life, making things happen that you never thought possible. And that is what obedience is about. Obedience is when God does it IN YOU! It's when the Spirit of Life in Christ Jesus begins to SET YOU FREE from the law of sin and death, and you can feel it and see it and know that it's happening in your very own personal heart and soul and body.

So Paul says, "Let that attitude; let that kind of obedience be in you." Of course the obedience is not just in saying the right words, but in doing the right thing. And the right thing is in surrendering to God's will, surrendering to the troops of the Sanhedrin, surrendering to the Elders, and the Pharisees and the Sadducees, surrendering to the beatings, and the mockings, and the crown of thorns, and doing it with the right attitude; the attitude of surrender; like it says in Isaiah 53, "He was led as a Lamb to the slaughter, and He opened not His mouth." (Isaiah 53:7)

The only way we will be able to stand is if we are totally surrendered to Jesus so that His Holy Spirit so fills us that it is He who is doing the standing; it is He who is doing the enduring; it is He who is doing the obeying; 'cause I'm pretty certain that we can't possibly do things like that under our own power. Thank God we don't have to do something like that by ourselves, without Him being right there with us.

Service and Surrender

"SERVE." Service. Surrender. If you hang around with Jesus much at all you keep hearing this message, "Be humble. 1Don't just play like a servant [slave]; don't just act like a servant [slave]; *be* a servant [slave] in your heart. Be willing to surrender yourself, to give your life a ransom for others (whether by living or by dying)."

But in the situation we've been discussing, of serving Jesus, and serving others by letting Him live His life through us, 'whatever it takes' takes on a whole new meaning. Then it starts to mean something more; surrendering more; giving up more of yourself; sacrificing more of your time or your energy or your money or whatever Jesus asks of you, simply because it stops being about your plans and your design for your life, and it starts being about God's design and His plans for your life. You *want* to please Him; simply because you want to be more like Him; simply because "it is no longer I, but Christ, who lives in me." (Gal. 2:20) That's service. James 5:13-20, is about several things that people who believe in, who _trust in and surrender to_, Jesus, do. They are not exactly things that they're supposed to do, as a duty, but things that they do, because it's in their hearts and it _has to come out._ _(it's part of their nature)_ . . these things really are things we ought to do, because they really are part of what it means to serve, to be a servant, both to God and to others.

And if we surrender ourselves to Jesus, and line ourselves up with His teachings and most of all with His Spirit, we have the same direct line to God that Elijah had. It's not just that we CAN have what Elijah had, we DO have what Elijah had. All we have to do to fully realize God's power in us is to do what Jesus says in Luke 9:23, "Deny yourself, and take up your cross daily, and follow Me." Simple but not easy; it takes daily surrender.

So if we're talking about service, what does that mean? It means that we really are God's lights in the world. It means that we really are "the salt of the earth" whereby it is flavored, whereby it is saved from corruption. All we have to do is surrender to Him and let His Spirit use us to fulfill His purposes in the world.

So who is a 'righteous' person? A righteous person is one who has Jesus' righteousness in him because he has surrendered his whole self to Jesus. Not my righteousness but His righteousness is the only thing that is going to save me, the only thing that is going to make me holy, as God is holy. So if you want to have prayer that is powerful and effective what do you have to do? You have to surrender; not just once, but every single day, every hour, every minute. Most of the time we're too busy to do that; to think about that, to even consider that. But if you try to do it, and you keep on trying, eventually it gets to be a habit; you enter a zone where you're in constant contact with the Spirit that is in you; and you begin to 'pray without ceasing'; you begin to 'rejoice evermore'; you begin to 'give thanks in all things', because that really is 'the will of God in Christ Jesus for you'. (1 Thess 5:18) That's where 'righteous' comes from; and that's what it takes to be a servant, in the Biblical sense. Not me, but God. Christ in you, the hope of glory. (Col. 1:27)

Praying is an act of service. The prayer of a righteous person is powerful and effective. Who is righteous? Anyone who has surrendered to Jesus and let His Spirit come to dwell in their heart. No one else is righteous in God's eyes. If you want to have a powerful and effective prayer life, surrender your whole self to Jesus. Deny yourself, take up your cross daily (that means 'die to yourself' so Jesus can live His Eternal Life in you!), and follow Him. That's the ONLY way to have a powerful effective prayer life.

Elijah HAD a powerful effective prayer life. Even though he was a human being, even as we are, he was 'righteous in God's eyes' because he was totally surrendered to God; Elijah denied himself, so God's eternal Spirit lived in him. So when Elijah prayed, stuff happened in response to His prayers. (James 5:17-18) When you truly surrender to God, you understand and discern God's will so well that you get lined up with God and you're able to be obedient to pray for what God wants to have happen. Then it happens. I heard a pastor say that when you're praying and you're really 'in tune' with God, He begins to tell you what He wants you to pray for, and when you do, those things happen. (Rev. Jim Jackson)

So here we are. We've come to the end. We started out talking about drawing nearer to God, so He'll draw nearer to us; (James 4:8) hopefully so we can fulfill Jesus' Great Commission for us to 'make disciples', and baptize them, and teach them to observe all things that He commanded us to do. We've discussed six great themes of the Bible, all of which we hope will shed some light on this mutual design of ours for drawing nearer; and what have we learned?

Well, we've learned some interesting facts to know and tell. We've learned a little more about what it really means to have a relationship with God. But mostly, we learned that if you want to have a real, genuine, growing, developing relationship with God, you just have to give plumb up, completely surrender to Him, so He can do whatever He wants to with your (and my) life. We have to keep on doing it every day. We have to love, to humble ourselves, to be thankful, to trust, to obey, and to serve. In short, we have to "let this mind (this attitude) be in us, which was (and is) in Christ Jesus." (Phil 2:5)

So if love is about when you surrender your *self* to the one you love, and you quit worrying about what you want and you focus on what He wants; and if humble is when you surrender your *self* and become a servant (slave) for those around you;[23] (he who would be great, first let him serve); (Matt 20:26-27) and if thanksgiving is about surrendering so much that **you can and do give thanks in all things;** and if obedience is when you are obedient to the death of your sinful nature, so Jesus can live His Eternal Life in you; and if 'service' means to surrender your *self* so fully that Jesus' Spirit begins to flow through you, and God's righteousness begins to dwell in you; THEN Jesus has found Himself a disciple, a disciple who has counted the cost and is making disciples, and baptizing, and teaching, and living his/her life as the light and the salt for God.

We're back. How do you draw nearer to God? *You surrender to him* and He takes you in hand and fills you up with Himself, and gradually you begin to fulfill the Great Commission almost without really trying. Life becomes a day-to-day miracle, whether you're conscious of trying to do something for Jesus or not. He uses you when you're not even conscious of it. All of a sudden you notice that you're actually living the miracle of 'rejoicing all the time; praying without ceasing; and giving thanks in all things", just because it's in you and it has to get out; just because you know you're doing what God wants you to do because God is doing it in you; and you realize you're not just 'drawing nearer to God'; you've already accomplished the trip.

Conclusion of the Conclusion: Make Disciples

We started out talking about drawing near to God, so we could fulfill the Great Commission given by Jesus, just before He ascended into heaven. And we all know that the Great Commission is "Make Disciples." And as an underlying theme, "Make Disciples" is what this book is all about. So, in conclusion of the conclusion, we're going to talk a little about the best discipleship relationship in the Bible, the one between Paul and Timothy.

Paul loved Timothy. (And it's reasonable to deduce that Timothy loved Paul). Paul addressed his first letter to Timothy this way: "To Timothy, my true son in the faith." In the second letter, Paul addressed Timothy: "To Timothy, my dear son."

In 2 Timothy 1:5, Paul says, "I thank God, whom I serve, as my ancestors did, with a clear conscience, as night and day I constantly remember you in my prayers. Recalling your tears, I long to see you, so that I may be filled with joy. I am reminded of your sincere faith, which first lived in your grandmother Lois and in your mother Eunice and, I am persuaded, now lives in you also."

Then Paul says, "But you have carefully followed my doctrine, manner of life, purpose, faith, longsuffering, love, perseverance, . . . you must continue in the things which you have learned and been assured of, knowing from whom you have learned them, and that from childhood you have known the Holy Scriptures, which are able to make you wise for salvation through faith which is in Christ Jesus." (2 Tim 3:10)

The relationship between Paul and Timothy was no short term engagement. After their initial meeting, Timothy followed Paul all over the Eastern Mediterranean; he went where Paul told him to; he taught and preached and organized churches; he lived out his life as a disciple of Jesus by the hand of Paul. It is interesting to note that of the books in the Bible that we usually refer to as the "Pauline Epistles" (Paul's letters), two are written from Paul, Silas and Timothy, and three, Philippians, Colossians and Philemon are written from Paul and Timothy. That is good evidence that Paul, and probably many others, recognized Timothy as a leader in the Faith in the first Century. Even at the end of Paul's life, he's still talking about Timothy, and where he is, and when he's coming to visit. It's pretty clear that this friendship between Paul and Timothy was not just a casual acquaintance.

In Acts 16:1-3, the author Luke says, "Then he [Paul] came to Derbe and Lystra. And behold, a certain disciple was there, named Timothy, the son of a certain Jewish woman who believed, but his father was Greek. He was well spoken of by the brethren who were at Lystra and Iconium. Paul wanted to have him go on with him." That's how they met. And right away, a 'discipleship' relationship started. From Timothy's viewpoint: Timothy met Paul, and God told him he could learn to be a disciple of Jesus from Paul. So Timothy, without really trying (because God was in him, the Holy Spirit was guiding him) demonstrated to Paul that he had a sincere desire to learn from Paul how to be a disciple of Jesus. And Paul got it. He got the message from God, that Timothy was 'like-minded' with him, about the things of God, that Timothy was his own son, after the Spirit. Paul took Timothy with him and taught him. He made a disciple of Timothy, just like it says in the Great Commission; he taught Timothy to "observe all things that Jesus had commanded." He taught Timothy to surrender. He taught him to trust. He taught him to humble himself before the Lord. He taught him to obey. And he taught him to serve. And then Paul said to Timothy, "And the things you have heard from me before many witnesses, the same commit (teach, teach diligently) to faithful men, who shall be able to teach others also." (2 Tim 2:2)

In modern day English, Paul might've said, "I've taught you everything I know. I've showed you everything I know. I've poured my heart out to you over and over about all it means to me to know Jesus; to love and surrender to Jesus; to trust and obey and serve Jesus. So find some more people who God has touched, and teach them and show them, the things I have taught you. And don't just teach them to do it; teach them to _teach others also_." **That** is true, complete, discipleship. . . . Oh, and by the way, keep on doing that for the rest of your life. _**That is your Great Commission.**_

So in relation to this Paul-Timothy discipleship story, I've developed a motto, "**K**now a disciple, **B**e a disciple, **M**ake disciples, **T**each them to make disciples . . . **for Jesus**."

K.B.M.T. for JESUS

It makes me think of a graph, with a line along the bottom, and a line up the left side, and then a long curving line from the lower left-hand corner to the upper right hand corner. And up in the upper right hand corner is where God is. And down in the lower left-hand corner is where we all start out when we are 'born again'. Everybody who claims the Name of Jesus is on that curving line somewhere. Maybe real low and near the starting place; or maybe higher, nearer to God. You know, John the Baptist and Elijah and Moses may be pretty far up the line, pretty close to God and Jesus. Maybe Billy Graham or Martin Luther or Stephen the Deacon are half-way up the line. Oh, and by the way, there's some little children, that don't know com'ere from sickum, that are almost all the way to God. What God has been wanting for all of us; what Jesus was talking about all the time He was on the earth; what the Holy Spirit has been moving us toward, and guiding us toward, and encouraging us to reach out for; is to move on up that line toward God, every day of our lives; to enjoy more and more of the Presence of God, to know Him better, and surrender to

Him more, every day til we join Jesus in heaven. And all the time, we're supposed to be helping each other along the way, by sharing the love and mercy and grace, and humility, and trust, and obedience, and gratitude, and the servant's heart that the Holy Spirit is steadily putting in us. Hallelu Jah! Praise the Lord! from Whom all blessings flow!

THE END